Lessing and the Consequences

Robert Vellusig

Lessing and the Consequences

palgrave
macmillan

Robert Vellusig
Institut für Germanistik
Karl-Franzens-Universität Graz
Graz, Austria

ISBN 978-3-662-71872-8   ISBN 978-3-662-71873-5 (eBook)
https://doi.org/10.1007/978-3-662-71873-5

Translation from the German language edition: "Lessing und die Folgen" by Robert Vellusig, © Springer-Verlag GmbH Deutschland, ein Teil von Springer Nature 2023. Published by J.B. Metzler. All Rights Reserved.

This book is a translation of the original German edition "Lessing und die Folgen" by Robert Vellusig, published by Springer-Verlag GmbH, DE in 2023. The translation was done with the help of an artificial intelligence machine translation tool. A subsequent human revision was done primarily in terms of content, so that the book will read stylistically differently from a conventional translation. Springer Nature works continuously to further the development of tools for the production of books and on the related technologies to support the authors.

© The Editor(s) (if applicable) and The Author(s), under exclusive license to Springer-Verlag GmbH, DE, part of Springer Nature 2025

This work is subject to copyright. All rights are solely and exclusively licensed by the Publisher, whether the whole or part of the material is concerned, specifically the rights of translation, reprinting, reuse of illustrations, recitation, broadcasting, reproduction on microfilms or in any other physical way, and transmission or information storage and retrieval, electronic adaptation, computer software, or by similar or dissimilar methodology now known or hereafter developed.
The use of general descriptive names, registered names, trademarks, service marks, etc. in this publication does not imply, even in the absence of a specific statement, that such names are exempt from the relevant protective laws and regulations and therefore free for general use.
The publisher, the authors and the editors are safe to assume that the advice and information in this book are believed to be true and accurate at the date of publication. Neither the publisher nor the authors or the editors give a warranty, expressed or implied, with respect to the material contained herein or for any errors or omissions that may have been made. The publisher remains neutral with regard to jurisdictional claims in published maps and institutional affiliations.

This Palgrave Macmillan imprint is published by the registered company Springer-Verlag GmbH, DE, part of Springer Nature.
The registered company address is: Heidelberger Platz 3, 14197 Berlin, Germany

If disposing of this product, please recycle the paper.

In memoriam
Gisbert Ter-Nedden
(1940–2014)

Contents

Part I Writings	1
The Prodigal Son	3
The Young Scholar	7
Prudent Doubt	13
Theology of Laughter	19
The Virtuous Freethinker	25
The Compassionate Jew	31
Berlin: Friends and *Writings*	37
A "Domestic Tragedy": *Miss Sara Sampson*	43
A Correspondence on Tragedy	55
School of Intuitive Cognition: Fables	61
Letters on Literature (Primarily No. 17)	67

A War Drama: *Philotas*	73
Media Aesthetics of the Mimetic Arts: *Laocoön*	81
Hamburg: Aristotelian Dramaturgy	93
Composed in 1763: *Minna von Barnhelm*	105
A Modernised Virginia: *Emilia Galotti*	115
Wolfenbüttel: Fragments of an Anonymous Author	125
Anti-Goeze, No. 12: *Nathan the Wise*	135
Dialogues for Freemasons: *Ernst and Falk*	145
The Education of the Human Race	151
Part II Consequences	159
Lessing as a Public Figure	161
Pre-Classicist and Pioneer	169
Lessing and Goethe	175
An Unpoetic Poet	185
Lessing and Schiller	189
An Untragic Tragedian	203
Legislator of the Arts	211
Friend of Spinoza	221
Lover of Theology	227
"Lessingiasis" and "Nathanology"	235

Lessing Dies	247
Notes on the Bibliography	255
Bibliography	257

Part I

Writings

The Prodigal Son

In December 1747, shocking news reaches Johann Gottfried Lessing, scholar-clergyman and pastor in Kamenz: Gotthold, his highly gifted, promising son, is said to be neglecting his studies in Leipzig, consorting instead with actors and freethinkers. In 1741, after having attended Latin school in town up to the age of twelve, he had left his parental home for scholarly training at the 'Prince's School' of St Afra in Meissen, which was to prepare him for the study of theology. According to the school inspector's verdict, he proved to be "a good boy, though inclined to mockery" (RD, 10), and extraordinarily perceptive, as the Rector of the school remarked to his father: "This is a horse which needs a double ration of fodder. The lessons that are too hard for the others seem child's play for him. We hardly know what to do with him anymore" (KGL 1, 40).

Already during his years at St Afra, where religion and the classical languages (Latin, Greek, Hebrew) were the principal subjects taught, the son had pursued his own interests, received private lessons in philosophy and natural sciences from the mathematician Klimm, and made use of the holdings of the library to immerse himself, of his own accord, in ancient literature. He only returned to Kamenz twice during this time. In 1746, he had left the monastic precinct of the Prince's School to enrol at Leipzig University as a student of theology, the pursuit of which, however, he evidently did not take too seriously. To the horror of his pious parents, he had come into contact with Caroline Neuber and her theatre instead.

When the parents are informed by a well-meaning friend that their son has shared his Christmas cake from home "with a number of actors, accompanied by a bottle of wine", the mother tearfully declares her child "lost to this life and to eternity" (KGL 1, 73). The father takes drastic measures. Under the pretext that the mother is on her deathbed, he brings their son home: "On receipt of this, take the mail coach at once and come home. Your mother is mortally ill and wishes to speak to you before she dies" (B 11/1, 10). Half frozen, the prodigal returns home; a confrontation ensues. It does not change Lessing's mind, however: In the autumn of 1748, he will give up his studies for good and follow his step-cousin, journalist and editor Johann Christlob Mylius, to Berlin, there to earn his living as a freelance writer and make a name for himself as a journalist.

The story of the prodigal's return is more than anecdotal; it gives a clear impression of the social and cultural milieu into which Lessing was born. Lessing is one of a number of pastor's sons turned poets. His first biographer, Karl Lessing, recounts that his brother "was instructed to pray as soon as he could babble" (KGL 1, 27). His first religious education was provided by his father: "As early as in his fourth and fifth year, he already knew what, why and how to believe" (KGL 1, 27). In his parental home, Lessing was faced with the traditional Protestant hostility towards the theatre; his father, far from allowing him to participate in the performances of the Kamenz school theatre, would intervene against them. As a learned man, he would have appreciated it had his son pursued an academic career after dropping theology – what he had no understanding for, in contrast, was his son's preference for the theatre.

When Johann Gottfried Lessing had studied philosophy and theology in Wittenberg, university as an institution had still been the centre of literary culture, and the world of books had been the exclusive domain of academically educated scholars. In Leipzig, however, his son was not only introduced to the theatre and the classics of modern drama, Molière's comedies and Voltaire's tragedies – the Saxon metropolis also offered him an opportunity to escape from the narrow world of academic scholarship and tap into the abundance of modern literary culture. Leipzig was the hotspot of printing in Germany, and therefore of the medium that turned out to be the actual driving force behind the process of cultural revolution in the 18th century already referred to by contemporaries as the Enlightenment.

Leipzig is where Zedler's *Complete Universal Lexicon* (1731–54) was published, a 64-volume compendium of "all the sciences and arts", which turned the idea that scholarship consists simply in knowing what is written down in books into a media-historical anachronism. Leipzig is where the German translation of Pierre Bayle's *Dictionnaire historique et critique* (Rotterdam 1695/97) came out, a unique lexicon which, rather than collect established facts, subjected traditional book-learning to a critical review in countless, endless footnotes. None other than the renowned literary reformer Johann Christoph Gottsched was responsible for this translation, although he did feel compelled to soften Bayle's criticism of scholarly tradition by providing the book "with annotations, especially for offensive passages".

At Leipzig University, everyday life was very different. The scholars Lessing encountered were traditional: Their means of knowledge – their proficiency in classical languages, mastery of rhetorical techniques, knowing all about things written in books – dominated over the purpose of knowledge. Lessing found this practice of academic scholarship problematic, which explains the paradox of the most learned among the 18th-century German poets rejecting his own erudition with such vehemence: "I am not learned – I have never intended to be learned – I would not want to be learned, even if a dream would make this possible" (B 10, 240), as he put it in an often-quoted note from his unpublished writings.

At St Afra, Lessing had found a mentor in Klimm, who made fun of his colleagues' pedantry and showed him a way out of the narrowness of traditional book-learning. In Leipzig, it was the mathematician Abraham Gottlieb Kästner who made a profound impression on him. Lessing attended his colloquium on philosophical disputation, and Kästner proffered advice and assistance during his work on the comedy *The Young Scholar* (*Der junge Gelehrte*). It was performed with great success on Caroline Neuber's stage in January 1748 – just before Lessing's father tricked his prodigal son, who had already seemed lost, into returning home.

The Young Scholar

Lessing gave his parents an account of the reasons that drew him to the theatre. The letters he writes from Berlin in the first half of 1749 are impressive in the candour with which he judges himself and the determination with which he stands up for himself. In the letter to his mother, he portrays himself as a young scholar who had tried to find "his happiness in books", but whose eyes were opened in Leipzig:

> Shall I say fortunately for me, or unfortunately? The future will show. I came to realise that, while books might well make me learned, they would never make me a human being. I ventured out of my chamber to mingle with my peers. Good God! what a disparity was brought home to me, between me and the others. A boorish diffidence, uncouth and undeveloped physique, total ignorance of manners and social life, and a truculent expression which others interpreted as contemptuous: those were the good

qualities that remained after honest self-judgement. I felt a shame I had never felt before. And the effect of it was a firm resolution to improve myself in this regard, whatever the cost. (Jan 20, 1749; B 11/1, 15)

The figure of Faust in his study – "I've studied now, alas!" – is, as it were, already prefigured here: The young scholar, who knows nothing but the world of books, is forced to realise how awkwardly and clumsily he moves among actual people – a nuisance to himself and others, who interpret his uncouthness as contempt. Lessing learns "how to dance, to fence, to vault", and goes on to set himself the task of "also learning how to live" (B 11/1, 15–16). This he learns in social intercourse and with the help of the mirror the dramatic stage holds up to him: "I got to know myself, and ever since, I have certainly ridiculed and mocked no one more than myself" (B 11/1, 16).

Ridicule and self-mockery – the comedy which caused a stir in Leipzig and made Lessing the talk of the town in Kamenz may be regarded as following this motto. It reveals something of the bitterness not unfamiliar to Lessing, which is personified throughout his literary oeuvre in the character of the misanthrope. Traces of this misanthropy are also evident in the preface to the third volume of his *Writings* (*Schrifften*) from 1754, in which Lessing's comedy is first published. In it, he says:

I must confess, regardless of the danger of being laughed at, that among all the works of wit, comedy is the first I ventured on. Already during the years when I only knew people from books – enviable who never gets to know them more closely! –, I was occupied by the imitations of fools whose existence meant nothing to me. Theophrastus, Plautus and Terence were my world, which I studied at leisure in the narrow confines of a monastic school. – How I wish I could have these years back; the only ones during which I have had a happy life. (B 3, 154)

"Vermin" is what he calls the "fools" amongst whom he has grown up and against whom he now aims his "satirical weapons" in *The Young Scholar* (B 3, 156). Not excluding himself: In his first comedy, the experience of his socialisation into literary culture serves as a substrate for laughter and mockery, not least about himself.

Like many a conventional comedy, *The Young Scholar* is about the comic complications that a young couple, Valer and Juliane, have to brave before they can finally get together. And just like in every romantic comedy, they have to assert themselves against parents and rivals. However, the focus of Lessing's play is peculiarly shifted: It is on the comic figure of the young scholar Damis, who only becomes the lovers' antagonist because his father, the merchant Chrysander, wants to marry him to his ward Juliane in order to get his hands on her fortune, which a lawsuit is promising her, and because the young scholar gets it into his head to suffer an exemplary scholar's fate and make himself deliberately unhappy by way of marriage to "a perfect devil of a wife" (I/6; B 1, 159).

The dramatic plot develops from the colliding interests of the characters involved. The merchant is all out for the money, the young scholar for glory and fame; the naïve foster daughter, out of obedience and loyalty to her foster father, is prepared to sacrifice her own happiness; Valer, who loves her, is collaborating with the maid Lisette on a letter intrigue to make the girl appear penniless and therefore unattractive as a bride. While the father is waiting for news about the lawsuit he intends to bring on behalf of his ward, to see whether it promises success, the son is waiting for news from Berlin: He has participated in a competition at the Prussian Academy of Sciences and has submitted a treatise on the Monadology, which, he hopes, is to bring him honour and recognition.

Damis mimics the lifestyle of a scholar: He lives according to the examples he reads about (cf. I/6; B 1, 156), making a show of being pensive, absent-minded and removed from the ordinary hustle and bustle (cf. III/7; B 1, 213), flaunting his Latinity and his comprehensive erudition, being rude when interacting with others, and showing nothing but contempt for the uneducated – who, in their turn, see nothing in him but a scholarly fool.

The play bears all the hallmarks of a satirical comedy, and yet it already hints at the path Lessing will take in his dramas. Damis does not merely embody a certain social defect which, being part of the game, does not warrant an explanation; his uncouth behaviour and foolishness do have a reason: Damis is a *young* scholar. His friend Valer, who has "laid his books aside", having "had the notion put into his head that one must give oneself the last finish by social intercourse and knowledge of the world" (II/12; B 1, 193), predicts that, "when you have more sense, you will repent of your follies":

> With your years, your body cannot yet be full-grown, and you think, nevertheless, that your mind has already attained its highest possible perfection? I should consider him my enemy who would deny me the privilege of increasing my intelligence day by day. (III/7; B 1, 214)

This is the central motif of the play in a nutshell. The Young Scholar's soul has not yet "attained its highest possible perfection", as the 1767 version will put it (B 1, 1074). Therefore, as Valer points out, it "takes some cruelty to make fun of such a pitiful fool" (III/7; B 1, 215). Valer defends the man against his own uncouthness, thus proving himself a true friend to the eponymous hero – just like another well-meaning friend in Berlin, who has held back Damis' treatise in order to protect him from making a fool of himself with it.

Damis and Valer are the first instance of a constellation that will turn up again as a blueprint for Lessing's comedies: the friendship between the misanthrope Alceste and the philanthropist Philinte from Molière's *Misanthrope*. Molière's comedy ends with Alceste's exile from society; Lessing's misanthrope Damis flees into the world with a curse: "Oh, ye stupid Germans! [...] I will leave my thankless fatherland" (III/15; B 1, 232) – which gives him the chance to acquire the worldliness that is expressed in Lessing's own wish of "learning how to live".

"Years know more than books," says an English proverb that Lessing once noted down (B 10, 658). It could also be a preface to the play about the Young Scholar, which bids farewell to a form of book-learning that has become obsolete in the age of periodicals and encyclopaedias, and which serves Lessing as a medium for reflecting on his personal liberation.

Prudent Doubt

In the great letter of justification Lessing sends to his father in late May 1749, he strikes religio-philosophical tones. To his mother, he had described the acknowledgement of his own shortcomings as an experience of existential crisis that would eventually turn out for the better or worse; in his letter to the learned theologian, he now defends his chosen way of life as the path of 'prudent doubt':

> Time will show whether I have respect for my parents, firmness in faith, and morals guiding my way of life. Time will show whether he is a better Christian who memorises and regurgitates the principles of Christian doctrine, who goes to church and participates in all the customs because they are the conventional thing to do; or he who has had prudent doubts (*klüglich gezweifelt*) and who, by the path of investigation, has arrived at conviction, or at least strives to do so. The Christian religion is not something one should simply accept from one's parents in good

faith. [...] As long as I do not see that one of the foremost commandments of Christianity, to *love thy enemy*, is better observed, I shall doubt whether those really are Christians who claim to be. (May 30, 1749; B 11/1, 26)

The letters to his parents formulate a resolution that Lessing will also rephrase shortly afterwards as a good wish for his younger brother Theophilus: that he may follow his "inner calling" and live the way he will eventually "wish that he had lived" (Feb 8, 1751; B 11/1, 34). Lessing scholarship has expressed doubts about Lessing having really pursued such an idea, arguing that his career paths are too erratic, his intellectual interests too diverse and disparate, and his life choices too much left to chance (cf. FV, 15). The concept of a continuous personal development, in the way that the 'Goethe generation' will pursue it, does not seem to figure in Lessing's biography (cf. HBN, 3–4) – but appearances are deceptive: The questions and issues that were to occupy him throughout his life, and to shape not only his way of thinking, are already clearly expressed in his letters to his parents. The question about the truth of religious tradition and a way of life accordant with this truth was to become the leitmotif of Lessing's life.

Lessing is one of the founders of the modern religion of intellectuals, poets and philosophers, who have detached themselves from the dogmas and rituals of an institutionalised church, claiming for themselves the right to interpret human life in an authentic and wholesome way. In the context of the controversy surrounding Lessing's edition of the biblical-critical fragments of the Hebraist Hermann Samuel Reimarus, Lessing will reject the idea of having to commit to a specific dogma as an intellectual imposition, asserting himself against his rival Goeze, head pastor of Hamburg, both confidently and polemically as a "lover of theology":

> I am a lover of theology and not a theologian. I am not committed to any one dogma. Nothing obliges me to speak any language other than my own. I pity all honest men who are not so fortunate as to be able to say this about themselves. But such honest men should not try to tie the same noose around the horns of other honest men with which *they* are tied to the manger. If they do, my pity will cease; and I can do nothing but despise them. (B 9, 57–58)

The insistence on his own language is Lessing's answer to the thoughtlessness with which "nominal Christians" (B 9, 196) keep regurgitating the "statutes and formulas" of their religion. This corresponds to the courage to use reason publicly in religious matters, which Kant will declare as the "motto of Enlightenment" (IK 2, 53–54).

Lessing means it. It is one of his early certainties that the truth of religion not only proves its worth in lived practice, but that "firmness in faith" can only be considered true religious conviction if it prompts the right 'moral conduct'. "What good is it to believe rightly if you live wrongly?" (B 1, 941), he asks in the fragment *Thoughts on the Moravian Brethren* (*Gedanken über die Herrnhuter*, 1750). The question culminates in the insight that we are "angels, judging by our knowledge", but "devils, judging by our life" (B 1, 942). The pastor's son, who has fallen among actors and playwrights, claims for himself nothing more nor less than the right and duty to decide on his religion himself, and to take the path of 'prudent doubt', which Descartes had characterised in his *Meditationes de prima philosophia* (1641) as the willingness to methodically question all certainties.

A didactic poem entitled *On Religion* (*Die Religion*), which was probably written around the same time as the letter to his father, spells this out. The title indicates that Lessing is not talking about the "one and only true religion" (i.e., Christianity), but that it is "religion as such" (B 2, 264) he has in view. The unfinished poem imitates a soliloquy "on a lonely day of discontent" (B 2, 264). It methodically traverses the "labyrinths of self-knowledge", following the idea that self-knowledge has "always been the nearest", as well as the "safest", path to religion (B 2, 264).

The first (and only) canto is dedicated to the doubts "that can be raised against everything divine from seeing the inner and outer misery of mankind" (B 2, 264). The conclusion is sobering: We are created neither for truth nor for virtue. Human knowledge is finite, our ability to tell the future is limited; we do know what is good but are unable to act accordingly because, barely awakened to consciousness, we are guided by egocentric impulses.

Lessing translates the question about the truth of religion into a question about the right way of life, the success or failure of which is accessible to individual, subjective experience. Religion responds to an existential need for orientation by interpreting the individual human life from an absolute point of view, but it does not have the status of knowledge, neither in a historical nor in a metaphysical sense. Taking the Bible literally and believing to hear God in its wording (cf. B 2, 268), is naïve and self-deceived.

The young poet makes himself the spokesman of radical religious criticism, but he does so in the service of the religion's self-enlightenment. In what way the "misery depicted [in the first canto] must itself become the guide to religion" (B 2, 265), as announced in the introductory note, is left open by the poem – though it does already hint at the direction in which the solution is to be sought.

Lessing will find it in his treatise on *The Education of the Human Race* (*Die Erziehung des Menschengeschlechts*): It is founded on the acknowledgement that the human heart is "black" and that it would be "blasphemy" to see the divinity of creation realised in it (B 2, 276). The "selfishness of the human heart" (§ 80; B 10, 95) is the anthropological legacy that stands in the way of its own happiness; it is therefore in need of "purification" (B 2, 45) in order to be able to "love virtue for its own sake" (§ 80; B 10, 95). This is the conclusion Lessing will draw at the end of his life.

Both here, in this early didactic poem, and there, in the *Education* treatise, the question at stake is the question of theodicy, i.e. the vindication of God in light of the evident evils in the world, a term coined by Leibniz. The thorn in the young scholar's flesh is not physical but moral evil: the realisation of being a sinner while despising sin (cf. B 2, 276): "Such forceful desire, and yet such utter impotence, / Can a God imbue one soul with both at the same time?" (B 2, 270). This bitter question, however, does not mark the end of his path of reflection but its turning point. The young poet restrains himself, realising that his curious gaze into the abyss of the soul only increases the evil he seeks to control: "I am turning too black for me to regard myself any longer, / And curiosity gives way to melancholy horror" (B 2, 275). Methodical doubt must not lose its way in the labyrinth of self-knowledge if it is to point the way to religion. In a review written in 1753, Lessing delineates this problem very clearly:

> Man's noblest occupation is man. However, one can deal with this subject in a twofold way: Either one considers man individually, or generally. In the first case, the statement that it is the noblest occupation can hardly be made. Knowing man individually, what do we know? Fools and

villains. And what use is this knowledge? Either to strengthen us in folly and villainy, or to make us melancholy about the worthlessness of our fellow creatures. In the case of the consideration of man in general, it is quite different. Regarded in general, he reveals greatness and his divine origin. (B 2, 474–75)

The "consideration of man in general" places individual human life in the horizon of the species, and the species within an absolute horizon. In his *Theodicy*, Leibniz had attempted to consider creation from such a standpoint; Lessing follows him in this: Humans are "moral beings", capable of perceiving perfections and acting in accordance with them. This is a conviction we already find formulated in the early fragment *The Christianity of Reason* (*Das Christentum der Vernunft*, 1752/53), from which Lessing derives the maxim individual human life has to follow if it wants to fulfil its destiny. It reads: "*Act in accordance with your individual perfections*" (B 2, 407) – become the best version of yourself.

The person himself is regarded as a process, with adolescence being a necessary phase of this process. Education takes time. Even as a twenty-year-old, Lessing already knows this: "the future will show", "time will show". This conviction gives him the confidence to entrust himself to this process.

Theology of Laughter

Methodically doubting all certainties, questioning the truth of religion, searching for his own vocation, and turning to the theatre – all that is part of Lessing's resolution to learn how to live and act in accordance with his own perfections.

One of these perfections is an unbounded curiosity that will not be limited to any particular science. In a preface to one of his unfinished projects, he describes himself as a "learned vagabond" who, "unable to give a fixed direction to his intellect", roams "through all fields of scholarship" without settling down permanently in any one of them. And in doing so, he comes across "treasures" which "a happy accident along the way, more often the byway than the highway, allows him to find" (B 5/1, 449). To his father, he admits openly that he has "not the slightest desire" to become "the slave of an office" (Apr 3, 1760; B 11/1, 346); the fact that "being professorial" is not

Lessing's cup of tea is equally obvious to his brother Karl (Mar 18, 1775; B 11/2, 706).

Financial worries soon manifest themselves as a downside of this refusal to pursue an academic career. In Leipzig, Lessing stands surety for the Neuber troupe and is left with their debts when some actors make off; in Wittenberg, where he obtains his master's degree in 1752 with a thesis on the Spanish physician Juan Huarte (1529–88), he has to use his scholarships to clear his debts.

In Berlin, the world of modern periodicals becomes his intellectual and professional habitat. Lessing writes reviews, mainly for the *Privileged Berlin Newspaper* (*Berlinische Privilegierte Zeitung*), whose editorial office had been taken over by his cousin Mylius, and quickly establishes himself as a critic. "A new critic has arisen here," the philosopher Johann Georg Sulzer reports to Zurich in 1751, writing to his Swiss mentor, Johann Jakob Bodmer (RD, 42). Lessing is intent on making a name for himself. In retrospect, his Berlin years will appear to him as a time "in which curiosity and ambition had every power over me" (May 7, 1780; B 12, 326).

In October 1749, he and Mylius jointly launched their *Contributions to the History and Improvement of the Theatre* (*Beyträge zur Historie und Aufnahme des Theaters*), an attempt to survey the entire spectrum of European dramatic literature and make it accessible to the public via translations. The *Contributions* are not only the first German theatrical periodical, but also Lessing's first project in which he addresses the topic of "the right and wrong ways of imitation" (B 1, 728). He does this programmatically in a treatise on the Roman comic playwright Plautus, whose *Captivi* are translated and praised by Lessing as "the most beautiful play" that "has ever been seen on a stage" (B 1, 766). This treatise gives Lessing the opportunity to draft a moral philosophy of laughter, which understands laughter as the true alternative to penitent contrition and comedy as the true alternative to the pulpit:

> Either we consider vice as something that ill behoves us, that demeans us, that lures us into countless perverse transgressions; or we consider it as something that is against our duty, that arouses the wrath of God and thus must necessarily make us unhappy. In the first case, we must laugh about it; in the second, we will grieve about it. The best opportunity for the former is provided by a comedy; for the latter by the Holy Scriptures. He who only ever weeps over his vices and never laughs at them, does not, in fact, give me a very good impression of his disgust against them. Possibly, he will only be weeping over them out of fear that he might fare badly, that he might not be able to escape punishment. But he who laughs at vice despises it at the same time, proving that he is vividly convinced that God has not commanded us to avoid vice out of some despotic will, but that our own welfare, our own honour commands us to flee it. (B 1, 747–48)

Lessing's poetics of comedy is rooted in his moral and theological criticism. He dismisses the image of the divine despot whose punishment is the object of traditional fear of God and whose reward is the hope of traditional piety, and establishes a culture of self-care and cheerful unconcern with all human shortcomings.

In Plautus' comedy about the *captivi* (prisoners of war), he finds the very pattern that "comes closest to the intention of comedy" (B 1, 878), but that has not been followed since: It succeeds in making "virtue lovable" (B 1, 877) and "ennobling the play with sublime sentiments" (B 1, 878), without enfeebling it "by the all too tender emotion of love". Its hero is Tyndarus, a prisoner of war, who is ready to sacrifice himself for the sake of his co-captive master and friend by offering himself as a hostage, while the latter (supposedly as his servant) is sent off to arrange an exchange of prisoners.

In the eyes of his contemporaries like Christian Fürchtegott Gellert, whose *Treatise on the Sentimental Comedy* (*Abhandlung für das rührende Lustspiel*) Lessing translates from Latin and comments on in his *Theatrical Library* (*Theatralische Bibliothek*, 1754), love stories are "the main source [...] from which comedy draws its sentimental character" (CFG 5, 153); for Lessing, they are the surest means of ruining the actual purpose of the comedy. Plautus' *Captivi* becomes his model: The traditional goal of the comic plot, the lovers' reunion, is replaced with the reunion of fathers and sons who have been separated by war. Lessing takes this as an opportunity to declare the entire European comedy tradition as downright erroneous:

> What praise, now, does Plautus not deserve for not having enfeebled the purified morality, which prevails throughout the whole play, by the all too tender emotion of love! How many successors has he had in this? None. But how great would the benefit be if they had followed him? Infinite. If they had, the stage would have become the school of morality in the most literal sense. (B 1, 878)

The idea of the stage as a "school of morality" is, in fact, a conventional one; what is not conventional, however, is the explanation with which Lessing underpins this idea: The play about the *captivi* combines the comic with the sentimental and renounces the virtue-vice based moralism that underlies both the traditional and the sentimental comedy. The play is sentimental in that Tyndarus is willing to risk his life for a friend: "Whoever knows and has experienced virtue and the divine pleasure virtue pours over the soul, certainly would not want to be anyone but

Tyndarus" (B 1, 877). And it is comic in that, from this, Plautus develops scenes in which Tyndarus has to twist and turn in the most absurd ways so as not to be unmasked in his game of disguise.

After the success of *The Young Scholar*, Lessing had envisioned himself as 'a German Molière' (Apr 28, 1749; B 11/1, 24). He had to abandon this idea because it was not reconcilable with his moral philosophical convictions. Molière is the master of a type of comedy aimed at the aggressive ridicule of a social outsider. Its comic potential springs from a form of representation that is necessarily blind to the mental processes inside the comic figure – just as the comic figure must necessarily have no sense of their own shortcomings. Lessing could not adopt this elementary comic strategy; his aim was to establish drama as a medium of self-knowledge, insofar as it allows the viewer to recognise himself in the *dramatis personae* and their incongruous behaviours.

The Virtuous Freethinker

After practising the art of ridicule and self-mockery in *The Young Scholar*, Lessing turns to the conflicts with his parents and his experiences in "freethinking Berlin" (KGL 1, 81). He makes them the subject of a comedy that follows the tradition of the *Captivi* in demoting the love story to a side issue while introducing a serious element, namely the ideological conflict between rivalling groups. In the *Contributions* he had emphasised that "one can indeed dramatise the most serious philosophical truths, even religious disputes" (B 1, 883). His comedy about the virtuous freethinker (*Der Freigeist*) puts this contention to the test.

For his pious contemporaries, the concept of a freethinker was associated with the image of an atheist who leads a dissolute life, not having to fear punishment for his sins after death. Morality as a matter of duty becomes obsolete if "there is no just God, no virtue, no immortal soul, and thus no eternal reward or punishment" (CFG 6,

45), Christian Fürchtegott Gellert argues in his *Moral Lectures* (*Moralische Vorlesungen*). He warns against a society of freethinkers, which would be a "society of swindlers, of ingrates, of perjurers, of robbers, of murderers, of incestuals, of atheists".

This prejudice has nothing to do with the self-image of those who admit to not feeling affiliated with any church. In his *Discourse of Free-Thinking* (1713), the manifesto of the movement, Anthony Collins, an educated landed gentleman, defended the right to be independent from authorities in matters of religion, arguing that religion itself is too important to leave the examination of its doctrines to others, especially if its representatives are discrediting themselves through dogmatic disputes and their way of life. The same is true about Adrast, Lessing's freethinker. He has been financially ruined by clergymen (cf. I/2; B 1, 368) and therefore has every reason to view the representatives of the church with suspicion. In the house of Lisidor, his fiancée Henriette's father, he meets Theophan, a young clergyman who is betrothed to Juliane. At first glance, the play revolves around amorous complications: Juliane, a quiet girl, "shows signs of sensual love for Adrast" (B 1, 351), while Theophan is more drawn to the lively Henriette – and vice versa. However, the resolution of these complications is not the main point of the comic plot. The play combines the old comic device of two couples falling in love with the other's partner, respectively, and the ideological conflict between the two young men: Lessing's actual interest lies in their bond of friendship.

The theme of friendship is set out in the first dialogue between the two opponents and, referring to Anthony Collins, is explicitly distinguished from the Christian commandment of neighbourly love. Friendship is exclusive: It springs from a "certainly not arbitrary agreement of minds", and "this innate accordance with one single other being", which "alone constitutes true friendship", cannot, according to Theophan, be the object of a law: "Where it exists, it need not be enjoined; and where it does not exist, it would be enjoined in vain" (I/1; B 1, 367). While Theophan hopes to gain Adrast's friendship, Adrast cannot see the young clergyman as anything but a pious hypocrite – a prejudice that has its roots in contemporary literature: In his *Instructions from a Father to his Son on Entering College* (*Lehren eines Vaters für seinen Sohn, den er auf die Akademie schickt*), Gellert warns against getting involved with a person "who has too little goodness of heart to be a friend of God" – he will be "both incapable and unworthy" of true friendship (CFG 5, 303). In his eyes, the "honest man without religion" is a contradiction in terms and, therefore, definitely "a suspicious friend" (CFG 6, 261–62).

This prejudice is what Lessing's play is centred around. Adrast is far from a blasphemer, Theophan is far from prejudiced towards or disdainful of the freethinker. The original scenario describes the freethinker as a man "without religion, but full of virtuous sentiments"; Theophan is characterised as "as virtuous and noble as he is pious" (B 1, 348).

The social prejudices about the freethinker are personified in the two servant figures – "the very images of their masters, from the ugly side: freethinking has turned one of them into a rogue, and piety has made the other a blockhead" (II/4; B 1, 387), as the quick-witted maid Lisette attests. The pious Martin parrots what is preached by the pastor, who considers the freethinker a "changeling, lustfully begotten of hell with the wisdom of this world" (II/5; B 1, 388); and the freethinking Johann considers the satisfaction of his lusts – "courting, drinking" (II/5; B 1,

390) – his duty and suggests to his master that he dishonour the bill of exchange he has signed.

The caricature of a freethinker, as described by Martin and embodied by Johann, serves Lessing not only as a contrast to highlight Adrast's honesty (e.g., he indignantly rejects his servant's plan); the grotesque appearance of the servant figures also contributes significantly to the comic effect of the drama. This effect has free play in the intellectual and moral abysses that are revealed in the characters' speeches. It acquires a bitter taste in Theophan's cousin Araspe, whose entrance drastically expands the spectrum of comic nuances. This sentimental churchgoer has come to celebrate his relative's wedding and ruin the freethinker Adrast by presenting his bills for payment – in the pious conviction of acting in the interest of the salvation of Adrast's soul: "Difficulties may perhaps make him reflect more seriously" (III/1; B 1, 395).

Araspe is one of the numerous characters in Lessing's works who commit their evil deeds with the best of religious intentions. Araspe feels personally offended by the freethinker's refusal to profess Christianity – which will also be Goeze's reaction in the course of the Fragments Controversy, when he accuses his opponents of denying the gospel with malicious intent. Of course, the character is not aware of his wickedness; he does what he does in all good faith. But it is Theophan who proves to be the truly righteous man, for not only does he take care of Araspe's promissory notes, but he also stands surety for the freethinker with a bill broker (cf. IV/9; B 1, 426) who doubts his creditworthiness.

The comic effect of the drama grows from the dead seriousness of the ideological conflict that underlies the plot. After the fraud committed by his clergymen in-laws, which Adrast went through in the backstory, and now confronted with another clergyman in Lisidor's house, who is to marry his beloved Juliane, Adrast turns misanthropic and resentful: "What cruel destiny pursues me everywhere?" (I/2; B 1, 369). This lamentation escalates into an accusation against "deaf chance", "blind fate", "worthless life" (I/5; B 1, 376); it darkens his view of creation as a whole. "Grumbling against Providence" is how Lessing will describe this attitude in *Minna*, and already in *The Freethinker* he takes up this 'grumbling' as a motif on which he builds his tragicomic drama of misrecognition.

His *Freethinker*, too, aims at combining humour and sentiment and coming as close as possible to "human life" by depicting "both decency and incongruity" (B 3, 279). The true comedy, according to Lessing's conviction, which he develops from his study of Gellert's concept of a "sentimental comedy", imitates social reality, where "the wise and the fools [...] are mingled together" (B 3, 279). This imitation is successful if it "never forces our feelings to take a leap" (B 3, 278) but instead leads them slowly along: "Being suddenly torn from one extreme to the other is quite different from moving gradually from one extreme to the other" (B 3, 278). Therefore, Lessing's comedies (no different from his tragedies) need a virtuous protagonist who becomes entangled in a process of delusion in a way that is only too understandable.

Humour and sentiment arise from the contrast between Theophan's readiness to stand up for the honourable freethinker and Adrast's increasingly firm conviction that it is this righteous man who is behind all his misfortunes, while putting on a "mask of sanctity" and "mask of generosity" (III/7; B 1, 406). This escalation of mistrust starts out from Adrast's resolution, nourished by bitter experience, to "hate" Theophan "and all [his] order" (I/2, 368–69), grows into a conviction of being "able to hate [Theophan] from the bottom of my heart" (III/6; B 1, 405), should he cause his ruin, and culminates in the exclamation: "Hate him I will, even if he should save my life" (V/2; B 1, 430).

In the end, Adrast's eyes will be opened to himself: "Oh! if I am always in the wrong in the same degree as I have been in my conduct to you, Theophan, what a man, or rather, what a wretch I must be" (V/8; B 1, 444). And Theophan, in his turn, will recognise that where love is concerned, "the heart cannot be reasoned into anything", but "maintains its independence of the understanding" (V/3; B 1, 435). Not only the engagement of the pious man to the lively woman, and the engagement of the lively man to the pious woman (cf. V/7; B 1, 443), but also the friendship between the theologian and the freethinker thus follows the law of nature, which counteracts all ideological conflicts by establishing individual relationships between the conflicting parties. Lessing also attributes to nature the fact that the freethinker encounters religion with nothing but contempt – he is young, and in young years it is only too natural to become a freethinker "even contrary to inclination": "But then he is only so until the understanding has attained a certain state of maturity, and the boiling blood has cooled down" (III/1; B 1, 395).

The Compassionate Jew

The victory of friendly relationships over collective conflicts is also at the heart of another one of those comedies in which Lessing addresses the inevitable consequences of social group formation. After the atheist's conflict with the Christians, it is now the Christians' conflict with those of a different faith that is up for discussion. Again, the play is not centred around questions of Christian dogmatics, but around the core of the Christian doctrine: right action.

The plot construction of the one-act play is based on a text that could hardly be any more prominent: the biblical parable of the Good Samaritan. Jesus tells it in response to the question about correct conduct with which a lawyer had put him to the test: "Teacher, what shall I do to inherit eternal life?" (Luke 10:25). The answer is clear: It lies in the love of God and neighbour, as commanded by the Scriptures. What is under dispute, however, is who this neighbour is – the parable concretises this. It is about a man who was attacked by robbers and left half dead alongside the road. A priest who comes along sees him and passes by, unmoved; likewise a Levite; finally, "a certain Samaritan, as he journeyed", shows compassion, brings the man to an inn and pays for the costs of his recovery. "So which of these three," is Jesus' somewhat cumbersome question in return, "was neighbour to him who fell among the thieves?" (Luke 10:36). The lawyer has to give in and to acknowledge the Samaritan, though he is despised by the orthodox Jews, as the true benefactor.

The biblical parable challenges the rescued man and with him the orthodox Jews to recognise the true Jew in the representative of a disdained religious minority. While the Bible itself omits this after-effect, Lessing's drama displays it. A baron has been attacked by two men; a traveller has stood up to them to save him. The plot reveals the background of the happily averted crime: The Baron's bailiff and warden are identified as the real malefactors (they had used beards to disguise themselves as Jews), whereas the real benefactor turns out to be a Jew who has not only chased away the alleged Jews but also exposes them as criminals in the course of the play, thus saving the baron's life a second time. The typical happy ending of a comedy, however, does not materialise: The Baron, who wants to give his daughter's hand to his rescuer, sees his wish thwarted. Both the Christian and the Jewish religion prohibit exogamy, making a marriage impossible.

The lively young woman, who has taken a liking to her father's rescuer, cannot comprehend this unexpected turn of events: "Oh, what difference does that make?" (22; B 1, 486). The Baron and his rescuer, who had been fascinated by everything about the girl being "still just the way nature created it" (6; B 1, 458), are upset. Thus, the conventional comedy finale is replaced by the bond of friendship between the Christian and the Jew, who recognise their respective "thoughts and opinions" (6; B 1, 458) in each other. Initially, the rescuer had objected to the idea that a most natural act of assistance – "The common love of mankind obliged me to it" (2; B 1, 451) – should establish a friendship that would demand "only voluntary movements of the soul" (6; B 1, 419), but he is now moved by the magnanimity of the Christian Baron, who tries to offer him refuge from his supposed persecutors, and reveals himself as a Jew. This culminates in mutual recognition, expressed in a corresponding sigh: "Oh, how worthy of respect would all Jews be if they were all like you!" – "And how delightful the Christians, if they all had your character!" (22; B 1, 487–88). This appreciation of the Jew by the Christian and of the Christian by the Jew preludes the scene in *Nathan*, where the friar Bonafides recognises the true Christian in Nathan, and the Jew Nathan – himself a good Samaritan – recognises the true Jew in the Christian: "O Nathan, Nathan! You're a Christian soul! / By God, a better Christian never lived!" – "And well for us! For what makes me for you / A Christian, makes yourself for me a Jew!" (IV/7; B 9, 597).

The parable of the Good Samaritan is so eminent a text for Lessing because it allows him to assert the primacy of orthopraxy over orthodoxy as the true core of the Christian doctrine, and because he finds in it the idea of the *opus supererogatum*, the "work of supererogation" (B 10, 32), which will be at the centre of the social-philosophical dialogues between Ernst and Falk about true Freemasonry.

A work of supererogation is one that cannot be commanded by any community because it transcends the boundaries of the community. Even in traditional Judaism, the commandment of neighbourly love is limited to assisting a fellow believer in need; the biblical parable already polemicises against this interpretation, and it is this polemical potential that inspires Lessing's comedy, where the noble Jew proves to be neighbour to the Christian because his situation commands it. Already in the New Testament, it is explicitly stated that the traveller "had compassion" for the injured man, thus placing the basic emotion of compassion at the centre of neighbourly love. Not only Lessing but also the New Testament combines the satirical polemic with a moment of sentiment, which is fundamental to Lessing's theology of laughter and which his *The Jews* (*Die Juden*) translates into a sequence of comic misrecognition and relieving anagnorisis, i.e. revelation. It is not the representatives of two religions that meet in the Baron and the traveller, but two individuals who do not identify themselves as members of their group – and who, in this, recognise each other as "sympathising spirits" (B 10, 57). When, after the revelation of his master's identity, the traveller's servant is incredulous about there being "Jews" who "are not Jews" (B 1, 1163), he turns out to be a representative of that 'nominal Christianity' which Lessing portrays in the Christian mob as well as in the patriarch in *Nathan*. The Baron of his one-act play, on the other hand, is one of those Christians who are not Christians (any more), confirming to his friend as well as to the audience that he, too, is the exception to the rule.

There is an aftermath to Lessing's play that has significantly contributed to its impact on public awareness. In 1754, a review is published in the *Göttingen Announcements of Scholarly Matters* (*Göttingische Anzeigen von gelehrten Sachen*) by the prominent Göttingen theologian Johann David Michaelis, who praises Lessing's drama but critically objects that it is "too improbable, after all" that "such a noble mind should have been able to develop more or less on its own, in the midst of a people with such principles, lifestyle and education, and a people whom the negative attitude of the Christians must definitely have filled with hostility or at least indifference towards the Christians" (B 1, 490).

To this objection, Lessing responds with an argument that not only undermines the Christian prejudice but also questions the moral self-assurance of Christianity. First, he distinguishes between the *poetological* and the *lifeworldly* dimension of Michaelis' criticism. The poetological aspect is easily refuted: The play presents a rich, urbane, and well-read Jew – should such a Jew not be "honest and magnanimous" (B 1, 492), as well? With that, the lifeworldly core of the criticism becomes all the more apparent: Those who doubt that there can be honest and magnanimous Jews do not only degrade them to the status of "savage human beings", but place them "far below humanity" (B 1, 491). This prejudice is the actual scandal taken up by Lessing's play; and this prejudice discredits itself: By denying humanity to the Jews, it exposes the arrogance – "nothing but pride! mere pride!" (I/2; B 9, 494), as Nathan says – and the unkindness of those who harbour it. This, in fact, was what the play aimed to show: "Even if my traveller were a Christian, his character would still be very rare, and if the rare alone makes for the improbable, it would be very improbable" (B 1, 492).

Berlin: Friends and *Writings*

In his response to Michaelis, Lessing contrasts the urban milieu of Berlin with the limited horizon of Göttingen. In Berlin, he had the opportunity to "get to know the Jews more closely", rather than identifying them with "the slovenly rabble" that "wanders around the fairgrounds" (B 1, 492). Berlin is a metropolis of immigrants. Lessing roams the coffee houses and clubs, where he meets representatives of a modern Judaism, who – much to the rabbis' chagrin – were fascinated by the journalistic and social culture of the city. Among them were the Jewish doctor Aaron Salomon Gumpertz and a young man who had come to Berlin penniless at the age of 14 and who, after years of existential uncertainty, had found shelter in the house of a Jewish silk manufacturer: Moses Mendelssohn.

A letter from Mendelssohn to Gumpertz, in which he defends himself easily against the degrading insinuation that Jews are not capable of moral education, is published by Lessing together with his reply. Like Lessing, Gumpertz frequented the "Scholars' Coffee House" ("Gelehrtes Kaffeehaus") and was a member of the "Monday Club" founded in 1752, a forum for sociable intellectual exchange in close contact with the scholarly periodicals of Berlin and their feuilletons. It was probably Gumpertz who had introduced Lessing and Mendelssohn to each other in 1753.

Mendelssohn, though highly gifted, was an autodidact. As the son of a Dessau schoolmaster and Torah scribe, he could have taken the path towards the rabbinical elite; against his father's will, he decides to seek his fortune in Berlin and educate himself as a philosopher without any institutional support. At the end of 1754, Lessing meets Friedrich Nicolai, another autodidact. Nicolai had completed a bookseller's apprenticeship and, quite uncharacteristically for someone of his status, had dabbled in old and new languages and literature. His *Letters on the Current State of the Fine Arts in Germany* (*Briefe über den itzigen Zustand der schönen Wissenschaften in Deutschland*, 1755), which he had written due to a lack of conversation partners, attracted the attention of the scholarly world; the advance sheets aroused Lessing's interest in getting to know the author personally.

The runaway pastor's son, the homeless Jew, the learned bookseller – they all have escaped the social and intellectual ghettoes of their origins to find in each other the perfect conversation partners. In a letter to Michaelis, Lessing had described himself as a socially displaced intellectual who lived in Berlin solely because he "cannot live in any other big city" (Oct 16, 1754; B 11/1, 59). In retrospect, Nicolai will characterise the situation of the three friends and their exchange of ideas in a very similar way:

> These three deeply attached friends, who met at least two or three times a week, were alike in that they had no status,

no intentions, no connections, no prospects for promotion in the scholarly world, nor did they seek any; and even in the bourgeois world, they were without any connection or significance, nor did they desire any. Moses and Nicolai were young merchants, both still without households of their own. Lessing, indeed, had studied at universities, but not in the usual way, nor for any of the usual purposes, and was pursuing no intention in Berlin other than that of satisfying his thirst for knowledge. Their studies and their conversations had no purpose other than the expansion of their knowledge and the sharpening of their judgement. In consequence, they all hardly cared for any authority or other considerations, and prejudice did not count at all. (FN, 15–16)

Nicolai's portrayal depicts the cultural biotope in which Lessing's critical spirit unfolded, and it conveys a sense of the inevitability with which the three friends found each other: All three of them are equally passionate and lonely readers, and as such passionately dependent on conversation with other readers. Their debates were not only the place for an exchange of ideas about what they had read, but also the breeding ground for the texts in which they carried their "symphilosophising" (as the Romantics later called it) into the public sphere.

In a letter to the popular philosopher Christian Garve, Schiller identified "education through reading" (Oct 1, 1794; NA 27, 57) as the characteristic of his era, thereby joining Kant, who had answered the question about the nature of Enlightenment (1784) from a media theory point of view. Enlightenment is the cultural-revolutionary consequence of the "freedom to use reason *publicly* in all matters", and this public use is the use "that anyone as a *scholar* makes of reason before the entire *literate world*" (IK 2, 55). For an individual man to enlighten himself is difficult, if not impossible; but that a "public" should do so is "almost inevitable" (IK 2, 54). Enlightenment is the inevitable consequence of the media change that was dynamised in the 18th century by the periodic print media. Kant's "motto" of Enlightenment only draws the conclusion from the journalistic practice followed for decades, of making everything and anything the subject of daily public reflection, without being intimidated by social authorities. One of the most momentous consequences of this process was the distinction between the social and factual dimensions of communication, which is also discernible in Nicolai's portrayal: It depends on this distinction whether critical doubt is perceived as presumptuous disobedience or as factual dissent.

The journalist, critic and poet Gotthold Ephraim Lessing is one of the icons of this cultural-revolutionary process. In his scholarly skirmishes, Lessing will insist that dispute is always conducive to truth, as it nourishes "the spirit of investigation" and keeps "prejudice and authority in constant convulsion" (B 6, 717). In "religious matters" (IK 2, 66), particularly, he will make confident use of his licence to publish. In his debate with the Hamburg head pastor Goeze, which will darken the last years of his life, he emphasises that modern freethinkers – unlike the heretics of the past – do not cause any harm to Christianity because they do not wish to "form factions or sects", they only want "their whims to go to press" (B 9, 189). When Goeze wants to force him to conduct their dispute in the language of scholars (i.e., in Latin), Lessing is outraged, pointing out that the exclusion of the general reading public by the academic enclosure of the debate amounts to claiming sovereignty over the discourse and thus hindering the development of Christianity (B 9, 193–99).

In Berlin, Lessing begins to make a name for himself as an author. From 1753 to 1755, he publishes a six-volume collected edition of his own works, the *Writings*

(*Schrifften*). All the texts that have, so far, mostly been published anonymously or not at all – songs, fables, didactic and philosophical poems, literary-critical letters and scholarly studies, comedies and tragedies – are now to be seen as the work of one author – and they stir up emotions: "His writings are testimonies to his ignorance, his coarseness and narcissism. Yet, they are admired, praised, and read," the theologian Johann Gottfried Reichel rages in a letter to Gottsched: "This brazen, impudent young man has got to [...] be chastised" (B 2, 1197).

The third volume of the collection (1754) includes defences intended to do justice to scholars discredited in the *respublica litteraria*. These so-called *Vindications* (*Rettungen*) are not only outstanding examples of Lessing's vigorous critique of tradition, indebted to Pierre Bayle, but also of his supreme philological competence, which he had already demonstrated in a treatise on Christian Gottlieb Jöcher's *Concise Dictionary of Scholars* (*Compendieuses Gelehrten Lexicon*, 1751), in which he set himself the task of reducing "the countless errors therein" (B 2, 709) to the best of his ability.

The *Vindications* disprove the historical judgements about the anti-Lutheran Cochlaeus, about the astronomer Hieronymus Cardanus, whose autobiography Lessing appreciated very much, and about the anonymous author of the *Inepti religiosi*, a criticism of religion from the 17th century. The second volume (1753) had already contained – in the form of fictitious letters – a vindication of the poet Simon Lemnius, who had incurred the wrath of Luther and was persecuted by him. This is viewed by Lessing as a sign of a character flaw "welcome" to him, because it protects him from "deifying" the revered Luther: "The traces of humanity that I find in him are as precious to me as his most brilliant perfections" (B 2, 658).

The jewel in the crown of these scholarly defences, however, is the defence of Horace against the accusation of sexual excess. It was preceded by another vindication of the poet – the polemical dispute with Samuel Gotthold Lange, pastor in Laublingen, whose translations of Horace Lessing criticises almost furiously, compiling the corrections of Lange's "schoolboy errors" (B 3, 143) into a sensational *Vademecum* (1753): "A young local poet, Lessing, has wretchedly exposed poor Lange for his clumsy translation of Horace, and for his even clumsier defence of the same," reports the popular philosopher Johann Georg Sulzer to his Swiss mentor, the writer Johann Jakob Bodmer (RD, 66).

This time, Lessing does not aim at the vindication of the poetic work but the vindication of the poet – the accusation being that Horace had allegedly "*enjoyed his mistresses in a room full of mirrors, so as to find on all sides, wherever he looked, the voluptuous reflections of his happiness*" (B 3, 163). Lessing dismisses this with "Nothing else?" and praises Horace for not being one of those "coarse people to whom lust and gallantry are one and the same, and who are content with the satisfaction of a single sense in the dark" (B 3, 163) – only to go on to prove in a subtle philological argument that the source on which this questionable moral judgement is based, is questionable itself.

A "Domestic Tragedy": *Miss Sara Sampson*

In the sixth volume of his *Writings*, Lessing published a drama subtitled "bürgerliches Trauerspiel" (usually translated as 'a domestic tragedy'), which was to make literary history with its genre: *Miss Sara Sampson*. "A domestic tragedy! My God! Can you find a word about such a thing in Gottsched's *Critical Ars Poetica* (*Critische Dichtkunst*)?" (B 2, 389) With this comment, made in a self-review, Lessing polemically asserts himself against Gottsched, the great reformer of the German stage.

The conventional classicist tragedy, to which Gottsched dedicated himself, dramatises those historical-political subjects (Cato, Virginia, Julius Caesar, etc.) which are centred primarily around the struggle for political power; the domestic tragedy, on the other hand, dramatises conflicts between individual members of a "civil society", which in Lessing's case usually belong to the aristocracy. The term "bürgerlich", in many contexts equivalent to "bourgeois", is therefore not to be interpreted here as the opposite of "aristocratic" – it corresponds to the Latin "civilis" and refers to a person living in a community. Accordingly, the oldest bibliography of the "bürgerliches Trauerspiel", compiled by Christian Heinrich Schmid, states:

> It would, indeed, be more appropriate to call this genre of tragedies domestic (*häuslich*) tragedies or tragic family portraits, rather than bourgeois (*bürgerlich*) tragedies. [...] Citizens, in this context, are the opposite of the characters from heroic tragedies (rulers of great countries, war heroes of the past, knights of the Middle Ages, etc.), thus encompassing various ranks and classes of people. (CHS, 282–83)

The domestic tragedy is not primarily characterised by the rank of the *dramatis personae*, but by what the *conflicts* between the characters are about. The play focuses on the way the characters treat themselves and each other, and it shows how, in doing so, they put their happiness in life at stake. The de-heroisation of the *dramatis personae*, who thus become privatised and familiar individuals, serves to make the behaviour and fate of the characters comprehensible, giving the audience the opportunity to relate to them on a personal level. In his *Hamburg Dramaturgy* (*Hamburgische Dramaturgie*), Lessing will place particular emphasis on this point:

> If we have compassion for kings, we have it for them as people rather than as kings. If occasionally their rank makes their misfortunes more important, it does not therefore make them more interesting. Though entire populations may be enmeshed, our sympathy demands a single subject, and a nation is far too abstract a concept for our sentiments. (HD 14; B 6, 251)

Both Schmid, in speaking of "domestic tragedies" or "tragic family portraits", and Lessing, in quoting Marmontel that "the sacred names of friend, father, beloved, spouse, son, mother, of human beings in general: these have more pathos than anything else; they assert their rights always and forever" (HD 14; B 6, 251), highlight what Aristotle had already defined as the core of tragedy: In the 14th chapter of his *Poetics*, he emphasises that it is particularly tragic – seeing that it evokes fear and pity – "when the tragic incident occurs between those who are near or dear to one another – if, for example, a brother kills, or intends to kill, a brother, a son his father, a mother her son, a son his mother, or any other deed of the kind is done –, these are the situations to be looked for by the poet" (A, 19).

Lessing's first tragedy turned out to be an overwhelming stage success. The testimonies that have come down to us have significantly shaped our idea of the age of 'Sentimentalism'. Gleim refers to it as a tragedy "that, whenever it is performed, does not allow for anyone who has seen it to go home with dry eyes" (WA 1, 35). Frequently cited are the words of the poet Karl Wilhelm Ramler, who was present at the premiere of the play in Frankfurt an der Oder: "The audience listened for three and a half hours, sitting still like statues and weeping" (B 3, 1221). Friedrich Nicolai reports to his friend that at the Berlin performance, he cried "until the beginning of the fifth act" and afterwards was so moved that even his tears failed him (B 3, 667–68).

The tragedy is set in England and, at first glance, resembles Richardson's *Clarissa*, the epitome of the sentimental epistolary novel, sharing with it the motif of the harassed and seduced innocent. Clarissa, the eponymous heroine, has been lured from her parents' house by Lovelace, an erotic adventurer, and raped in an inn under the influence of narcotics. She languishes and dies the martyr's death of a Christian Lucretia.

Richardson is one of the inventors of the modern psychological novel (*Bewusstseinsroman*); and the same applies to Lessing in the field of drama. Although the ethos underlying Lessing's tragedy could hardly differ more strongly from Richardson's novel, it focuses equally on mental processes – the drama gains momentum from the inner conflicts and warring impulses of the characters entangled in this story.

Sara and Mellefont are on the run from Sara's father, Sir William, in whose house Mellefont has met Sara and whom they have betrayed with their elopement. Sir William has tracked down the fugitives in an inn, where they have been staying for nine weeks just before crossing over to France, and is trying to bring them back. The person who has informed him of the couple's whereabouts is Lady Marwood, Mellefont's "old love", who has come with their daughter Arabella to win back her lover.

Sir William is torn between his love for his daughter and his desire for revenge on her seducer; Sara has followed Mellefont out of love but is tormented by having deceived and left her old widowed father; Mellefont has found himself enchanted by Sara's innocence and has indeed renounced his libertine lifestyle for her sake, but he hesitates to commit himself to Sara once and for all, delaying the wedding under the pretext of inheritance matters; Marwood, on the other hand, is hurt and furious but has to force herself to display love and forgiveness in order to recapture her lover and bring her daughter's father back.

The dynamics of these psychological processes crystallise around the opposite moral poles of revenge and forgiveness (cf. GTN 3, 145–61). The revenge plot is established between the genders, the forgiveness plot between the generations; and these two alternative courses of action are also interpreted from a religio-philosophical point of view: Revenge and forgiveness correspond to different conceptions of God, which Lessing already addressed in his didactic poem on religion. On the one hand, there is the notion of a sadistic avenging demon whose "pleasure in being able to punish us is the first purpose of our existence" (I/7; B 3, 443–44), as Mellefont remarks critically. On the other hand, there is the idea of a being "whose preservation of miserable mankind is a perpetual forgiveness" and who finds in this forgiveness a "great insurpassable blessedness" (III/3; B 3, 476), as is assured by the faithful servant Waitwell, who brings Sara her father's letter of forgiveness.

The moral-psychological clou of this philosophy of religion lies in the insight that the experience of being able to forgive others and oneself is the heaven that religion speaks of; and that the tormenting desire for revenge and the bitter experience of not being able to forgive oneself is the hell where the suffering that people inflict on themselves and each other never ends. These two patterns of behaviour and their underlying psychodynamics form the matrix for the dramatic plot unfolding on stage.

In his uncharitable condemnation of Marwood as a "voluptuous, egoistic, shameful strumpet" (II/7; B 3, 462), Mellefont will prove himself to be a true "devil" who "lures feeble mortals into crimes and himself accuses them afterwards for these crimes which are his own work" (II/7; B 3, 463). He will become a "monster" in his own eyes because he does hesitate to marry Sara (IV/2; B 3, 489), and he will not be able to forgive himself for his share of the blame for Sara's murder: "It is not for me to undo what is done – but to punish myself for it is still in my power!" (V/10; B 3, 526).

Sara will beg Marwood, in her disguise as Lady Solmes, on her knees for the "justice not to place me and Marwood in one and the same rank" (IV/8; B 3, 508). Before her encounter with Mellefont's supposed relative, she had feared to find in Lady Solmes "one of those proud women, who are so full of their own virtue that they believe themselves above all failings" (III/2; B 3, 470); but in her conversation with her, she actually sets herself up as judge over Mellefont's "old love", even though she had recognised her in her oracular dream as "one who resembled myself" (I/7; B 3, 442).

What is this similarity? Marwood and Sara share one and the same fate: Both have given their hearts to a man who then hesitates to take them for his wife. Marwood has risked her good reputation; Sara is about to sacrifice her happiness for the man she loves. – That she has given herself to Mellefont is irrelevant for the play. "It was the error of a tender-hearted maiden" (I/1; B 3, 434), Sir William comments laconically. This cannot be stressed enough. Reducing morality to questions of sexuality, which is what Richardson does, is in itself morally questionable in Lessing's eyes. In his *Vindications of Horace*, he had indicated that sexuality, too, needs to be cultivated: In his notes on Edmund Burke's *Philosophical Enquiry into the Origin of Our Ideas of the Sublime and Beautiful* (1757), he appreciates "venereal lust" as a form of love, because like love, it is characterised by the fact that the happiness and pleasure of one person cannot be distinguished from the happiness and pleasure of the other. Even if it does not necessarily require "true love", "in the short moments" of its duration the lustful union really is love, "and perhaps the most intimate love in all of nature" (B 4, 451). It is not *carnal love* that shakes the moral world – it is the *lovelessness* springing from the egocentricity that comes so naturally to the human heart.

Lessing found the inspiration for his drama among the ancients: Sara and Marwood are Medea figures. Marwood's words when she threatens the unfaithful man with killing their child, "Behold in me a new Medea!" (II/7; B 3, 464), explicitly point to that. Such "key quotes", as Lessing scholarship has called them (GTN 3, 45), cannot be resolved in terms of character psychology; they must be read as philological hints, with the help of which the dramatist draws his audience's attention to the logic of his play.

In appropriating his literary templates, however, Lessing took all the liberties that he had granted to the modern poet in his contemporaneously written treatise on the tragedies of Seneca (1755): Unlike the ancient Greeks, whose tragedies were based on the myths handed down mainly in Homer's epics, he is not compelled to "stick to the traditional story"; "he can change whatever he wants" (B 3, 563–64), and he should imitate the patterns to which he orients himself "not slave-like, but like a head thinking for itself" (B 3, 554). Such a practice, a creative art of 'modernisation' (cf. B 3, 759), is also evident in Lessing's first tragedy; indeed, it actively wants to be seen as a testimony of a conscious appropriation practice. He was inspired by Euripides' *Medea* and Ovid's *Heroides*, which in turn owe themselves to a critical reading of Euripides.

Euripides had developed the myth of the magic-endowed barbarian into a revenge tragedy. His *Medea* is the tragedy of a woman who avenges herself on her unfaithful husband by murdering the children she has with him, thus plunging herself into misery. Medea, the daughter of King Aeëtes, has helped the Argonaut Jason to steal the Golden Fleece and has fled with him from her home country. When Jason sees an opportunity to marry into the royal family of Corinth, she is abandoned by him – her consequent revenge is an act of blind self-assertion, in which the self-destructive potential of the Greek ethos of being "terrible to one's enemies and well disposed to one's friends" (E, 67), which Lessing had discovered in his philological studies (cf. B 5/2, 44), becomes apparent in a particularly drastic way. In

Euripides' play, the chorus takes the side of the "mortals" by pointing out to Medea the self-destructive consequences of her desire for revenge (E, 67). This other, humane ethos is something Lessing himself feels committed to, as he finds in it the commandment of love of one's enemies and the renunciation of judging and avenging, which is at the centre of what he called the "religion of Christ" (B 10, 223): "You have heard that it was said, 'You shall love your neighbour and hate your enemy.' But I say to you, *love your enemies* [...]," it is said in the Sermon on the Mount (Mattew 5:43–44). And: "Judge not, that you be not judged" (Matthew 7:1).

Euripides' *Medea* is an ancient revenge tragedy par excellence. The murder of the children, committing which Medea makes herself "the most unhappy of women" (E, 67), is the tragic finale of a dynamics of escalation where the man's lovelessness drives the woman into a vengeful furore. For the sake of triumph over the unfaithful lover, this furore does not even stop at her own self-destruction. All of Lessing's tragedies visualise such fatal processes of escalation that lead the parties involved into lose-lose situations.

Lessing found his idea of interpreting the stories of the "young widow" (IV/8; B 3, 502) Marwood and the "tender-hearted maiden" Sara as two phases of the same female fate prefigured in Ovid (cf. GTN 3, 126–30). In his *Heroides*, fictional letters from female mythical figures to their lovers, Ovid gives a voice to two Medea figures: Medea, the "puella simplex" (epist. 12,89–90; O, 116), the "naïve girl" who has been beguiled by Jason's words – and Hypsipyle, Queen of Lemnos, with whom Jason had fathered two children before he set off again for Colchis to steal the Golden Fleece and flee across the sea with Medea. Hypsipyle's curse is directed at the other woman; she herself would be a Medea to Medea: "Medeae Medea forem!" (epist. 6,151; O, 62).

Lessing appropriates this idea: His Marwood is modelled after Ovid's Hypsipyle, who transforms into a "new Medea" after being humiliated by Jason. This allows him to assign to Sara the fate of a Medea figure who has not yet embarked on that flight across the sea, which she recoils from so strongly at the beginning of the play (cf. I/7; B 3, 445), and to let her suffer the fate of Creusa, a fate she herself provokes by arrogantly and self-righteously belittling Mellefont's former love. With this "rashness" (IV/8; B 3, 508), so characteristic of Lessing's tragedies, she tempts Marwood into surrendering blindly to the triumph of revenge: "I must not recover my reason nor she hers" (IV/9; B 3, 510) – and thus, into actually becoming a murderer who "will not escape her fate" (V/10; B 3, 523).

The overwhelming stage success of this tragic "*Lehrstück* about revenge and forgiveness" (GTN 3, 127) was only short-lived. Already in the 18th century, the play disappears from the repertoire of the theatres. As early as 1775, Johann Martin Miller, author of the sentimental bestseller novel *Siegwart*, writes: "Today, *Sara*, which in itself is a mediocre and boring play, was performed particularly boringly and poorly. I really would have thought *Sara* was better than that, but on the stage, she is a terrible nuisance and offence" (RD, 338). This has a lot to do with the fact that Lessing's first tragedy is written not only for being performed on stage, but also for quiet reading. When Lessing makes his characters speak about their feelings so extensively and reflect on their sensations so intensively, he does so for two reasons. On the one hand, the characters' speeches are supposed to automatically guide the actors' acting: "The dramatist must give the actor the opportunity to show his artistry", and the actor can do this best when the script puts him in a "certain state of mind, following which this or that change of the body occurs automatically, of its own accord". The more in detail the emotions that are to be represented are outlined by the playwright, "the more imperceptibly the actor himself gets drawn into them" (Sep 14, 1757; B 11/1, 249–50). On the other hand, the speeches of the *dramatis personae* are supposed to give the reader the opportunity to bring the reality experienced by the characters to life on their own mind's stage. Lessing deliberately accepted the disadvantages of this "untheatrical", or "overly theatrical", procedure (Sep 14, 1757; B 11/1, 251). Moses Mendelssohn remarks in passing that *Sara* contains some "indeclaimable" passages that are "too philosophical" for the stage, observing that "the most excellent thoughts escape the listener unnoticed, which have most entertained the reader" (Aug 11, 1757; B 11/1, 233) – but Lessing is undaunted: For the very reason that these thoughts are of a philosophical nature, he is not going to delete them, "at least not as long as more people read tragedies than see them performed" (Aug 18, 1757; B 11/1, 239).

These philosophical passages include the finale of the play, when Sara dies the death of Socrates. Like the philosopher after drinking from the cup of hemlock, she is fully conscious while going through the numbing of her limbs and actively reflects on the experience of dying: "This hand hangs as if dead by my benumbed side. If the whole body dies away as easily as these limbs – [. . .] if that which I feel is the approach of death, then the approach of death is not so bitter. Ah!" (V/7; B 3, 518–19). With the fading of her physical strength, her egocentric desire for self-assertion dissolves, too:

> Let me not hear of revenge! Revenge is not ours. [. . .] Alas, Mellefont! Why are we less prone to certain virtues with a healthy body, which feels its strength, than with a sick and wearied one? How hard are gentleness and moderation to you, and how unnatural to me appears the impatient heat of passion! (V/5; B 3, 516–17)

Sara's dying overturns the notion of death as "the wages of sin" (Romans 6:23), in which Paul the Apostle sums up the myth of the Fall of Man. The idea that even a natural death is an act of divine revenge will pose a problem for Lessing in his treatise on the representation of death in antiquity. In it, he will point out to his readers that the ancients did not portray Death as a skeleton but as a beautiful youth, as "Sleep's twin brother" – Hypnos and Thanatos (B 6, 723): "There have been philosophers," Lessing remarks, "who considered life a punishment; but to consider death a punishment is an idea that simply would not have entered the head of anyone who just used his reason, had it not been for revelation" (B 6, 778). It is not death that is terrible, according to Lessing's conviction, but dying or rather: the way in which someone gets to die (cf. B 6, 760–61). The fearsome spectre, however, of which the medieval *Danse macabre* bears witness, is merely the image of a misunderstood religion: "Only misunderstood religion can estrange us from beauty; and it is proof of the true, of the correctly understood true religion if it will always bring us back to beauty" (B 6, 778). Here too, therefore, Lessing's philosophy of religion and his aesthetics converge in the most natural way.

It is a beautiful death that Sara dies, and a terrible suicide for her lover Mellefont. What is it that makes the former death beautiful? Nothing other than the acknowledgement that the desire for revenge is self-destructive, and that foregoing judgement and condemnation is its own reward, as it gives to the soul the "serenity and mildness" that Christ Crucified calls "heaven". What is it that makes the latter death terrible? Nothing other than the desire for revenge, which in the case of Mellefont vents itself in the curses showered on Sara's murderer Marwood, and nothing other than the despair of being partly to blame for

Sara's death and not being able to forgive himself for his share in it.

Lessing's translation of the ancient revenge tragedy into a psychological drama with a religio-philosophical perspective finds its telos in Sir William's willingness to adopt Arabella, the daughter of his daughter's murderer, as his own child. – This motif will eventually be at the centre of Lessing's *Nathan*.

A Correspondence on Tragedy

The aplomb with which Lessing goes about his philological studies, as attested to by his modernised *Medea*, is just as evident in a correspondence with his friends, in which they explore (to quote Schiller) the "reason why we take pleasure in tragic subjects". In October 1755, Lessing had left Berlin to move to Leipzig. What exactly he was looking for there is unknown – he may not have known himself. Already in the preceding spring he had resigned his position as editor of the *Privileged Berlin Newspaper*; in a letter to his father, he hints at feeling drawn "to Moscow", where a university had been founded at the beginning of the year (Apr 11, 1755; B 11/1, 65).

With the physical separation, the writing of letters became his primary medium of intellectual exchange and friendly intercourse. Lessing, as Moses Mendelssohn testified, was "never the most vigorous letter writer" (MM 2, 333) when the sole object was keeping in touch; but he did rely on a lively exchange with like-minded people, because only a life lived in thought seemed to him a life lived intensively (cf. B 8, 137). After finishing his work on *Sara*, he had "jotted down a lot of disordered thoughts about the domestic tragedy" (Jul 20, 1756; B 3, 663), which he sent to his friends for review.

This correspondence was preceded by a collection of fictitious letters *On the Sentiments* (*Über die Empfindungen*, 1755), in which Moses Mendelssohn tried, among other things, to get a grasp of the nature of the so-called "mixed emotions", and a *Treatise on Tragedy* written by Friedrich Nicolai. Mendelssohn had defined compassion as a sentiment in which our goodwill towards a person is mixed with our suffering in witnessing their misfortune (cf. MM 1, 85–86). This definition was supposed to resolve the strange paradox that the audience enjoys seeing someone else's suffering represented on stage – a phenomenon that had already occupied Aristotle, whose *Poetics* was one of the authorities of early modern dramatic theory. The traditional interpretation of the *Poetics*, however, was challenged by the autodidact Nicolai, who, though he did declare the arousal of passions to be the aim of tragedy, rejected the idea that this involved a purification of the emotions, let alone a moral education (Aug 31, 1756; B 3, 664).

Nicolai's criticism of Aristotle gave Lessing the welcome opportunity to develop an alternative understanding of this educational mission Aristotle attributes to tragedy. The crux of his argument lies in the question of which passions are aroused. He distinguishes between the passions represented by the actors and the emotional states experienced by the audience: The characters in the play can experience all kinds of passions, be it joy, love, anger, vengefulness – but these do not automatically become the passions of the audience. The only passion that can be said to be directly "*felt*" by the spectator "himself, and not just felt as being felt by another" (Nov 1756; B 3, 669), is compassion. Terror and admiration, which Nicolai had mentioned besides, are for Lessing merely part of this process – in particular, he dismisses admiration as "compassion become superfluous". A hero who is "so far above his misfortune" and even "proud" of it, gives the audience no reason to pity him (Nov 1756; B 3, 670) and is therefore discarded by Lessing. "Do not stage any of the Christian tragedies written to date," is his consequent advice, with which he will open his *Hamburg Dramaturgy* in 1767 (HD 2; B 6, 193).

Already the Scottish moral philosophers, notably Francis Hutcheson, whose posthumous *System of Moral Philosophy* Lessing translates towards the end of 1755 (cf. B 3, 744–53), had not attributed moral feelings to social disciplining, but understood them as a part of human nature. Lessing adopts this idea. He interprets our capacity for empathetic participation in the suffering of others (and being prompted towards prosocial behaviour by it) as the elementary human ability cultivated by tragedy, and which tragedy can only cultivate if at the same time, it also entertains the audience. Benefit and pleasure – *prodesse et delectare*, as the formula goes in Horace's *Ars poetica* – cannot be found without each other:

> *The most compassionate human being is the best human being*, the most inclined to all social virtues and every kind of magnanimity. Thus, whoever makes us feel pity makes us better and more virtuous, and the tragedy which does the former also does the latter – or rather, by doing the former it is able to do the latter. (Nov 1756; B 3, 670)

Such is Lessing's apologetic alternative to Nicolai's criticism of Aristotle. Moses Mendelssohn cannot agree with this: He regards the element of admiration, so disparaged by Lessing, as the "mother of virtue", as a higher feeling, the "glow" of which "penetrates the mind" (Nov 23, 1756; B 3, 676), because it prompts us to emulate what we admire.

Mendelssohn's objection forces Lessing to contour his theory of compassion. He does so by differentiating between the empathetic ability to comprehend immediately how and what someone is feeling, and the more basic phenomenon of emotional contagion (or mood transmission). To this end, he distinguishes between the mere resonance with the feelings of others (which he terms "communicated sentiments", because they respond to the expressive behaviour of the literary characters) and "original sentiments", which arise from the viewer forming an idea of the situation in which the characters find themselves (Feb 2, 1757; B 3, 713–14). The audience, therefore, are not limited to the characters' horizon of perception and knowledge but, additionally, they always react to the circumstances in which said characters find themselves and to the fact that they misjudge their situation. Thus, already in his Correspondence on Tragedy, Lessing makes it clear that the compassion cultivated with literary means includes the spectator's power of judgement, and that the emotional participation in the literary characters' suffering also relies on a certain distance from their perspective.

This focus on the situational context of empathetic participation is also due to a more in-depth engagement with Aristotle's *Poetics*. In it, Lessing comes across the theory of the "middle character" and the *hamartia*, the error of the virtuous protagonist, which inspires him because it fits in with his aversion to the 'stiff-necked' heroes of the stoic endurance tragedy (*Bewährungstragödie*)

(Nov 28, 1756; B 3, 680) and corresponds to his processual thinking. Even the virtuous hero must not be without faults if his misfortune is to move us – not because the misfortune of a faultless man would evoke revulsion, Lessing declares, but "because without the fault that brings the misfortune upon him, his character and his misfortune would not constitute a *whole*, because the one would not be founded on the other, and we would think of each of these two pieces separately" (Dec 18, 1756; B 3, 701). It would lack motivation if disaster struck the hero out of the blue, like a bolt of lightning or a collapsing palace; such a disaster would not be a part of his story but a stroke of fate, which, liable to hit anyone, would arouse "horror and revulsion" rather than pity (Dec 18, 1756; B 3, 701).

The Correspondence on Tragedy is an unfinished project. Nevertheless, it is one of the most impressive instances of a joint reflection on questions of art and has been perceived as part of Lessing's oeuvre since its first publication in Lessing's *Collected Writings* (*Sämmtliche Schriften*, 1794). The epistolary conversation, which gave the friends the leeway to let their thoughts *"ripen under the pen"* (Dec 18, 1756; B 3, 693), is fascinating in the determination with which it was conducted, and the willingness to understand controversy as an amicable favour: "You are my friend; I want my thoughts examined by you, not praised" (Nov 28, 1756; B 3, 683), Lessing writes to Moses Mendelssohn, as well as:

> *Dearest friend!* You are right; I have rambled on quite a lot in my letter to you. [...] Let me now try and see whether they [my thoughts, R. V.] have ripened thanks to your objections and admonitions. I am wiping the whole slate clean, and do not want to have declared myself on the matter of admiration yet. Back to square one! (Dec 18, 1756; B 3, 693)

Mendelssohn will go on to place his contributions within the framework of his theory of "theatrical illusion", and to agree with Nicolai that tragedy is capable of arousing not merely sentiments of compassion in the viewer (Dec 1756; B 3, 689–90); Lessing will withdraw from the debate in the spring of 1757. Presumably, he felt compelled to make a new approach due to his more in-depth engagement with Aristotle's *Poetics*. Already after reading his *Rhetoric* and *Nicomachean Ethics*, he realises that the Greek *phobos* should not be translated as "terror" (*Schrecken*) but rather as "fear" (*Furcht*) (Apr 2, 1757; B 3, 716). With this insight, all his reservations lose their philological basis. In the *Hamburg Dramaturgy*, he will continue to follow this lead, rethinking and redefining the relationship between *eleos* and *phobos*. The new formula is "pity and fear".

School of Intuitive Cognition: Fables

In the Correspondence on Tragedy, Lessing had advised his friends to "go and learn from the ancients" (Nov 28, 1756; B 3, 681). The ancients also became his benchmark in his critical engagement with contemporary fable production, particularly the German imitators of Jean de La Fontaine. It is not against him, "this peculiar genius", that Lessing's qualms are directed, but against La Fontaine's "blind worshippers" (B 4, 399). Lessing treats with scepticism the verse and the casual tone that La Fontaine had cultivated in his fables; in his view, this form of presentation contradicts the "precision and brevity" (B 4, 398) that originally characterises the genre and that is alone appropriate to its nature.

Aristotle had discussed the fable not in his *Poetics* but in the *Rhetoric*, following the intuition that fables only acquire their meaning in a specific context of speech and interaction: Fables use stories that represent a specific situation to interpret specific situations; they are –

comparable to proverbs – narrative patterns for interpreting experiences. Lessing reminds himself and his contemporaries of the original function of the genre, and the return to the sources is marked by a critical demarcation between literature, rhetoric, and philosophy.

He had already taken a similar approach in a treatise co-authored with Moses Mendelssohn on Alexander Pope's *Essay on Man* (1734), in which he had rejected the prize-essay topic posed by the Berlin Royal Academy of Sciences, a question about the philosophical content of this didactic poem, with the argument that the language of poetry must not be measured by the standards of discursive cognition: As a poem, Pope's poem is "perfect sensuous speech" (B 3, 617), as Lessing says, and this inherent logic of verse and imagery obstructs the conceptual precision and compelling argumentation to which philosophical reflection commits itself.

The same applies to the fable: Even though it is one of the fashionable literary genres of the 18th century, its original place in the world was not the written but the spoken word. Fable compilations such as those handed down under the name of Aesop were not primarily intended for quiet reading, but served as mnemonics for the speaker who could draw on them in the appropriate *context*. In a process of literarisation, the fable gained its status as a text among *texts*, and La Fontaine's achievement lies in establishing fables as small narrative works of art, and in imbuing them with a lightness that imitates the art of social conversation and is therefore also suitable for self-sufficient reading.

Lessing disagrees. He understands the fable as a narrative that makes a moral truth intuitively recognisable (B 4, 376). Moral truths are truths about questions of individual and interpersonal actions, insofar as they are guided by values, and the fable makes such truths accessible to the imagination by visualising these actions. Thus, fables follow a moral-philosophical intention which the art of versification is detrimental to, since it distracts from the essentials. The famous fable of the carved bow, which breaks because the artist has adorned it with hunting scenes, illustrates this by referring in an Aristotelian manner to the "skopos" of the genre, i.e., the goal inscribed into it: If you want to hunt, you need a usable bow, not pictures of hunting.

Lessing follows Aristotle not only in his agenda of gaining perspectives for the optimisation of literary practice by questioning the main features of the genre, but also in his method of intertwining empirical evidence and general reflection. All general definitions are derived from the analysis of successful examples, which, conversely, are supposed to train the eye for essentials. Lessing's own fables are meant to be read as a case in point, which is why his advice is to "judge the *fables* not without the *essays*" (B 4, 299). – He will then proceed in the same way in his studies on the epigram, which draw upon a logic of "*expectation and resolution*" (B 7, 188) to develop criteria for a successful text.

Lessing's method can be exemplified by a study of a fable entitled *The Miser* (*Der Geizige*), which explicitly points out that it is to be understood as a rewrite of the homonymous fable by Aesop: "Fab. Aesop. 59." (B 4, 967). In this older version, a miser has converted his assets into cash and bought a lump of gold for it, which he buries by his wall. In doing so, he is spied on; the gold is stolen. When he discovers and laments the theft, a well-wisher advises him to bury a stone in the place of the stolen treasure: "Do not be sad, my friend, but take a stone, put it in the same place and imagine that your gold is there. Because, at the time it was still there, you did not make use of it either" (Ae, 219). The *fabula docet* remarks that, "The story illustrates that possession is worthless unless use is made of it, too" (Ae, 221).

Obviously, the lesson that Aesop's fable teaches the miser is not suitable to visualise the nature of avarice. Possession is not worthless, quite the contrary: It is worth more to the miser than any benefit he might derive from it. Considering this, the advice is short-sighted, showing no insight into the first-person perspective of a miser, but judging it only from the outside perspective of common sense. Therefore, Lessing problematises the proposed solution, developing from it his new version:

> Unfortunate man that I am! a miser complained to his neighbour. Last night, someone stole my treasure, which I had buried in my garden, and put a goddamned stone in its place. You would never, replied his neighbour, have used your treasure. Only, therefore, imagine the stone to be your treasure, and you will be nothing the worse. Even supposing I was nothing the worse, replied the miser, is not somebody else the better? Somebody else the better! I shall go mad! (B 4, 322)

Lessing's fable takes the miser's perspective seriously and translates it into a plot, that is, "*a sequence of changes which together constitute a whole*" (B 4, 357). Such changes are not necessarily of an external nature – "every inner conflict of the passions, every sequence of different thoughts where one supersedes the other" (B 4, 363) is a plot in Lessing's sense. The "whole" of this plot is the moral concept of avarice, illustrated in the fable by a study of its psychodynamics: The lament turning into anger shows that avarice and envy are, in fact, two sides of the same coin. The miser hoards his fortune because he begrudges it both to himself and others.

Lessing's fables are not embedded in a context of face-to-face communication; they are not intended to be used moralisingly on a given occasion, but to be perceived as written texts in their own right that support conceptual, or in Lessing's words, "symbolic" cognition (B 4, 373). The vividness of presentation they strive for, which becomes evident in *The Miser*, is not a superficial characteristic of the genre but its aesthetic core, as it "*endows*" a general case "*with reality*" (B 4, 376), as Lessing puts it. To gain the status of "reality", a moral-philosophical thought experiment must be concretised in an I with its Here and Now: "Reality only belongs to the particular, the individual; and no reality can be conceived without individuality" (B 4, 371). The moral insight conveyed by the fable is, therefore, dependent on the suggestive power of the literary representation. Fables are instructive to the extent that they succeed in initiating a process of imagination that allows moral behaviour to be not only seriously considered but also understood from the inside.

This can be observed once again in Lessing's rewrite of the fable of the miser: The insight that possession in itself is worthless is the insight of common sense, to which Aesop's original refers; the moral deficiency of the miser, which consists, in fact, in begrudging possession to anyone else, gives Lessing's new version a critical punchline and, thus, its wittiness. His fable conveys a sense of what it is like to be miserly. It is not a means of reading the riot act to a miser or exposing him to ridicule and scorn; it is meant to reveal a moral-philosophical truth to the thinking mind.

As he did in his apologia for comedy and tragedy, Lessing again makes it clear in his theory of the fable that the insight offered by the genre is inseparable from its aesthetic appeal. Like comedy and tragedy, he contours the fable as a representation of psychological processes (*Bewusstseinspoesie*) – even though the fable, unlike the former, cares about its characters' fate only insofar as the characters are part of the moral maxim illustrated by it: The fabulist does not need to take an interest in their story, he can "leave them behind en route" (B 4, 367).

Lessing's fables are exercises in the art of making the poetic representation of human actions a model of moral cognition (cf. GTN 2). In this respect, they pursue the same goal as Lessing's plays. And just like them, they also demonstrate a practice that wants to be recognised as such: the art of moral-philosophical reflection occasioned by and underlying the construction of the plot.

Therefore, the fable finds its actual, "*heuristic* benefit", as Lessing puts it, in teaching: It is supposed to teach students to "rise from the particular to the general just as easily as descend back from the general to the particular", and thereby bring them up as "a *genius*" (B 4, 408). Students are not only to read fables but also to practice the fabulous "*principle of reduction*" by inventing fables themselves, or at least by being guided by the teacher to familiarise themselves independently with the treasure trove of fable tradition, just as Lessing demonstrates it in the second volume of his fable collection.

Letters on Literature (Primarily No. 17)

In 1759, Lessing, Mendelssohn and Nicolai launch a journalistic project that brings a new tone to literary criticism. Nicolai recalls that "almost all" journals at that time were "frosty, shallow, partisan, full of compliments" (B 4, 1086); their own project was to take the openness of their conversations to the public: "Often, it has been said among us in jest: One should simply write the way we talk" (B 4, 1086). The *Letters Concerning Recent Literature* (*Briefe, die neueste Literatur betreffend*) were based on the principle of an unbiased exchange of ideas, such as had already characterised the Correspondence on Tragedy. They allowed themselves to "not be tied to a specific purpose", to determine the beginning and end as they liked and to choose their subject at will (B 4, 1087). Above all, they did not take into account the prominence of the authors. In a letter to Frederick II (Mar 10, 1761), the lawyer Johann Heinrich Gottlob von Justi will accuse the authors of "treating the most famous scholars far and wide in the most impertinent and irresponsible manner" and "having no respect for either God or men" (as cited in GEL, 344–45). In particular, Lessing's contributions, with their conciseness, elegance and sharpness, were perceived by contemporaries as symptoms of a new beginning. He appeared under the ciphers O. Fll. L. E. G. A. (research has identified these as an anagram for the Latin "flagello", 'I scourge'; cf. HBN, 252) and made polemics his creative principle. In the *Hamburg Dramaturgy*, he will advise the critical writer to start by "looking for someone with whom he can argue; in this manner he will gradually get into the subject matter, and the rest will sort itself out" (HD 70; B 6, 535).

With the *Letters on Literature*, Lessing established himself – as Johann Gottfried Herder remarked in his obituary – as the "*first* critic in Germany" (St, 127). His polemics were directed against authors as prominent as Christoph Martin Wieland or Klopstock, whose sensational attempt to translate the New Testament into an epic (*The Messiah*) had already been critically commented on by Lessing in his *Writings*. Particularly vehement was Lessing's dispute with *The Nordic Guardian* (*Der nordische Aufseher*), a moral weekly which had disparaged the morality of freethinkers in several articles. Here, again, he targeted Klopstock.

The one *Letter on Literature* that was to gain outstanding significance in literary history, however, was no. 17 (Feb 16, 1759), in which Lessing presents himself in the manner of Odysseus as a "nobody" who dares to doubt the merits of the Leipzig theatre reformer Johann Christoph Gottsched: "'nobody', say the authors of the *Library of Belles-Lettres*, 'will deny that the German stage has Professor Gottsched to thank for a great part of its improvement.' I am this nobody; I deny it outright" (B 4, 499). – All the improvements introduced by Gottsched, according to the tenor of the letter, were actually deteriorations: The banishment of Harlequin from the theatre, acted out in collaboration with Caroline Neuber, was itself a Harlequinade; the orientation towards the French classicist tragedy a mistake; his own theatrical productions the clumsy work of a plagiarist. So harsh an attack would not have been necessary, seeing that in 1759, Gottsched's star was already waning. However, Lessing's polemical rejection of the literary programme represented and established in Germany by Gottsched was to be epoch-making.

Gottsched's dramaturgy misunderstood itself as rational because it saw itself as in line with the principles of Aristotelian *Poetics*, though in fact, it only considered the epiphenomena of tragedy (such as the three unities). Against this form of modernisation of the ancient heritage, Lessing brought into position an alternative drama tradition, which impressively met the actual goal of tragedy without adhering to conventional dramaturgical rules – the Shakespearean theatre, despised by Gottsched:

> Even judging by the models of the ancients, *Shakespeare* is a far greater tragedian than *Corneille*; although the latter knew the ancients very well, and the former knew them hardly at all. *Corneille* comes closer to them in the mechanical arrangement, and *Shakespeare* in the essential aspects. The Englishman accomplishes the purpose of tragedy almost every time, no matter how peculiar and idiosyncratic his ways; and the Frenchman accomplishes it hardly ever, even though he follows the well-trodden paths of the ancients. After *Sophocles' Oedipus*, no play in the world can have more power over our passions than *Othello*, than *King Lear*, than *Hamlet*, etc. (B 4, 500–01)

In his public debate with the Hamburg head pastor Goeze, Lessing will insist that it is possible to be a Christian without having read the Bible (cf. B 9, 73–75) – here, he puts forward the same argument: It is possible to be an Aristotelian without having read Aristotle. The quality of a drama is not determined from its conformity with dramaturgical conventions, but from the actualisation of the aesthetic intention, from which the specific conventions become understandable in the first place. In Sophocles' *Oedipus*, Gottsched had found an illustration of the moral maxim that "God does not leave unpunished even the vices committed in ignorance" (JCG, 611), and pondered on the fact that considering the oracle, the tragic hero should have avoided committing manslaughter altogether: "For he should always have thought: What if this were my father!" (JCG, 607–08). He justified the concept of the unity of time by arguing that it was unlikely for "someone to see dusk falling several times on the stage, and yet remain seated in one place the whole time, without eating, or drinking, or sleeping" (JCG, 614). Such considerations are not, to use Hamlet's words, "sicklied o'er with the pale cast of thought" – and they are revealing for that very reason: They convey an idea of how much Lessing's criticism, and his claim to show German drama the way forward via a return to the ancient origins, raises the level of theoretical reflection.

In the *Hamburg Dramaturgy*, he will point out how nonsensical it is to want to measure the unity of time in hours, and argue for a distinction between "physical" and "moral" time (HD 45; B 6, 406). This distinction is helpful in understanding the Attic tragedians' practice of limiting the story duration to one day: Man is but a creature of a day, an *ephemeros* – "for a day can humble all human things, and a day can lift them up" (S, 23), Sophocles says in his *Aias*. Thus, the limitation of the story duration to a short period of time has mimetic qualities, and it also has a potentially tragic dimension, because tragedy arises out of rashness and oversight.

This is also discussed in a scene that Lessing anonymously presents to the reading public as a test case: the draft of a Faust play, which was to remain unfinished but turned out to be no less influential than the *Letter on Literature*, no. 17 itself. It shows Faust in conversation with seven devils – the fastest of them is to be his servant. The first four devils disqualify themselves because they conceive of speed only in the dimension of measurable time: They are only at home in the physical world. The last three, in contrast, enter the sphere of the moral world: One is "as fast as human thoughts", another "as fast as the avenger's revenge", the last one as fast as "the transition from good to evil" (B 4, 63). To the fifth devil, Faust replies that human thoughts, "when truth and virtue call them", are in fact quite "sluggish" (B 4, 63). In the sixth devil, he recognises the blasphemous demon of revenge, who has created a god for himself in his own image – he, too, is slow, because the "avenger's revenge" is nothing but the natural consequences every action yields. Finally, the seventh and last is Faust's devil. Why? Because evil is, essentially, rashness. The idea that there is nothing faster in the moral world than the "transition from good to evil" is an insight of moral and religious philosophy: Reflection needs time, and evil is good that gets missed in the heat of passion.

The reason why the Faust fragment is such an eminent text is that here, the central idea of Lessing's tragedies is presented in a particularly trenchant way: the Fall of Man. All of Lessing's tragic or potentially tragic heroes are fallen virtuous heroes (cf. GTN 3). In his *Education of the*

Human Race, he will still emphasise: The danger of failing to do right is our anthropological heritage (cf. § 74; B 10, 94); nevertheless, in our ability to follow moral laws there lies a "happiness" as is only given to moral beings (§ 75; B 10, 94).

A War Drama: *Philotas*

On August 29, 1756, Prussian troops invaded Saxony, thus opening a war that began as the Third Silesian War, lasted seven years, resembled a first world war and was fought with more than just military means: The Seven Years' War was the first war in human history that not only affected the ruling classes and the disputed territories but also saw the passionate involvement of the international media. It was a war that, contrary to Lessing's hopes at the beginning of the *Letters on Literature*, was not merely "a bloody trial involving independent heads" that "leaves all other social classes undisturbed" (B 4, 456). In his autobiography *Truth and Poetry* (*Dichtung und Wahrheit*), Goethe later recalls the debates at the family table and the fascination that the Prussian king held for him, as for so many of his contemporaries (cf. TaP II/2; MA 16, 52–55).

Lessing himself was directly affected by the outbreak of war. As companion of the Leipzig merchant's son Gottfried Winkler he had embarked on a journey in May

1756 that was to take him to England. In Amsterdam they were surprised by the war – Winkler cut the journey short to see to things in Leipzig, Lessing had to accept the situation: "Thanks be to the King of Prussia!" he writes to Moses Mendelssohn. "We were just about to cross over to England when we had to rush back all at once" (Oct 1, 1756; B 11/1, 109).

Lessing maintained a critical distance towards the war – in Prussia he was considered a Saxon, in Saxony a Prussian. While his friend Johann Wilhelm Ludwig Gleim, poet and secretary of the Halberstadt Cathedral chapter, was drawn into engaging in the war with his *Martial Songs by a Prussian Grenadier* (*Kriegslieder eines preußischen Grenadiers*) and stirring up public opinion in favour of Frederick, Lessing was more reserved. He did preface and publish Gleim's poems with his publisher in Berlin, Christian Friedrich Voss (1758), and also included his ode *To the Muse of War* (*An die Kriegsmuse*), in which the Prussian grenadier celebrates the victory at Zorndorf, in the *Letters on Literature* (no. 15); some passages, however, he commented on very critically, nor could he restrain himself from telling his friend Gleim that "at various points, his hair stood on end in horror" (Dec 16, 1758; B 11/1, 305).

Gleim had stylised Frederick in his *Martial Songs* as "The Anointed" and "Messenger from God" and referred to the opposing army as "savages" whom the King's "avenging sword" was mowing "out of [his] God's world" (JWLG, 39). Lessing thought this sacralisation of the war as a battle between the powers of good and the powers of evil was scandalous – not only because, as he confessed in a letter to Gleim, patriotic feelings were alien to him (cf. Feb 14, 1759; B 11/1, 311), but even more so because this sacralisation embraced a patriotism that failed to appreciate the suffering this war caused on both sides.

The short war drama *Philotas* can be read as a public response to his contemporaries' war fever, as conveyed by the media. It counters their patriotism with a metapolitical and "cosmopolitan" perspective. Lessing had reproached Gleim, saying that the patriot in him was unduly "shouting over" the poet (Dec 16, 1758; B 11/1, 305). His own war drama sheds light on the blind spots of patriotism and is devoted to political enlightenment: It contrasts the unconditional fighting morale that escalates armed conflicts with an ethos of political conflict reduction (cf. GTN 3, 202–03).

Lessing's *Philotas* is published in 1759 in a luxury edition. The title page identifies the one-act play as a "tragedy", but omits the usual indication "in one act" that is common in Lessing's works. In fact, the play is so condensed and boiled down to a few scenes that it would be more appropriate to describe it as a parabolic thought experiment. The *"principle of reduction"* (B 4, 408), which is at the centre of the fable essays, equally reigns over the play about the heroic martyrdom of young Philotas. Lessing's war drama cannot be understood if read as a direct representation of an actual conflict; it translates the war into a parabolic model that makes visible the logic of armed conflicts – just as the Ring Parable will demonstrate the logic of religious conflicts.

The conflict between revealed religions stems from the claim to exclusivity raised by all of them. *Philotas*, too, is based on a mirror-image construction of this kind: Two kings (Philotas' father and Aridaeus), two princes (Philotas and Polytimet), two soldiers (Parmenio and Strato) face each other in a war, the genesis of which is only hinted at. Friends in their younger days, the kings have been alienated by mistrust, Philotas' father having evidently been the first to draw the sword. His son is a child of war. Barely out of childhood, he has been taken prisoner during his first battle because he had charged too far ahead of his army. Now, his war fever threatens to be his father's downfall, because the capture of the son has made the father vulnerable. In the same battle, however, Polytimet, Aridaeus' son, has also been taken captive, so that the original balance is restored. Aridaeus takes this as a stroke of good fortune: He wants to use the exchange of prisoners as an opportunity to restore the former peace; his plan, however, does not work out, because Philotas now sees himself in a position to help his father to victory through the sacrifice of his own life. He consequently dies for his fatherland, and the topoi surrounding this death, drawn from Greek antiquity, are quoted extensively in the drama, which also plays a prominent part in contemporary literature – for example in the war drama *Cissides and Paches* (1759) by Lessing's friend, the Prussian officer Ewald von Kleist. To quote from this play, "a death for the fatherland is worthy of eternal / veneration" (EvK, 152). "Dulce et decorum est pro patria mori" (carm. 3,2,13; H, 116), is the corresponding formula by Horace, which echoes through Lessing's drama: "Ha! It must be a glorious, a grand sight: a youth stretched on the ground, the sword in his breast!" (6; B 4, 28).

The sequence of scenes is structured by three long monologues of the eponymous hero, which reflect his state of mind and path to suicide. In the first, the opening monologue (1), he struggles with his fate of captivity that has made him the "worst enemy" (2; B 4, 15) of his loving father. In the second, the decision monologue (4), he marvels at the graciousness of the gods, who have played into his father's hands through the capture of Polytimet – but in the same breath, he presumptuously declares that Providence is "all too indulgent" and that a "god" is thinking within him that it is now up to him alone to help his father to victory by taking his own life and leaving his father without a son. Lastly, the third monologue (6) prepares the "second rashness" (5; B 4, 23), which makes Philotas a tragic hero: He has stalled for time and delayed the exchange of prisoners by one crucial day, and is now picturing the heroic death he will die in the finale (8).

From the perspective of the son sent to war by his father, this is most consistent. However, the perspective of the young war hero is not the perspective of the play, which sheds light on the dynamics of escalation in warfare, rooted in the mirrored structure of the conflict. From a non-partisan perspective, the young hero's self-sacrifice is tragic: Philotas forfeits his chance to devote his life to "the welfare of the state" and thus "fulfil [his] end" (4; B 4, 20), because he is deaf to the offers of peace Aridaeus makes to him. If the latter were to pay like with like, sacrificing his own son in return, the prince's self-sacrifice would remain no more than a meaningless episode in a never-ending war. Philotas' success as a peacemaker, as he envisages himself with his dying breath, is owed to Aridaeus' willingness to give in for the sake of his own son's life. This alone prevents an outcome where everyone loses everything in the end.

The eponymous hero's monologues follow the logic of the *Trugrede*, a speech of deception which Lessing had discovered in his studies on Sophocles, namely on the *Aias* tragedy (cf. GTN 3, 204). They depict a young man who becomes entangled in contradictions and gets carried away to act against his better judgement. The art of tragic irony that Lessing practises here consists in making visible his character's perspective blindness, and this blindness lies (just as in the case of Mellefont) in the hero's inability to forgive himself: "May I forgive myself all the errors which Providence seems to pardon me? Shall I not judge myself more severely than Providence and my father judge me? All too indulgent judges!" (4; B 4, 19).

When Lessing has his hero shake his head over himself with the words "And how easily I delude myself!" (4; B 4, 19), the attentive reader is to comprehend just this tragic deception: In Philotas' self-condemnation, we are not to hear the voice of his "impartial self", and in his decision to commit suicide not a thought "which a god thought within me" (4; B 4, 20). In both instances, all we see is the blind egocentrism of a youthful hero, who is tempted by the idea of triumphing over the enemy, making him vulnerable by his own death – a circumstance that he had previously experienced as an injustice imposed by the gods (2; B 4, 14).

The tragedy of Aias serves as template, in a broader sense, for Lessing's parabolic play. It is centred around the dispute over Achilles' armour, in which Aias turns against Odysseus and the Greeks. To protect the Greeks from his fury, Athena casts "tyrannous fancies" (S, 17) upon his eyes and makes him vent his hatred on a herd of cattle, which he mistakes for the Greeks. In his finale, Lessing provides a rewrite of this scene: Philotas believes himself surrounded by a superior enemy force and avoids the "disgrace" (8; B 4, 33) of being captured by stabbing himself in the chest.

In the case of Aias, too, it is ignominy that drives the hero to suicide after he has come to his senses. Aias, too, is unable to bear the thought of returning home in disgrace and facing his father "without that meed of valour" (S, 47). In this tragedy of the war hero, it is Odysseus, the despised adversary, who assumes the task of having pity on the madman (S, 23) and of standing up to Agamemnon as the dead man's advocate, in order to avert the disgrace of an honourable burial being denied him.

In Lessing's war drama, it is Aridaeus who gives voice to compassion and political common sense. Aridaeus is also the one who counters the blasphemous interpretations of the "strange fortune of war" (3; B 4, 16) by which Philotas tries to disguise his thirst for glory, with the insight that the will of the gods becomes clear in whatever reason and humanity command: "The gods – I am convinced of it – watch over our virtue, as they watch over our lives. To preserve both as long as possible is their secret and eternal work" (3; B 4, 16). The best way to honour their will and prove oneself worthy of it is, therefore, "grateful joy" (3; B 4, 17). – Minna will see it just the same.

Like all of Lessing's dramas, this parabolic play about the honourable death for the fatherland is grounded in religious philosophy; the political enlightenment to which Lessing feels committed cannot be separated from his enlightened religious philosophy. Already in *Sara*, he had discovered the political art of Greek tragedy in the Christian ethos of forgiveness and underpinned this ethos with his moral psychology. In the same way, *Philotas* cultivates a non-partisan view of the logic of interpersonal conflicts and exposes the reasons for which they escalate: The reasons lie, as the *Education* treatise calls it, in the "selfishness of the human heart" (§ 80; B 10, 95) and in the allegiance of the individual to the selfish interests of their group.

The natural endowments of the human heart, however, include the ability to overcome this selfishness by tears and laughter. Aridaeus confesses to this ability, saying, "I am a human being, and I like to cry and laugh" (7; B 4, 31). Laughing and crying are part of the natural emotional capacity of humans, which Lessing's play defends against the morality of heroic self-assertion. "Do not let the rough soldier so soon stifle in you the loving child!" (3; B 4, 22), is the warning given by the experienced warrior Parmenio to the inexperienced prince. In vain, however. Like all of Lessing's youthful heroes, Philotas lacks one experience that would mature him into a man more than any other:

the experience of being a father himself (cf. 3; B 4, 22). Aridaeus emphasises this, too: "What is a king, if he be not a father? What is a hero void of human love?" (7; B 4, 31). The love of fathers for their sons, or of parents for their children, opens the heart to love for humanity; it is the epitome of non-exclusive love in Lessing's eyes.

Media Aesthetics of the Mimetic Arts: *Laocoön*

On June 8, 1768, the renowned antiquarian Johann Joachim Winckelmann is murdered in Rome. This news and the circumstances surrounding his death stir up public emotions. Lessing is deeply affected – he writes to his friend Nicolai that he would "gladly have given a few years of my life" to Winckelmann (Jul 5, 1768; B 11/1, 526–27).

Indeed, Lessing held Winckelmann in the highest esteem, even though, or possibly because, the latter's writings, notably his *Thoughts on the Imitation of Greek Art in Painting and Sculpture* (*Gedancken über die Nachahmung der Griechischen Werke in der Mahlerey und Bildhauer-Kunst*, 1755), provoked his contradiction. In it, Winckelmann had described the ethos of Greek art as "noble simplicity" and "quiet grandeur" and recommended it to the Germans for emulation: "Just as the depths of the sea always remain calm however much the surface may rage, so does the expression of the figures of the Greeks reveal a great and composed soul even in the midst of passion" (B 5/2, 17). The work of art in which Winckelmann saw this attitude exemplified was a group of figures discovered in 1506, which depicts a scene from the Trojan War: Laocoön, flanked by his two sons, wrestling with two snakes that have been sent by the gods siding with the Greeks to strangle the priest who was warning about the wooden horse. In Virgil's *Aeneid*, which sings about this episode of the Trojan War, Laocoön roars like a bull, and his screams echo to the stars: "clamores [...] horrendos ad sidera tollit" (II, 222; V, 76). But not so in the Laocoön Group: There, the tormented man does not emit "a terrible cry". "For the opening of his mouth does not permit it; it is rather an anxious and troubled sighing," Winckelmann comments: "Laocoön suffers, but he suffers like Sophocles' Philoctetes; his pain touches our very souls, but we wish that we could bear misery like this great man" (B 5/2, 17).

Lessing takes this description as a starting point for an elaborate contradiction, which aims at redefining the boundaries between the representational possibilities of painting and literature. It bears witness to an intellectual energy that impressed his contemporaries and continues to interest posterity: "One must be a young man," Goethe recalls,

> to render present to oneself the effect which Lessing's *Laocoön* produced upon us, by transporting us out of the region of scanty perceptions into the open fields of thought. The so long misunderstood *ut pictura poesis* was at once laid aside, the difference between plastic and speaking art was made clear, the summits of the two now appeared sundered, however near their bases might border on each other. (TaP II/8; MA 16, 341)

The conceptual framework Lessing develops here is not new – central distinctions have already been introduced into the aesthetic debate (cf. MF 1, 241–42); but what continues to fascinate to this day is the ease with which Lessing takes up these arguments and weaves them into a text that so clearly bears his own signature. It is the signature of an author who actively involves his readers in the process of developing his thoughts by "presenting the occasion for each reflection, as it were, before their eyes," as Johann Gottfried Herder aptly observes: "We see his work *come into being*" (as cited in B 5/2, 709).

First of all, Lessing's treatise "on the limits of painting and poetry (*über die Grenzen der Malerei und Poesie*)" is a vindication of Virgil, who is belittled by Winckelmann. Lessing shares Winckelmann's view on the aesthetic appeal of the Laocoön statue, but he disputes the reasons he puts forward. To express one's physical pain does not indicate weakness of character for the Greeks – quite the contrary: "To suppress all pain, to meet the stroke of death with unflinching eye, [...] to lament neither their own faults, nor the loss of their dearest friends," these are characteristics of "the old heroic courage of the north," and of a barbaric state of mind to Lessing (B 5/2, 20–21). Lessing's reservations about the stoic endurance of suffering are both of an ethical and an aesthetic nature: The suppression of pain is not only barbaric, it is also (as has already been argued in the Correspondence on Tragedy), incapable of moving us:

> All stoicism is untheatrical; and our sympathy is always proportioned to the suffering expressed by the object which interests us. It is true if we see him bear his misery with a great soul, this grandeur of soul excites our admiration; but admiration is only a cold sentiment, and its

inactive astonishment excludes every warmer feeling as well as every distinct idea. (B 5/2, 21)

Therefore, if it is short-sighted to attribute the art of visual representation to a specific ethos, it must obey other principles. Lessing's argument is that Laocoön sighs "not because a shriek would have betrayed an ignoble soul, but because it would have produced the most hideous contortions of the countenance" (B 5/2, 29); like all Greek artists, the unknown sculptor was committed to the law of beauty and therefore felt compelled to "soften shrieks into sighs". Thus, the beauty of the figure can transform the "annoyance" that is excited by the sight of pain "into the sweet feeling of compassion" (B 5/2, 29). For the poet, the situation is quite different: When Virgil makes his Laocoön roar like a bull, he does so because it is only too human, and he is free to do so because the verbal representation of pain does not force the reader to picture a countenance distorted into a grimace.

This insight makes it necessary for Lessing to make some fundamental distinctions, for which he is indebted to the *Poetics* of Aristotle. Aristotle raises the question of the 'first definitions' of poetry; philosophical reflection should, he argues, promote artistic practice by making us aware of what matters in poetry. The basic idea is this: Poetry is mimesis – the imitation of something in a certain medium and in a certain way. Poetry imitates "human action", using language, rhythm and melody, just as painting uses "form and colour". Lessing's "unarranged collectanea" (B 5/2, 15) follow this methodical procedure. According to the starting point of his considerations, all mimetic arts are mimetic re-presentations of reality, which make "what is absent seem as if it were present, and appearance take the form of reality" (B 5/2, 13); but they do so with their own specific means and in their own specific ways. Poetry imitates human life with the help of language: "Articulated sounds in time" are its medium of expression (B 5/2, 116), and therefore, actions are its appropriate subject. For painting, the medium of representation is "form and colour in space" (B 5/2, 116); therefore, its appropriate subject are bodies. If the "succession of time" is thus "the department of the poet", and "space is the department of the painter" (B 5/2, 130), this also marks the limitations of the two arts. Poetry can only represent bodies by hinting at them in the actions of their characters; painting can only indicate actions by allowing us to "gather" what is taking place from the positions of the bodies (B 5/2, 116). Although the contemplation of a painting also unfolds over time, this process is external to the represented object and, as such, does not enter our consciousness (B 5/2, 124). Different is the case with poetry: It represents actions, that is, a structured sequence of movements oriented towards a certain goal, and the recognition of this process is a structured process in itself.

With this differentiation, Lessing corrects an old poetological dogma attributed to Simonides of Ceos, according to which painting could be regarded as "dumb poetry", and poetry as "speaking painting" (B 5/2, 14). The most influential expression of this idea is found in Horace's *Ars poetica*, condensed into a formula about how poetry should resemble painting: "ut pictura poesis", which had not only been invoked by the Swiss critics Johann Jakob Bodmer and Johann Jakob Breitinger. It also legitimised the tendency of poets to place special value on descriptive passages. In Lessing's opinion, this "mania for description" (B 5/2, 15) in contemporary poetry has become a problem. When he (reluctantly) speaks of a "poetical painting", he does not mean a structure that could also be painted, i.e., transformed into a "material painting", but rather a structured whole represented by verbal means:

> Every feature, every combination of several features, by which the poet makes his object so palpable to us that we become more conscious of this object than of his words, is referred to as a painting, because it brings us nearer to that degree of illusion of which material painting is especially capable, and which is most readily called forth by the contemplation of such painting. (B 5/2, 113)

Therefore, the centre of Lessing's theory of aesthetic illusion – or deceptive *phantasia*, as he calls it in a footnote (B 5/2, 113–14) – is the immersive quality of the representation. We are more aware of the subject than of the words if a text succeeds in involving us and recentring us in the Here and Now of the represented reality. A poetical painting re-presents human actions in so suggestive a way that we personally relate to it, laughing and crying, hoping and fearing.

Lessing's media aesthetics of the arts embeds Aristotle's poetics in a comprehensive theory of imagination, with not only the reader's imaginative ability up for debate, but also the imaginative ability of the literary genius. Poetry is the mimesis *of* human beings *by* human beings *for* human beings: The literary work is a thinking mind's imaginative achievement that has taken shape, and a template for the imagination of a reader who is able to recognise it.

The drawing of boundaries for the mimetic arts and the formulation of criteria by which the success of a representation can be measured enable Lessing to identify the representational techniques with which the arts achieve their goals in their respective ways. Painting masters the challenge of imitating actions by showing a particular moment that allows the imagination free scope: Lessing calls it the most "fruitful" or "pregnant" moment (B 5/2, 32, 117). The fruitful moment is when both "what has already taken place" and "what is about to follow" become immediately apparent (B 5/2, 117): "The longer we gaze, the more must our imagination add. The more our imagination adds, the more we must believe we see" (B 5/2, 32). Poetry, on the other hand, masters the challenge of imitating bodies by resisting the temptation to describe them, and only naming those features of their objects that are significant for the context of the action.

In Homer's *Iliad*, Lessing not only finds examples for his philosophical considerations of art; Homer's masterful practice actually points the way for such reflections: "Homer describes nothing but progressive actions, and when he paints bodies or single objects, he does it only as contributary to such, and, then, usually only by a single touch" (B 5/2, 117). For example, he refrains from describing Agamemnon's clothes: "We see the garments, whilst the poet is describing the operation of putting them on" (B 5/2, 119); he also refrains from describing Agamemnon's sceptre: "Instead of the appearance, he gives us the history of the sceptre" (B 5/2, 120). And the same applies to the shield of Achilles: Homer refrains from describing the shield with all its ornaments; he "paints" it "as it is being wrought":

> Thus, he here also makes use of that knack of art I have already commended, by which he changes that which, in his subject, is coexistent into what is consecutive, and thereby converts a tedious painting of a body into a vivid picture of an action. We do not see the shield itself, but the divine craftsman who executes it. (B 5/2, 134)

The *media-aesthetic* differentiation between the spatial and temporal arts with their respective laws of representation also has a *semiotic* implication. This is only hinted at in the first book of *Laocoön*, but is already systematically taken into consideration. Not only does language consist of words and rules for linking them, with the help of which a speaker can translate the multidimensional variety of his processes of consciousness into a one-dimensional sequence of signs; linguistic signs, as Lessing says, are also "arbitrary": They are based – unlike "natural signs", which are intrinsically related to what they signify – on convention (B 5/2, 123).

This makes language particularly suitable as a medium for representing facts: It transforms the world as we perceive it into a world of concepts, so that its representational space is not limited by the conditions of *sensory perception* (cf. B 5/2, 60). However, from an aesthetic point of view, this is quite precarious, as the "arbitrariness" of linguistic signs (a well-known expression since Ferdinand de Saussure's *Cours de linguistique générale*) is not a specific characteristic of poetry; it is "a peculiarity of language and its signs generally, and not in so far as they are most adapted to the aim of poetry" (B 5/2, 123). Linguistic signs are adapted to the representation of actions when they possess Gestalt qualities, that is, when they come together to form a "whole": *Imaginative representations* or "ideas", as Lessing says, only become "lively" if, "from the rapidity with which they arise, the same impression should be made upon our senses which the sight of the material objects that these conceptions represent would produce", and if, "in this moment of illusion", we pay more attention to them than to the means of representation (B 5/2, 124). Even if the individual linguistic *sign* is "arbitrary", the linguistic *utterance* is not: It follows a process of articulation that is directed at something. Language becomes the medium of poetry to the extent that the representation succeeds in prompting a process of imagination, that is, an *immersive* representation of personal and interpersonal *reality*.

Lessing's magnum opus in the field of art philosophy remained a fragment. The announced second book and a third book, both existing as drafts, were never published. They were intended to develop the "collectanea", which Lessing had arranged around Winckelmann's interpretation of the Laocoön Group, into a general theory of the arts. A letter to Friedrich Nicolai from 1769, in which he brings up once again the subject of the relationship of the arts, gives an idea of the direction Lessing's argumentation would have taken. It says:

> Poetry simply must strive to elevate its arbitrary signs to natural ones; and only in this way does it distinguish itself from prose and become poetry. The means by which it does so are tone, words, the position of words, metre, rhetorical figures and tropes, similes, etc. (May 26, 1769; B 11/1, 609–10)

These sensual-sensory qualities of poetic style "approximate the arbitrary signs to the natural ones" (either by modelling the syntactic process of articulation, or by stimulating non-conventionalised processes of understanding), but they do not fully transform them into such. Arbitrary linguistic signs become fully natural only in dramatic poetry: Here, "words cease to be arbitrary signs and become *natural* signs of arbitrary things," as Lessing says (B 11/1, 610). – How is this possible? How is drama predestined to transform the arbitrary signs of speech into natural signs? The reason is as simple as it is compelling: Drama presents characters in action by making them speak. Thus, speech in drama is itself the object of mimesis – regardless of whether or not the act of speaking is performed on stage, as Lessing had already emphasised in the Correspondence on Tragedy (cf. Dec 18, 1756; B 3, 703). The playwright's *text* is a mimetic re-presentation of the realities of life, which is essentially an interpersonal reality. Mimesis of speaking, however, does not simply mean the reproduction of direct speech – speaking only becomes truly mimetic if it shows a character in action.

In his writings on dramatic theory, Lessing spelled this out, exemplified by a critique of the translation of a drama by Mme de Graffigny (cf. HD 20; B 6, 280–81). The speech under discussion is a reply in which "kind-hearted" Dorimond wards off the objection that, rather than giving away his belongings, he should enjoy them himself. He says: "J'en jouirai, je vous rendrai tous heureux" – "I shall enjoy it, I shall make all of you happy." In these laconic words, Lessing discovers the character of the person:

> Superb! Precision in every word! The truly effortless brevity of a man, for whom benevolence has become second nature, speaking of his own benevolence, if speak of it he must! To enjoy his own good fortune, to make others happy: both are one and the same to him. One is not merely a result or a part of the other; for him, one is entirely the other. In the same way that his heart does not recognise any difference between them, his mouth cannot create a difference. He speaks as if he said the same thing twice, as if both sentences were true tautological sentences, perfectly identical sentences, without the slightest conjunction. (HD 20; B 6, 280)

This is, succinctly, a representation of a way of speaking where language makes a person tangible and thus ceases to be a system of arbitrary signs. The translation criticised by Lessing destroys these characteristics of the text. It reads: "Only then will I begin finally, truly to enjoy my wealth – when I will have made you both happy through it." – Lessing expresses his dismay:

Unbearable! The sense is perfectly translated, but the spirit is gone: A torrent of words has suffocated it. This "only then" with its tail of "when"; this "finally," this "truly," this "through it": blunt specifications that give outpourings of a heart the ponderousness of deliberation and transform a warm sentiment into frosty speech. (HD 20; B 6, 280–81)

The "language of the heart" is a convincing form of poetical expression, a form of poetic speech that is destroyed if the "rules of grammar" are considered and the speech is "equipped with all the cold perfection and boring clarity that we demand from a logical sentence" (HD 20; B 6, 280). As a temporal art, poetry establishes itself to the extent that it becomes the mimesis of a speaking person.

The first book of *Laocoön* is published in 1766. The origins of the project date back to a phase of Lessing's life that is perhaps one of his most uncertain: Without saying goodbye to his friends, he leaves Berlin in November 1760 for Breslau, there to serve as a secretary under the fortress commander Friedrich Bogislav von Tauentzien – only to regret this step at once: In the few letters he writes to Moses Mendelssohn, he speaks of the "folly" of his decision (Dec 7, 1760; B 11/1, 356), calls it "a rash deed" and complains about misanthropic moods: "Oh, dearest friend, your Lessing is lost! In a year and a day, you will no longer know him. He is no longer himself. Oh my time, my time, my all I have – to sacrifice it thus for I don't know what intentions!" (Mar 30, 1761; B 11/1, 368).

Lessing's time in Breslau is not only a time of daily business, but also of contemplation and entertainment: In his spare time, Lessing devotes himself to his scholarly studies, in the evenings he goes to the theatre and, to stir the blood, he seeks the company of gamblers. When he recovers from a severe illness in 1764, he finds himself at a threshold in life: "The serious epoch of my life draws near;

I am beginning to be a man, and I flatter myself that I have burnt off the last traces of my youthful follies in this high fever. Fortunate illness!" (to Karl Wilhelm Ramler, Aug 5, 1764; B 11/1, 415).

The Breslau interlude ends in April 1765. Bringing along with him the drafts for *Laocoön*, Lessing returns to Berlin; here, his analysis, originally conceived as a systematic study, gains contour as an alternative interpretation to Winckelmann's. It ends with the fiction of a reflective pause in a process that is not yet concluded: "Winckelmann's History of Ancient Art has appeared, and I cannot venture a step further before I have read it" (B 5/2, 183).

Lessing's professional future remains uncertain. In a letter to his father, he emphasises that he has "not given up my formerly chosen way of life", and commits himself to "withdrawing myself from any service that is not completely to my liking" (Jun 13, 1764; B 11/1, 408–09). This is a decision in favour of existential uncertainty. In April 1767, he will leave Berlin, too, and seek his fortune in Hamburg. His path leads him back to the theatre and to the questions of dramatic theory that he had so passionately discussed with his friends in Berlin. At their centre stands the founding text of European literary theory: the *Poetics* of Aristotle.

Hamburg: Aristotelian Dramaturgy

"Pity and fear" (*Mitleid und Furcht*) – the formula with which Lessing translates the central terms of the Aristotelian *Poetics* (*eleos* and *phobos* in the original Greek) is one of the most often-quoted and memorable formulas of poetics ever. Whenever and wherever pity and fear are mentioned, Lessing is involved. Lessing's reading of Aristotle takes the study of the *Poetics* to a new intellectual level. Its basis is an ingenious philology that attempts to place Aristotle's treatise, which has not merely come down to us in fragments but was only roughly drafted in the first place, in the overall context of his thinking and interpret it from this perspective.

This undertaking was not planned. When Lessing takes up the position of journalist at the newly founded Hamburg National Theatre in April 1767, he is expected to comment on the theatre business week after week. The reviews themselves soon fade into the background – the actors, particularly Madame Hensel, the resident diva, had forbidden Lessing's criticism. Instead, he turns his attention more and more to general questions of dramatic theory, and – as already in *Laocoön* – he does so by approaching the matter as a lover of the theatre, as a philosopher and as a critic. The vivid combination of penetrating observation of specific phenomena and generalising aesthetic reflection, philological erudition and methodical comparison gives the *Hamburg Dramaturgy* its special character. Anyone who reads as a whole what arose from one specific occasion, giving rise to far-reaching poetological considerations, is faced with a text that seems to lose itself in detail while always keeping the fundamental in mind. Just as Lessing expects from the "good writer" that he "always has the best and most enlightened people of his time and place in mind" (HD 1; B 6, 191), he also expects his readers to follow him into the ramifications of his thinking and to abandon all hope of "droll" entertainment (cf. HD 50; B 6, 429).

The discussion of Aristotle's *Poetics* is the centrepiece of an ethical-aesthetic programme that understands poetry as a contribution to the cultivation of human consciousness. Poetry is mimesis – imitation of intra- and interpersonal life in its more or less lucky, more or less happy moments. In order to cultivate human consciousness, poetry must not simply imitate the phenomenal reality, "what is visible in nature," as Lessing puts it; it must also pay attention to "the nature of our feelings and thoughts" (HD 70; B 6, 533). Its foremost goal is to cultivate the ability to "direct one's attention at will" (HD 70; B 6, 534). The poetic representation interprets human life by contouring it and making it easier for the audience to fix their attention. Lessing has pinpointed this ability of literature to create models of human life, which has already been a crucial point in his fable essays, in his formula about artwork as a "silhouette of the totality made by the immortal creator"

(HD 79; B 6, 577). This silhouette itself, if it is to show the nature of things authentically, must be a structured whole in which everything has its natural consequences.

Here, too, it becomes apparent how closely aesthetic, religio-philosophical and ethical reflection are intertwined in Lessing's work. What is visible in nature is only instructive for an infinite spirit; finite spirits like human beings are supposed to perceive themselves in the drama as *moral* beings who take care of their own happiness in life, thus always running the risk of missing it. The theatre thus turns out to be a playground of theodicy: It presents the characters as moral beings and defends God and his creation against the idea that things might not be quite right in the moral world.

Drama only fulfils this task if it displays the reality it represents as a process, and if it succeeds in involving the audience in this process. This requires the art of perspectival representation, as Lessing programmatically developed it in the first essay of the *Hamburg Dramaturgy*. It consists in

> being able to shift oneself from the perspective of narrator to the authentic position of each and every person; to avoid describing passions and instead to let them develop before the eyes of the audience and grow smoothly with such illusory continuity that the audience must sympathise, whether it wants to or not. (HD 1; B 6, 187–88)

As he already did in *Laocoön*, Lessing makes it clear again that poetry is a temporal art. Its subject is human actions, in the case of tragedy sequences of events that produce a tragic outcome. Tragedy requires empathetic participation on the part of the audience in a process where people are drawn into an egocentric delusion, destroying their own happiness. The elaboration of a "plot" (HD 70; B 6, 532), as Lessing calls it, is therefore the foremost task of the tragedian. This applies especially when he takes his subject matter from history. History merely provides him with a repertoire of facts; translating these facts into a concatenation of causes and effects, which evolve from the psychodynamics of the characters entangled in them, is the creative task the poet is faced with:

> Dissatisfied with basing their possibility merely on historical authenticity, he will try to construct his characters in such a way as to make the events that set these characters into action arise necessarily from each other; he will try to measure the passions of each character precisely and to develop these passions through gradual steps; he will do all this so that overall, we perceive nothing but the most natural, orderly course of events. With every step his characters take, we would have to acknowledge that in the same heat of passion, the same state of affairs, we ourselves would have done the same. Nothing in all this would disconcert us except the imperceptible approach of an end from which our imaginations recoil. Once there, we find ourselves full of the sincerest compassion towards those who are carried away by such a fatal current, and full of terror knowing that a similar current could carry us away to commit deeds that in cold blood we imagine to be completely farfetched. (HD 32; B 6, 338–39)

Lessing's formula for tragedy is already explicated very clearly in this characterisation. Fear (*Furcht*), as he will later translate the Aristotelian *phobos*, is "compassion directed at ourselves" (HD 75; B 6, 557): "It is the fear that we ourselves could become the pitied object" (HD 75; B 6, 556). If we are to be able to sympathise with the disconcerting actions of the characters on stage, we must recognise in them an alter ego, and we must be able to perceive the evil deed as a final catastrophe, that is, as the end of a process. Therefore, Lessing eliminates the figure of the villain from the *dramatis personae*. Malice is not a motive. People do harm each other, no doubt about that – but they do not do so because they are wicked, but because they are deluded. This has already been considered in the Faust project, and this is what the programmatic first essays of the *Hamburg Dramaturgy* are about. The poet, according to Lessing's conviction,

> must never think so unphilosophically as to imagine that a person could want evil for evil's sake, that a person could act according to vicious principles, recognise the viciousness of those principles, and even boast about them to himself and others. Such a person is a monster, as hideous as he is uninstructive, and he is nothing but the miserable last resort of an insipid mind who thinks glittering tirades are the highest achievement in tragedy. (HD 2; B 6, 196)

Lessing defends the perpetrator against his deed. The evil deed is not a result of his wickedness; it is evil he does against his better judgement. The real evil is the dynamics of passions in which someone gets entangled, and the concatenation of their passionate actions into a plot, which in the extreme case is so diabolical that – as Lessing says about his *Faust* project – we might think it was "arranged by Satan" (as cited in RP, 45).

The fact that Lessing banned the villain from the stage is not only motivated by his anthropology and religious philosophy, but also by his moral convictions: The idea that "a person could want evil for evil's sake" is evil itself. The interpretation of social conflicts as a struggle between virtue and vice arises from a projection mechanism that nourishes these conflicts and escalates them. Therefore, the *Hamburg Dramaturgy* dismisses all those plots which represent the struggle of personified good against evil incarnate – first and foremost, the "Christian tragedy" in the form of the martyr tragedy. In it, Lessing finds exemplified the principle of the stoic endurance tragedy, against which he had already spoken out in the Correspondence on Tragedy.

In the Correspondence, he had spoken of the "stiff-neckedness of virtue" (Nov 28, 1756; B 3, 680), meaning a virtue that does not deserve its name because it has lost all sense of human proportion. In the *Hamburg Dramaturgy*, the martyr's heroic self-sacrifice becomes a nuisance to him because it testifies to pious frenzy, and he questions the very possibility of a Christian tragedy, since the "character of the true Christian" is completely "untheatrical":

> Do not his most characteristic traits – quiet tranquillity and consistent gentleness – somehow conflict with the entire business of tragedy, which seeks to purify passions through passions? Does not his expectation of a rewarding happiness in the next life contradict the selfless altruism with which we wish to see all great and good actions on the stage undertaken and performed? (HD 2; B 6, 193)

Just as evil personified springs from a primitive stage of moral development, so, too, is the figure of the martyr a distorted image of the true Christian. Already the Earl of Shaftesbury, whom Lessing particularly appreciated, had criticised this ethos in his *Essay on the Freedom of Wit and Humour* (1709) by describing the "*disinterestedness*" of human behaviour as a sign of moral enlightenment (EoS, 98), and Lessing himself will emphasise in the *Education of the Human Race* that actions can only be considered truly good if they are not aimed at a reward in this life or the next (cf. § 85; B 10, 96).

In lieu of the struggle between evil personified and virtue ready for unconditional self-sacrifice, Lessing therefore prefers stories that interpret the "Fall of the virtuous hero" (GTN 3, 305). They are ideally suited to arouse pity and fear, and to cultivate these social virtues by giving them a proper measure in the sense of the *Nicomachean Ethics* (cf. HD 78; B 6, 574).

What applies to tragedy also applies to comedy. The latter should equally train our self-perception, which it can only do by refraining from making the comic figure the object of ridicule. This goes against our egocentric tendencies. We like to laugh about people and their shortcomings; the art of comedy, therefore, essentially consists in inventing characters that overwhelmingly embody what makes us laugh. Comic characters are products of the imagination; they testify to the skill of the author in using his licence to exaggerate in the most ingenious way possible.

The conviction that laughter is triggered by deviations from ideal behaviour is shared by Lessing: "Every absurdity, every contrast between imperfections and reality is laughable" (HD 28; B 6, 322). A behaviour is imperfect in relation to human measure (what Lessing calls "reality"), from which it deviates in exaggeration. – However, he cannot reconcile himself with mockery. Just as the hero of tragedy must be "cut from the same cloth as we are" (HD 75; B 6, 599), the hero of comedy must not be without qualities we appreciate. Therefore, Lessing differentiates between laughter and derision: "We can laugh about a person, and on occasion laugh at him, without deriding him in the least" (HD 28; B 6, 322–23). The refusal to empathise that is typical of the derisive comedy (*Verlachkomödie*), which caters to our crude delight in mockery and schadenfreude, is replaced with laughter about a character we sympathise with, i.e., a character in whom we can recognise our own comic entanglements and delusions.

Drama is supposed to serve as a mirror of our own imperfections in a way that arouses either pity or amusement. However, tragedy and comedy also differ in terms of the importance of plot or character in them. In the case of tragedy, it is the playwright's task to develop the tragic sequence of events from the dynamics of the characters entangled in it; in the case of comedy, the sequence of situations "exists merely to get [the characters] going and to allow them to express themselves" (HD 51; B 6, 437). However, this behaviour should not arise from the imagination of our social prejudices but from a subjectively comprehensible reason.

Therefore, comedy, too, requires the art of perspectival representation that takes the reality experienced by the characters seriously and makes it accessible to understanding empathy. And therefore, comedy, too, must think of the dramatic character as a process, that is, as a character who unfolds his behavioural tendencies in the play, thus getting caught up in situations in which he loses his poise, but without being made contemptible. The kind of laughter trained by comedy is an art of living: The "true and universal value" of comedy "lies in laughter itself": "in the exercising of our ability to identify the laughable" (HD 29; B 6, 323) and thus to reconcile ourselves with the imperfections of human existence.

The *Hamburg Dramaturgy* elaborates in detail what has already been hinted at in the Correspondence on Tragedy, and what is explicitly discussed in the fable essays and *Laocoön*: It turns its back on the old European model of *prodesse et delectare* ('benefitting and pleasing') in favour of the question of the specific purpose of the respective medium and genre: Tragedy relies on compassion to cultivate a sense of justice, comedy relies on laughter to cultivate a sense of purity and personal integrity. Both transform elementary human "passions" into "virtuous dispositions" (HD 78; B 6, 574). The human ability to recognise in the other an alter ego, and to relate to this alter ego, becomes a virtue when it succeeds in setting conscious limits to moral feelings.

Therefore, the cultivation of morality is an ethical project. It trains the ability to question traditional moral concepts and thus counteract their destructive and self-destructive tendencies. These include the powerful desire for revenge and retribution as well as the very human habit of judging and condemning self-righteously, but also the seductive impulse to expose and shame all apparently deviant fellow creatures through ridicule and scorn. This dark side of morality turns out to be a problem in need of solving for Lessing.

The *Hamburg Dramaturgy* is one of the most influential writings on dramatic theory of the 18th century. In 1769, it was already available in a two-volume edition, with a vast number of imitations following in its wake. Numerous writings focused their interest on the art of acting, which Lessing had only considered in the first essays of the *Dramaturgy* (cf. WFB, 33–45). All of them – like the *Letters on Theatre* (*Briefe über die Schaubühne*) by Joseph von Sonnenfels, proponent of Enlightenment in Austria – are forgotten today. For Lessing himself, the venture was a fiasco. His attempt to establish a publishing house in conjunction with Johann Joachim Christoph Bode had failed; obviously, Lessing's expectations were exaggerated, his economic ideas unrealistic, his aesthetic demands too costly (cf. JPR, 30–31). The *Hamburg Dramaturgy* fell victim to printers of pirated editions. After hardly a year, it was discontinued with an essay in which Lessing accounted to himself and his audience for his literary practice and defended the principle of criticism, as he had practised it in the *Dramaturgy*, as a creative principle of his dramatic work.

> I am neither an actor nor a playwright. [...] I would be very poor, cold, and shortsighted, had I not to some extent learnt how to unobtrusively borrow foreign treasures, warm myself at foreign fires, and strengthen my eyes through the glasses of art. As such, I was always ashamed or upset when I read or heard something against criticism. It is said to stifle genius, and yet I flattered myself that I had obtained from it something that comes very near to genius. [...] If, with its help, I can bring something into being that is better than what someone with my talents would do without criticism, yet nonetheless it costs me too much time; I must be free of other business and uninterrupted by external distractions, I must have all my reading at the ready, and I must, at every step, be able to calmly rifle through all of the observations I have ever made regarding customs and passions. As such, no one in the world could be less suited than I to labour to entertain the theatre with novelty. (HD 101–104; B 6, 680–81)

This self-portrait can hardly be valued too highly – even if it did give the 19th century occasion to belittle Lessing's poetic ability. Lessing was not a playwright like Shakespeare or Molière; the theatre was not his primary medium for expressing and conveying his ideas, however important the status it held in his life. It was part of a broader reflection of the cultural, especially the religious heritage to which his critical attention was directed. If he encounters the contemporary cult of genius with scepti-cism, he does so with the proudly modest claim of being a genius himself: a genius of learning and of criticism. But his willingness to learn was not limited to the field of literature, nor could the playwright, according to Lessing, stop at having studied dramatic principles. To his brother Karl, who dabbled in literary matters and whose dramas he critically commented on, he wrote: "Do not take my objections badly. Study morality diligently, learn to express yourself well and correctly, and cultivate your own char-acter – without this, I cannot imagine a good playwright" (Oct 28, 1768; B 11/1, 559).

Composed in 1763: *Minna von Barnhelm*

On February 15, 1763, Prussia, Austria and Saxony sign the Treaty of Hubertusburg. According to its title page, Lessing's *Minna von Barnhelm, or the Soldier's Fortune* (*Minna von Barnhelm, oder das Soldatenglück*) was composed in this year. That is fiction and part of the game. After *Philotas*, the comedy about Major von Tellheim, who is in Prussian service, and his Saxon fiancée Minna von Barnhelm is Lessing's second reflection on the Seven Years' War and its consequences. While *Philotas*, parabolically condensed, is set in an indeterminate Greek past, the curtain in *Minna* rises to reveal an inn in Berlin, where six months after the peace treaty (on August 22, 1763), Fräulein von Barnhelm arrives in search of her missing lover.

Lessing has worked on the comedy for four years. The play premieres on September 30, 1767 at the Hamburg National Theatre; Lessing's theory of comedy, which he develops in the *Hamburg Dramaturgy*, has prepared it. Its success overshadows even the sensational success of *Sara*. And the further stage history of *Minna* is a success story, too: Still in the same year, the play is performed in Frankfurt am Main, Wetzlar, Vienna and Leipzig (cf. US, 18–21): "Where to find a theatre that does not play it?" Christian Heinrich Schmid asks in his *Chronology of the German Theatre* (*Chronologie des deutschen Theaters*) from 1775 (as cited in B 6, 811).

Goethe attributed the success of the play to its "specific temporary value" (TaP II/7; MA 16, 304), and research has not ceased to point out this topicality and relevance of the drama, which subsequently inspired a whole series of now forgotten soldier plays – Karl Hayo von Stockmayer (1898) actually identified 260 of them (KHS, 101–20; cf. MF 2). But Lessing's *Minna* is not a soldier play in the strict sense of the term: It does not depict a class of society as such, and it goes beyond the current events of the war. Once again, it is a play grounded in religious and moral philosophy. By its nature, this play is also literature made of literature and a prime example of a dramatic production that owes itself entirely to criticism. In it, Lessing ingeniously combines Molière's comedy about the misanthrope Alceste (*Le Misanthrope*, 1666) and Shakespeare's tragedy about the Moor of Venice (*Othello*, 1604) – and he does not fail to refer to these two templates explicitly in the play itself.

The centre of the drama is a good deed with its ambivalent consequences: Tellheim has proved magnanimous in the collection of contribution payments and has not only agreed with the Saxon representatives on the smallest negotiable sum but even advanced the missing money himself. When he wants to claim reimbursement after the end of the war, he is suspected by the Prussian authorities of having been bribed with the money (cf. IV/6; B 6, 83). Now, he is de facto under house arrest in the King of Spain

Inn. If convicted, he will face imprisonment; he would be socially discredited. On the other hand, it is this very good deed, which threatens to drive the war hero into social ruin, that has earned him Minna's love: "I loved you for this even though I had not yet met you" (IV/6; B 6, 83).

The trial against Tellheim is already decided at the beginning of the on-stage action. The King himself has quashed it. There is a good reason for Tellheim's not knowing: A letter to this effect does not reach him at first because he has had to vacate his room for the two young ladies from Saxony (cf. V/6; B 6, 96), and moreover, Minna's uncle, Count of Bruchsall, arrives in Berlin a day after his niece due to an accident (cf. II/2; B 6, 34). This *one* day gives the dramatist Lessing the necessary space for his psychological drama. It is the drama of the honourable man who has proved himself a true philanthropist in war and who, in the face of the situation he now finds himself in, is in danger of losing faith in humanity and the world: He dismisses his loyal servant Just, pushes away his friend Paul Werner, and passes on the suspicion of treachery, which is directed against him, to his beloved. Before the finale effects his awakening from this "nightmare" (V/12; B 6, 107) of misanthropy, he will accuse Minna of having come to Berlin merely to break up with him (cf. V/10; B 6, 104) and thus risk making himself utterly miserable.

In this play about good fortune, Minna's role is to keep her eyes on this fortune, while Tellheim's part is to lose sight of it and to "grumble against Providence" (I/6; B 6, 19), as he says in conversation with his friend Marloff's widow. Tellheim's grumbling, accordingly, has its counterpart in a prayer that Minna sends to heaven after she has found her lover again. This prayer expresses the religio-philosophical insight that true prayer is nothing less than the blissful experience of gratitude and the reflection on this gratitude:

> I have him again! ... Am I alone? I don't want to be alone for nothing. *She folds her hands.* I am not alone! *looking up* One single, thankful thought directed to heaven is the most welcome prayer. I have found him. I have found him! *She flings her arms wide.* I am happy, what can be more pleasing to God's eyes than a joyful creature. [...] Unhappiness is good, too. Perhaps heaven took everything away from him just to give him everything back in the shape of myself. (II/7; B 6, 41)

The whole of reality encompasses both: an inseparable intermingling of happiness and unhappiness. True happiness consists in being able to perceive this; true unhappiness consists in sinking into depression in the face of misfortune, becoming blind to the experience of happiness. In the great reunion scene, Minna will remind her Tellheim of it. When he reveals his true situation to Minna and the audience, he breaks into a laugh, in the bitterness of which Minna recognises the "terrible laughter of the misanthrope":

> Your laughter is killing me, Tellheim! If you believe in virtue and Providence, Tellheim, then don't laugh! I have never heard curses more dreadful than your laughter. [...] Providence, believe me, always indemnifies the man who is honourable, and very often ahead of time. [...] You know that I came uninvited to the first party at which I thought I should find you. I only came because of you. I came with the firm intention of loving you – I loved you already! –, with the firm intention of possessing you, even if I had found you as black and ugly as the Moor of Venice. You are not as black and ugly, nor, I think, as jealous. But Tellheim, Tellheim, you do have a lot in common with

him. Oh, these wild inflexible men who can fix their obstinate eyes on nothing but the ghost of their honour and who steel themselves against any other feeling! (IV/6; B 6, 83–84)

With this reference to misanthropy and to the Moor of Venice, the two master dramas that underlie Lessing's play about the soldier's fortune are prominently mentioned, and the "ghost of honour" is also intended as a reference to Lessing's templates and his creative intention in dealing with them: Molière's Alceste is an "homme d'honneur" (I/1; M, 8); Shakespeare's Othello turns into an "honourable murderer" (V/2; WS, 393). The former hates people because they are insincere or do not have the decency to hate the insincere (I/1; 16–17), and unluckily falls in love with a young woman who brilliantly masters the courtly roleplay he so despises; the latter gets caught up in an intrigue that destroys his faith in the world because he believes he has been betrayed by his beloved: "If she be false, O then heaven mocks itself" (III/3; WS, 299).

In the comedy about the "Cantankerous Lover" (such is the subtitle of Molière's comedy), Lessing recognises the potential tragedy of the virtuous war hero Othello, and he links these two figures into one story. To do so, he has to give to the character, who, as a comic figure, is defined by his misanthropy, a personal background that turns an unfounded social defect into the natural consequence of a character and his dispositions. He does this by depicting Tellheim as a philanthropist who proves his philanthropy in wartime, and letting him get caught up in a process that reveals his dark side: Only someone who values honesty and personal integrity as highly as Tellheim can turn bitter upon losing his honour, that is, his "irreproachable character" (IV/6; B 6, 86); only someone who lives in the certainty that there are "no completely inhuman people"

(I/8; B 6, 23) can darken when he realises that he is being misunderstood and slandered by his own people for a "noble act" (IV/6; B 6, 83).

Molière's misanthrope is a comic figure because he finds himself in the awkward situation of falling in love with an actress, and because his sincerity exceeds any reasonable measure; but his story is potentially tragic because in the finale he not only pushes away his friend, but also the woman who cannot bring herself to leave Paris and exile herself from society for his sake.

In the *Hamburg Dramaturgy*, Lessing has defended Molière's comedy about the virtuous hero against Rousseau's accusation that it makes an honest man contemptible. He rejects this objection with the argument that "the laughter which derives from the situations the playwright puts him in" does not diminish our "admiration" for the character (HD 28; B 6, 323). We may doubt whether this actually applies to Alceste, but it certainly applies to Lessing's new version of this character: Tellheim is "the honest man in the play" (HD 28; B 6, 323).

Minna's reference to the "ghost of honour", on which "wild inflexible men" fix their "obstinate eyes", outlines the course that the play will take. Tellheim's furious confession to misanthropy – "Bile is the best thing we have" (V/11; B 6, 105), he will reply to Paul Werner – marks the end of a process which, accelerated by the 'ring intrigue', plumbs the depths of his character. This is the point of the psychological processes in Lessing's comedy. The tragedy of Othello allows him to present the character of the philanthropist turned misanthrope. While in *Othello*, it is the handkerchief of the beloved that is passed on to the Moor of Venice as proof of her infidelity, here it is the engagement ring pawned by Tellheim, which Minna acquires from the innkeeper to return to her lover. Othello falls victim to an intrigue that shakes his relationship to the world; Tellheim gets entangled in a game of his lady, who takes the mischievous joke too far and thus risks being misjudged by him. – In either case, nothing less is at stake than the question of whether things are quite right in the moral world.

In his study of Terence's comedies, Lessing has defined the "collision of characters" (HD 99; B 6, 670) as the centre of comedy. The play does not need to aim at the moral improvement of the characters; it is only meant to make the characters more socially acceptable: "No one changes, but each reins in the other just enough to keep him safe from the disadvantages of excess" (HD 99; B 6, 671). This is also put into practice in *Minna*. The "continuing play among the characters" is meant to make it impossible for the audience to guess the playwright's "twists and turns" (HD 99; B 6, 671), even when the plot itself has come to an end. The external obstacle that prevents Tellheim from taking Minna for his wife has been dissolved (like the trial that Molière's Alceste has been dragged into by his adversaries); but the collision of the characters only comes to an end when they have shown both their bright and dark sides to the audience: Tellheim in his generosity and his misanthropy, Minna in her cheerfulness and her mischief. Her "No, I cannot regret having caught a glimpse of your whole heart!" (V/12; B 6, 106) is echoed in Tellheim's "You actresses! I should have known you better than that" (V/12; B 6, 107).

Minna catches a glimpse of his whole heart when she pretends to Tellheim that she has been disinherited because of him. Her alleged misfortune arouses Tellheim's pity – a pity that he had not only shown towards the enemy in war, but also towards Just's father (I/8) and Marloff's widow (I/6) – and sets him free to be himself: "Vexation and stifled rage had clouded my whole soul [...]. I feel the urge for self-preservation because I have something to preserve which is more valuable than myself and which has to be preserved by me." (V/5; B 6, 95). – Tellheim's apologia for pity corresponds to Minna's praise of laughter: "Laughter keeps us more reasonable than melancholy" (IV/6; B 6, 82), because it sets a cheerful perspective against a pessimistic view of the situation.

The play among the characters is not limited to the collision between the actress Minna and the honest Tellheim. Lessing distributes different psychological dispositions among the various characters of the play and 'nuances' them, as he occasionally says (cf. HD 52; B 6, 439). This allows him to contrast and contour the characters against each other. Traits of an honourable man are also to be found in Just, a simple baggage carrier, who shames Minna's maid Franciska by telling her about Tellheim's former servants (cf. III/2; B 6, 47–50), who all turned out to be rogues. The character of the gambler, taken to the extreme, is embodied by Riccaut, a character in the tradition of the boastful 'miles gloriosus', whose maxim of "*corriger la fortune*" (IV/2; B 6, 75) is opposed to Minna's art of cheerfully changing perspectives and recognising fortune in misfortune, but with whom she still shares the characteristic of "pride". It is her pride or "egotism", as Minna says, that tempts her to give Tellheim "some of his own medicine" after his rude rejection (III/12; B 6, 68). She does so despite the objection of the strictly "moralising" Franciska (IV/1; B 6, 69), who, in her turn, is unwilling to admit that every character has its "*individual perfections*" (B 2, 407). The art that Lessing's comedy demonstrates is the art of learning to live with their dark side: "My dear girl, you have such sympathy for good people, but when are you going to learn to put up with the bad ones? – After all, they are people too... and often not nearly such bad people as they seem to be. You simply have to find their good side" (IV/3; B 6, 76).

Lessing's *Minna* is another theatrical theodicy, and therefore more than just a couple's love story. It opens up a whole panorama of relationships (between Tellheim and Just, Tellheim and Marloff, Tellheim and Paul Werner), which have been forged in the war and are now in danger of being broken up by the return to civil order, with its distinction between "'mine' and 'yours'" (II/2; B 6, 35). That the attained peace does not "destroy" this good (II/1; B 6, 30) is the true happiness represented in the comedy.

A Modernised Virginia: *Emilia Galotti*

In Hamburg, Lessing had also worked on a tragedy project that had occupied him ever since the late 1750s. The title had long been decided: *Emilia Galotti*. So had the underlying concept. Already in a letter to Friedrich Nicolai dated January 21, 1758, there is a mention of a 'domestic Virginia', 'separated' from any political interest (B 11/1, 267): "So you will see that it is nothing more than a modernised Virginia, freed from all political interest," he says after the completion of the play in a letter to his brother Karl (Mar 1, 1772; B 11/2, 362).

Virginia is the legendary virgin from the third book of Livy's *History of Rome*, who is stabbed to death by her father Virginius because the tyrant Appius Claudius has his eye on her and tries to make her his sex slave under false pretences. Emilia Galotti, Lessing's eponymous heroine, will explicitly refer to this character in the finale of the tragedy, as she asks her father to stab her into the heart with a dagger:

> Long ago there was a father who, to save his daughter from disgrace, took the first steel that came to hand and plunged it into her heart – and brought her thus to life a second time. But all such deeds are of long ago! There are no such fathers anymore! (V/7; B 7, 370)

This father, Odoardo Galotti, is the actual protagonist of the drama. His Fall is at the centre of the tragedy. As in his earlier dramas, Lessing sets himself the task of modernising an ancient subject, that is, of tracing its inner logic and critically examining it. The reference to the template, which is intended to enable the viewer and reader to understand the reinterpretation of the story, is part of this programme. Its goal is not the depoliticisation of a political myth – quite the contrary: Lessing's modernisation of the Virginia story is committed to political enlightenment. It exposes the pseudo-political dimension of a historiography that tells the story of a struggle for political power as a story of ruthless sexual desire:

> His present subject is a domestic (*bürgerliche*) Virginia entitled *Emilia Galotti*. For he has separated the story of the Roman Virginia from everything of interest to the state, in the belief that the fate of a daughter killed by a father who values her virtue more highly than her life is tragic enough in itself, and sufficiently able to stir the heart in general, even if it does not lead to the overthrow of the entire political constitution. (To Nicolai, Jan 21, 1758; B 11/1, 267)

Thus, Lessing's concept is already outlined at an early stage. It consists in transforming an act of political heroism, which brings down a lecherous tyrant and puts an end to the Decemviri, into a moral catastrophe. The political myth of the victory of chastity (*pudicitia*) over lust (*libido*) is not continued by Lessing, but radically reconsidered.

A Modernised Virginia: *Emilia Galotti*

When he speaks of a "domestic Virginia", what he has in mind is – as it was in the case of *Sara* – a tragedy in the sense that it represents a story in which interpersonal conflicts escalate in a self-destructive manner. This has little to do with the question of political power struggle, which is at the centre of the Republican Tragedy, and equally little with the question of a power struggle between estates, let alone social classes in the 19th-century sense.

Lessing translates the political conflict between the decemvirs, patricians and plebeians into a conflict between private individuals, whose difference in status – high nobility on the one hand, simple landed gentry on the other – has no political implications whatsoever. The *dramatis personae* all come from the social class which Lessing's *Dialogues for Freemasons* (*Gespräche für Freimaurer*) will refer to as "good company": "princes, counts, gentry, officers, councillors of every description, merchants, artists" (B 10, 53) – excluding the merchants. There is no trace of a social, let alone an ideological division between *the* nobility and *the* bourgeoisie.

This transformation of the original story is part of an even broader modernisation strategy. In order to transform a myth from political history into a tragedy, Lessing first rewrites the roles that are to be filled:

The ruthless despot (Appius Claudius), who is seized by a sensual passion (*libido*), becomes a prince (Hettore Gonzaga), who loves "in all sincerity" (I/6; B 7, 300) and nearly loses his mind when he learns that the young woman (Emilia), whose "gaiety and wit" have "entranced" him (II/4; B 7, 313), is as good as married. The father (Virginius), who saves his defenceless child from the grasp of this lecherous despot by resorting to the only means left to him in order to save her honour, becomes an "adolescent hothead with grey hair" (Odoardo) (V/2; B 7, 359), who considers the Prince a "libertine" (II/4; B 7, 313) and suspects him of having his eye on Emilia only "to shame him" (II/5; B 7, 314). The betrothed (Icilius) who defies the ruler becomes a young nobleman (Appiani), who has come to court to serve the Prince of his own free will, and who is now so melancholy about leaving that on his wedding day, he allows an insult to make his "blood boil" (II/11; B 7, 325) and himself to mortally offend the Prince's chamberlain. The willing henchman of the despot (Marcus Claudius) becomes a status-conscious courtier (Marinelli), who pursues his own goals in the game of intrigue because the loss of his honour obliges him to get rid of his insulter. Finally, the silent victim of despotic desire (Virginia) becomes a young woman (Emilia) who submits to her mother's will in everything (cf. II/6; B 7, 317) and who eventually tempts her father to murder her in order to protect her from her own susceptibility.

Lessing not only rewrites the roles of the template but also expands them by two female figures for which there is no equivalent in Livy: the Prince's former mistress (Orsina), who uses the father of the new flame as an instrument for her revenge by suggesting to him that the Prince and his daughter have already been lovers for some time; and a mother (Claudia) fighting like a lioness for that same daughter, who knows about her child's innocence, and implores her husband to remember his role as a father.

Lessing thus expands and densifies the network of characters entangled in the conflict. And he focuses the representation on the psychodynamics of humiliation and resentment, bias and prejudice. Since this is what nurtures all conflicts and escalates them, he cannot be content with rewriting and expanding the *dramatis personae*; he also has to turn the template into a psychological drama and, as he expresses it in the *Hamburg Dramaturgy*, "shift himself from the perspective of narrator to the authentic position of each and every person" (HD 1; B 6, 187).

This art of perspectival representation is actualised in the art of arranging the characters' speeches across the scenes in such a way that the viewer recognises what they are "blind and deaf" to (cf. GTN 1, 12): Because of a conflict over Sabionetta, the Galottis' country estate, Odoardo believes that the Prince "hates" him (II/4; B 7, 312), while the Prince in fact esteems him: "An old soldier, proud and rough, otherwise upright and good!", even though he is "no friend of mine" (I/4; B 7, 297). The hatred Odoardo attributes to the Prince prompts Appiani to keep his wedding a secret from the latter, while the Prince declares it "would have pleased me greatly, had I been able to secure [Appiani's] services" (I/6; B 7, 302). The interplay of perspectives is most strikingly demonstrated in the accounts of the encounter between Emilia and the Prince at church. Emilia is so utterly terrified by the flattering words with which the Prince approaches her during Mass that she begs her "guardian angel" to "strike" her "deaf" (II/6; B 7, 315), only to actually fail to hear what the Prince is telling her: "Her fear was contagious; I trembled with her and finally begged her forgiveness" (III/3; B 7, 331). Such is his story as he tells it to Marinelli. In all Virginia dramas predating Lessing, it is taken for granted that innocence is being defended against evil incarnate. Lessing not only dissolves this narrative but translates it into a prejudiced perspective. The Prince is not a "libertine who admires, covets" (II/4; B 7, 313), as Odoardo puts it, he is not "a man of the world" (II/6; B 7, 318), as Claudia suspects, but an innocent lover who is caught in an exceptional psychological situation. The play secures him that minimum amount of benevolence necessary for him to not be denied the audience's sympathy.

In order to develop the final catastrophe from the psychodynamics of the characters involved, Lessing must give each character a sore point that makes him or her "go mad"

(I/6; B 7, 304) when touched: "Utter your accursed 'the same' once more and drive the blade into my heart!" (I/6; B 7, 303), the Prince cries out when Marinelli reveals to him that Emilia is about to be married to Count Appiani. "That is just the spot where I could be hurt most mortally!" (II/4; B 7, 813), Odoardo Galotti knows when he learns that the Prince has taken a liking to his daughter. "Heaven and Hell!", "Death and damnation!" (II/10; B7, 324), are the words with which Marinelli reacts to Appiani calling him a spiteful and cowardly jackass, which has been provoked by his contemptuous utterance about the Galotti family. Last but not least, the lovelessness and neglect with which the Prince encounters Orsina – he has "not even read" her letter (IV/3; B 7, 345) – make her "foolish" (I/6; B 7, 301) and prompt her to come to Dosalo with dagger and poison (cf. IV/7; B 7, 355), i.e., with the intention of murder and suicide.

The logic of character portrayal is explicitly reflected on in the Conti scene. The Prince accuses the painter, who brings him Orsina's portrait, of having transformed "pride [...] into dignity, scorn into smiles, a tendency towards gloomy reverie into gentle melancholy" (I/4; B 7, 296). This accusation fails to make any impression. Conti is an "artist who thinks" (I/4; B 7, 296); he paints "with the eyes of love" (I/4; B 7, 297), meaning that he is able to perceive the "individual perfections" (B 2, 407) of a character in their outward appearance. This is a variation on the Laocoön theme: What painting, which can only capture a single moment, vaguely alludes to, poetry translates into a process in which the character unfolds their typical tendencies. The drama shows the viewer how the Prince's lovelessness drives Orsina into a frenzy of revenge.

The characters' vulnerability is the prerequisite for the catastrophes staged in Lessing's psychological drama. As evil emerges from rashness, Lessing deliberately chooses the traditional unity of time to advance the psychodynamics of the action. "Yes, if only time were outside of us! – If a minute by the hand of the clock were not able to expand in us into years!" (II/8; B 7, 320): With this lamentation, Appiani gets to the heart of the psychological and moral dimension of time – "being one last step away from the goal or not having started out yet, is actually the same thing" (II/8; B 7, 321). His melancholy reflection on the one step through which (as already in ancient tragedy) human happiness is at stake, is echoed in Odoardo's warning of the one step that is "enough to turn into a false step" (II/2; B 7, 309). The Prince experiences this moral dimension of time through the immediate need to act that Emilia's imminent wedding puts him under. The hasty "With pleasure!" (I/8; B 7, 307), with which he agrees to sign a death sentence in the Camillo Rota episode, already hints at the pattern of rashness leading to catastrophe.

Prejudice and thoughtless reaction cause the characters to miss the right moment to act, so that their rashness and oversight form a fatal concatenation: Appiani has failed to inform the Prince of his wedding plans because he is biased by Odoardo's insinuation that the Prince is his enemy, and he is carried away to mortally offend Marinelli, who has now stepped between him and the Prince. The Prince, in despair over the news of Emilia's imminent marriage, is tempted to give Marinelli free rein and thus the leeway to take his revenge on Appiani. Emilia fails to tell Appiani about her encounter with the Prince at church because her mother, from painful personal experience, advises her to keep it a secret from her fiancé. And Odoardo fails to speak to Emilia because he is so beside himself over the news that she has enchanted the Prince that he cannot wait for her return from church.

These instances of rashness and oversight culminate in a series of coincidences that tragically pile up in the finale and are discussed by the characters themselves. Almost blasphemously, Orsina comments on the fact that the Prince has turned up in Dosalo, though not in response to her written invitation. When she informs Marinelli that "the word *coincidence* is blasphemy", when she recognises in the Prince's presence the "immediate act" of "all-loving Providence" (IV/3; B 7, 347), she makes Heaven an accomplice to her murderous intentions – not unlike what Odoardo will do when he interprets Emilia's appearance as a sign that Heaven has chosen him to murder his daughter in order to save her from becoming the Prince's whore:

> What if this were the usual deception? What if she is not worthy of what I plan to do for her? – *pause* Do for her? And what do I plan to do for her? – Have I the heart to tell myself? – Here I am, thinking a thing! A thing that can only be thought! – Monstrous! Begone, begone! I cannot wait for her. No! – *heavenward* He who plunged her, in her innocence, into this abyss, let him draw her out again. What need has he of my hand to help him? Begone! *He starts to leave and sees Emilia coming.* Too late! Ah! he wants my hand, he wants it! (V/6; B 7, 367)

The murder of the child by her own father is the telos at which Lessing's tragedy is aimed. From the beginning, he has identified it as the true catastrophe of the traditional story. Therefore, he had to translate the narrative of an honour killing into an act of self-destruction. The solution Lessing found for this problem is a prime example of his art of pattern recognition and combinatorics. The finale combines the Virginia myth with the tragedy of the Moor of Venice, which also inspired the finale of *Minna*. And here, too, it is the motif of honour that allows Lessing to cast the character of the tragic murderer Othello in the role of the republican virtuous hero Virginius. This turns Odoardo – the father, reminded of his father role by all the characters in the play (Appiani, the Prince, Orsina, Claudia), without being able to live up to it – into the actual tragic figure of the finale.

For Lessing, Othello is the epitome of the tragic hero because in delusional blindness, "rash as fire" (V/2; WS, 382), he destroys what is dearest to him, and thus his own happiness in life. Just as the intriguer Iago "poisons" the unsuspecting Othello with the suspicion (cf. III/3; WS, 302) that his beloved has been unfaithful to him, Orsina poisons Odoardo with the idea that the Prince and his daughter are in league with each other: "Is it taking effect, old man? is it taking effect?" (IV/7; B 7, 355). Othello is the "honourable murderer" (V/2; WS, 393), who avenges creation by killing Desdemona, this "cunning'st pattern of excelling nature" (V/2; WS, 373) degenerated into a "strumpet" (V/2; WS, 378). Odo-ardo, literally 'burning with rage' (*odio ardo*), does the same. For him, too, the order of creation is at stake: He presumes to destroy the "masterpiece of nature" (I/5; B 7, 300) formed from too fragile a clay, and to break the rose "ere the storm scattered its petals" (V/7; B 7, 370) – another quote from *Othello* (cf. GTN 3, 377–78).

The finale is centred around the motif of seduction: "Brute force! Brute force! Who cannot defy brute force? What we call brute force is nothing: seduction is the only true force" (V/7; B 7, 369). Emilia is talking about being seduced into sensuality – the true seduction, however, which takes tragic form in Lessing's play, is being seduced into violence. With her invocation of the sanctified women who committed suicide – "To escape a fate not worse than that, thousands have leaped into torrential waters and are saints!" (V/7; B 7, 369) –, and with reference to the honour killing by Virginius – "Long ago there was a father who, to save his daughter from disgrace, took the first steel that came to hand and plunged it into her heart" (V/7; B 7, 370) –, Emilia seduces her father into protecting her from her own sensuality, and makes him an accomplice to her suicide. All this is to be read as an instance of self-destructive delusion.

In fact, the finale of *Emilia* is not only a prime example of Lessing's art of criticising narrative patterns, but also for the difficulties that every reading of Lessing is faced with; we cannot understand it from interpreting the characters' speeches psychologically. Lessing's dramatic language follows a different logic: He always has his characters cite the sources that are under discussion in the drama. This includes, among others, the *City of God*, in which the Church Father Augustine mentions the rumour about the virgins jumping into the floods for fear of sexual violence. Augustine takes this as an opportunity to reject the suicide of Lucretia, reported by Livy in the first book of his *History of Rome*, as the error of a soul driven by the desire for "fame" (AA 1,19; 45). Emilia's reference to her and her father's will is – no different than in the case of Philotas – an expression of tragic irony: She fails to perceive what is truly good. Her act of self-assertion will leave all those entangled in the tragedy devastated.

The tragedy, which Lessing had begun working on in the autumn of 1757, was completed in February 1772. Lessing is under time pressure: It premieres on March 13 on the occasion of the birthday of his sovereign, Duchess Philippine Charlotte, in Wolfenbüttel – "with extraordinary applause," as *The Wandsbeck Courier* (*Wandsbecker Bothe*) reports: "You know what Lessing usually writes for the theatre, but it is said throughout that he has outdone himself this time" (JB 1, 352).

Wolfenbüttel: Fragments of an Anonymous Author

In December 1769, Lessing was appointed librarian of the Herzog August Bibliothek (ducal library) in Wolfenbüttel. This marked the end of a long period in which he had tried to gain a foothold in a profession – without becoming "the slave of an office" (Apr 3, 1760; B 11/1, 346) after all. Frederick II had been reluctant to appoint Lessing as Royal Librarian in Berlin – an unfortunate conflict with Voltaire, who had accused the young Lessing of having stolen one of his manuscripts, had soured the King's relationship with Lessing. The Hamburg enterprise had failed, the founding of a publishing house had brought Lessing to the brink of ruin.

In Hamburg, however, he had befriended the König couple. Engelbert König, a wealthy merchant and entrepreneur, dies in December 1769 on a business trip to Venice. Lessing becomes a close friend of his widow Eva, an educated woman, to whom he becomes engaged in September 1771. The wedding is preceded by a long period of waiting and hesitation, documented in a correspondence that stands out as one of the most significant testimonies of the 18th century, which is so rich in significant correspondences already. The wedding takes place in October 1776, but the happiness of the married couple is only brief: On December 25, 1777, Lessing's wife gives birth to a son, and the son dies, as Lessing writes to his brother, as a result of "the cruel way in which he had to be dragged into the world" (Jan 5, 1778; B 12, 117). Eva Lessing survives him only for a short time, for "the little rascal" leaves his father doubly bereaved, dragging "his mother away after him" (to Eschenburg, Dec 31, 1777; B 12, 116), and she dies on January 10, 1778.

Lessing's letters to his friend Johann Joachim Eschenburg, professor in Brunswick, are among the most poignant testimonies available about his life. Their laconic style has equally affected his contemporaries and posterity.

> Dear Eschenburg,
> My wife is dead, so I have now made this experience, too. I am glad that I cannot have many such experiences left to make; and I am feeling quite at ease. – I also find it comforting that I can be assured of your, and our other Brunswick friends', condolences.
> Yours, Lessing.
> Wolfenb., January 10, 1778. (B 12, 119)

The death of his wife and son occurred at a time when Lessing's professional existence was also at stake. The reason for this was a manuscript passed on to him by Elise and Albert Hinrich Reimarus, children of the highly esteemed Hebraist Hermann Samuel Reimarus. For decades, and purely for his own "peace of mind", Reimarus had devoted himself to questions that had arisen to him while reading the Old Testament and comparing the Gospels. They concerned the credibility of the biblical tradition and touched on the core of Christian doctrine by replacing unconditional election with the "chance of birth" (Saladin):

> We must all admit that we have not chosen Christianity over other religions through our own insight and free choice. The mere accident of our parents already being Christians, and of this sect, brought us to it. Had we been born of Jewish or Turkish parents, as could naturally have happened, our parents' religion and sect would have been instilled in us in childhood, and accordingly, we would have believed just as firmly that we, through a special grace of God, were born in the bosom of the orthodox church, the only one where we could hope to be saved, while all those of a different faith would be eternally damned. (HSR 1, 41–42)

Lessing's plan to publish the *Apologia or Defence of the Rational Worshippers of God* (*Apologie oder Schutzschrift für die vernünftigen Verehrer Gottes*) in its entirety failed due to the publisher's reservations. In January 1777, he published parts of the manuscript in *On History and Literature. From the Treasures of the Ducal Library in Wolfenbüttel* (*Zur Geschichte und Literatur. Aus den Schätzen der Herzoglichen Bibliothek zu Wolfenbüttel*), the magazine he edited without censorship. The publication of these 'Fragments of an Anonymous Author' marks the beginning of philological Biblical criticism and the quest of the historical Jesus.

Reimarus considered himself a deist, that is, a representative of a faith that limits itself to believing in the existence of God, the immortality of the soul, and a just connection between moral behaviour and personal well-being in the next life. His *Treatises on the Principal Truths of Natural Religion* (*Abhandlungen von den vornehmsten Wahrheiten der natürlichen Religion*, 1754) are an attempt at reconciling revelation and reason. In fact, however, he was not committed to the Christian doctrine. Already in a fragment Lessing had published in advance, *On the Toleration of Deists* (*Von Duldung der Deisten*, 1774), Reimarus complains about the hostility of orthodox theology towards the representatives of a "natural religion" (cf. B 8, 118–19), and distinguishes between the teachings of the Jewish itinerant preacher Jesus of Nazareth and what the Apostles, Evangelists and Church Fathers made of them (cf. B 8, 116). That the "religion of Christ" should be distinguished from the "Christian religion" (B 10, 223): in this point, Lessing agreed with Reimarus. What aroused his opposition, however, was an idea elaborated in the further fragments, that with Biblical criticism, Christianity itself was discredited.

The five fragments selected by Lessing (B 8, 175–311) have a clear argumentative structure: The first two defend (1) the authority of reason in matters of religious orientation, and doubt (2) the possibility of a revelation directed at all of mankind; the following three concretise these general reflections on the relationship between reason and revelation by exemplifying (3) the implausibility of the stories in the Old Testament (e.g., the crossing of the Red Sea by the Israelites), by denying (4) even the character of revelation to the Old Testament, and by concluding (5) from the evident contradictions in the different accounts of the story of the resurrection, that Jesus' disciples secretly removed his body from the tomb and spread the rumour of his resurrection. A truly scandalous thesis, which is elaborated even more comprehensively in a fragment *On the Aims of Jesus and his Disciples* (*Vom Zwecke Jesu und seiner Jünger*; B 9, 224–340), edited by Lessing in May 1778.

Lessing provided the five fragments with a number of *Counter-propositions of the editor* (*Gegensätze des Herausgebers*; B 8, 312–50), in which he subjects Reimarus' Biblical criticism to his own criticism. The questions that had arisen to Reimarus were inescapable for Lessing; his answers, however, were not. His main objection consisted in an argument that was also directed against the 'neologists', representatives of contemporary Protestant theology who attempted to reconcile revelation and reason: Lessing maintains that "objections to the letter, and to the Bible, need not also be objections to the spirit and to religion" (B 8, 312). He had already argued along those lines in the debate about the doctrine of eternal punishment, which posed a problem for theology because it was difficult to explain why temporal sins should entail eternal punishments in hell. The theologian and philosopher Johann August Eberhard, whom Lessing esteemed, had argued against the eternity of damnation in his *New Apology for Socrates* (*Neue Apologie des Sokrates*, 1772), limiting it to "an indefinite, but by no means infinite duration" (B 7, 498). Lessing cannot agree with this interpretation – he finds it both too radical and too harmless. In a letter to his brother Karl, he writes: "The hell that Herr Eberhard does not want to be eternal does not exist at all, and the hell that does exist is eternal" (Jul 14, 1773; B 11/2, 567). Thus, he distinguishes again between the letter and the spirit of the Holy Scriptures, pointing out that the concepts of heaven and hell are metaphors and trying to get at their core. Thinking in terms of reward and punishment is childish; the punishments with which the Bible threatens us are punishments only for a naïve moral mind. If we recognise, in the sense that Leibniz did, that "nothing in the world is isolated, nothing is without consequences, and nothing is without eternal consequences" (B 7, 491), we will see in eternal punishment nothing but the natural and permanent consequences of actions: "It is enough that no delay along the road to perfection can ever be made up in all eternity, and it therefore punishes itself throughout all eternity by its own agency" (B 7, 493). – However, if someone cannot think of heaven and hell but as places that forever separate the good from the bad, they may, according to Lessing, "continue to cling to the letter alone": It is for them that the letter of revelation is intended (B 7, 496).

Lessing's criticism of a literal understanding of religious tradition is also directed at the Fragmentist, who, like others, questions the truth of the letter instead of the truth of religion itself. Lessing counters that,

> the religion is not true because the Evangelists and Apostles taught it; on the contrary, they taught it because it is true. The written records must be explained by its inner truth, and none of the written records can give it any inner truth if it does not already have it. (B 8, 313)

In contrast to the contemporary neologists, proponents of a *"reasonable Christianity"* that identified revelation with reason – only that, as Lessing polemically states, "one does not really know what is reasonable, nor what is Christian about it" (B 8, 134) –, he insists on the peculiarity of the religious tradition and its metaphorical character. The inner truth of religion is not presented and present in the Scriptures as philosophical truths are; it is adapted to the comprehension of an unenlightened consciousness. The translation of its truths into "truths of reason" (B 8, 319), therefore, must consider the status of religious language as a language of images and parables.

Consequently, the proper alternative to the Biblical criticism practised by Reimarus lies in liberating religion from the "yoke of the letter" (B 9, 50). The fact that the Protestant orthodoxy was not willing or able to accept this idea became evident in a dispute known as the Fragments Controversy, which definitely made the publication of the fragments an event of historical significance. The Controversy is opened with a counter-proposition by Johann Daniel Schumann, headmaster of the grammar school in Hanover, in which he invokes the *Proofs of the Truth of Christianity* (*Beweise für die Wahrheit der christlichen Religion*, 1777), namely the Old Testament "prophecies" in which the life and death of the Messiah are foretold, and the "miracles" of Jesus, of which the New Testament bears witness. Against this "proof of the spirit and the power", Lessing brings up the irrefutable fact that "fulfilled prophecies of which I have only historical knowledge that others claim to have experienced them" and "miracles of which I know only from history that others claim to have seen and assessed them" can never be more than second-hand prophecies and miracles, never actual, authentic experiences (B 8, 439–40).

Naturally, Lessing considers the belief in miracles, which Schumann regards as the rock on which the Christian religion is built, to be highly questionable. However, he engages with the other's convictions in order to test them for their consistency – and to show their inconsistency. The "nastily broad ditch" (B 8, 443) between what may have happened historically and what is comprehensible to rational thinking is insurmountable: "*Contingent truths of history,*" as Lessing says, in reference to Leibniz, "*can never become the proof of necessary truths of reason*" (B 8, 441), and to trace the latter back to the former would be a category mistake (cf. B 8, 443).

The consistency of Lessing's arguments even targets the biblical text itself. Lessing's religious-historical studies had made him realise that the writing of the Gospels was preceded by a phase of oral tradition, so that "Christianity existed before the Evangelists and Apostles wrote about it" (B 8, 312). The thesis he developed, namely that the Evangelists themselves had relied on a now lost written source, is one of the most outstanding and lasting merits of his studies in religious history (cf. B 8, 738); it is as revolutionary as the question he already pursued in his Breslau years (1763/64) about the historical conditions that made it possible for Christianity to 'be fruitful and multiply' (cf. B 5/1, 426–45). Even though Lessing's *New hypothesis on the Evangelists as merely human historians* (*Neue Hypothese über die Evangelisten als bloß menschliche Geschichtsschreiber betrachtet*; B 8, 629–54) was only published posthumously in 1784 by his brother Karl, the ideas developed in this draft are already omnipresent in his *Counter-Propositions* to Reimarus' Biblical criticism.

In December 1777, the Hamburg head pastor Johann Melchior Goeze enters the debate. Goeze is a proponent of an orthodoxy that considered itself, in line with the practice of 'Elenchus', obliged to defend the purity of the doctrine against the controversial voices raised against it. Goeze identifies religion with the Bible. Lessing's assertion that there is a Christian religion without the Scriptures is an outrage to him. Accordingly, his journalistic attacks are not primarily directed against the anonymous fragmentist who criticises the Bible, but against his editor, who had "hostilely" questioned its authority and thus unsettled many believing souls:

> I would tremble at the prospect of my death if I had to fear that, in consequence of the spread of these essays, so malicious and highly dangerous to many souls, and detrimental to the honour of our great Redeemer, an account of it would be demanded from me on that day. (B 9, 20)

Lessing's criticism of theological literalism is interpreted by Goeze as the religious mockery of a playwright who, with the help of poetic sleight of hand, evades his obligation to speak plainly on dogmatic matters (cf. B 9, 121–22). Since it is impossible to debate with an opponent who does not say what he recognises as religious truth, he calls on Lessing to make a "complete confession of faith" (cf. B 9, 371). The idea that he might be demanding exactly what Lessing cannot do, for reasons of principle, does not occur to Goeze at all. The core of Christian doctrine is the commandment of love of God and of one's enemies; and this is what the student of theology who has fallen among the actors has already committed to in his great letter of justification to his father. Following this commandment is a salvific practice: "Dear children, love one another!" he makes John the Evangelist say in an apocryphal testament, assuring the congregation that "this alone, if it is done, is sufficient, quite sufficient" (B 8, 451). The idea that religion consists in such a lived practice, the salvific reasons of which are intelligible – regardless of what beliefs about the creation of the world or the identity of the Jewish itinerant preacher Jesus of Nazareth one is willing or able to accept –, remains incomprehensible to Goeze.

The debate gains particular vehemence because Goeze not only denies the moral integrity of the fragmentist and his editor, but also because he is not willing to even allow a dispute about the truth of religion. In his eyes, dissenting opinions on this question are nothing more than deliberate obstinacy and blasphemous refusal to acknowledge the truths of faith revealed in the letter of the Scripture. The mere fact that Lessing rejects his demand to conduct the theological dispute in Latin contradicts his self-image as a guardian of doctrine. Therefore, it is only natural for him to hope that "sovereigns and other authorities" will finally put a "bridle and bit" on the "newspaper writers" who "spread the most destructive principles among the masses" (B 9, 37). And he does not hesitate to demand such intervention from the state.

Anti-Goeze, No. 12: *Nathan the Wise*

On July 6, 1778, the Duke of Brunswick withdraws Lessing's privilege of freedom from censorship "in religious matters" (Aug 17, 1778; B 12, 187), forcing him to put his public dispute with Goeze to rest. Lessing continues the debate with other weapons: The dramatic poem about Nathan the Wise, to quote Friedrich Schlegel, is his "*'Anti-Goeze', no. twelve*" (St, 183).

This shift from theoretical to aesthetic discourse is more than a stopgap; the question of the authentic interpretation of religious tradition finds its authentic expression in drama. In a letter to Elise Reimarus, Lessing famously refers to the stage as his true "pulpit" (Sept 6, 1778; B 12, 193), arguing that we need the aesthetic representation of human life to display the religious insight that this life is not wholly in our own hands. Therefore, the motto of the play confidently says: "Introite, nam et heic Dii sunt!" (B 9, 483) – "Enter, for here too there are gods!"

Nathan is "*Lessing's Lessing*" (St, 183) – his most famous play and his religio-philosophical legacy, written with the intention of casting doubt on the "evident truth and universality" of revealed religions (to Karl Lessing, Apr 18, 1779; B 9, 1184) and of showing religion *as such* in its true light. In the announcement of *Nathan*, Lessing points out that the drama has been composed in one of those "moments of vexation, when one would always like to forget what the world really is like", but it is not at odds with the vicissitudes of life – on the contrary. Lessing writes: "The world as I imagine it is an equally natural world, and it may not be owing to Providence alone that it is not equally real" (Aug 8, 1778; B 9, 445).

Lessing's *Nathan* (just like his *Minna*) is a happily averted tragedy. At its centre, there is a good deed that nearly is the benefactor's undoing. After a pogrom in which he, like the biblical Job, lost his wife and his "seven hopeful sons", Nathan had been "lying / In dust and ashes, weeping unto God", he had "argued, stormed" with God, "cursed" himself and all the world and "swore against the Christian world a hate / Irreconcilable", until the "gentle" voice of reason made itself heard within him and enabled him to free himself from this nightmare:

> But bit by bit my reason found return.
> With gentle voice it spoke: "And yet God is!
> That too was God's decree! Up then, and come!
> Now practise what you long have understood;
> And what is scarcely harder to perform
> Than just to comprehend, if you but will.
> Arise!" – I stood and cried to God: I will!
> If Thou wilt, then I will! (IV/7; B 9, 596–97)

The deed that the "god-fearing" Nathan "forces himself to do" (IV/7; B 9, 596) is a mental process: a conscious decision based on the insight that the proper reaction to bitter suffering cannot be to increase the same but only to accept it as part of a reality whose meaning eludes all human "notions about God" (III/1; B 9, 543). "Profound submission to God's will" (III/7; B 9, 559) is what this attitude will be called in the Ring Parable. Man is supposed to want "what God wants him to want", according to Thomas Aquinas' *Summa Theologiae* (19,10; TA, 137); "the ultimate intention of Christianity," Lessing says in his *Anti-Goeze*, no. 4, is not "our salvation, but our *salvation by means of our enlightenment*" (B 9, 196) – and this salvation is identical with enlightenment because it frees the spirit from the prison of its struggle and strife. The whole-hearted acceptance of reality opens Nathan anew to this reality and allows him to receive the Christian child, which is brought to him by his friend's horseman in this moment of need, as a gift.

This very deed, which is covertly mentioned already in the opening scene – "wrong 'fore God" (I/1; B 9, 487) according to Nathan's housekeeper, Daja; "of all sins[...] / The greatest sin" (IV/7; B 9, 594) according to the Patriarch; the result of "virtue" (I/1; B 9, 486) according to Nathan himself – this deed threatens to get the Good Samaritan burnt at the stake. He has committed the mortal sin of apostasy, cheating the saved child out of the salvation of her soul, declares the Patriarch, according to whom it would have been better for the Christian child to perish than to be saved "for her damnation everlasting" (IV/2; B 9, 578).

The adoption of the orphaned Christian child by the widowed and orphaned Jew is not the only deed where one person becomes a neighbour to another. Nathan's adopted daughter, the supposedly Jewish girl Recha, is saved from a burning house by a Christian Templar; and before that, this rescuer had to be rescued himself: by a Muslim Sultan,

Saladin, who recognised in the captured enemy the features of his missing brother and therefore pardoned the man who had already been condemned to death. In the opening scene of the play, Nathan identifies this wonderful concatenation of good deeds as true miracles and mocks Daja's superstitious belief in miracles, which she is passing on to Recha: The idea that an angel should have saved her from the fire is "nothing but pride! mere pride!" (I/2; B 9, 494), and the idea of being chosen through this miraculous rescue "is either nonsense or it's blasphemy" (I/2; B 9, 495) – a blasphemous belief in which the three monotheistic religions all resemble each other.

All of these three good deeds are a reward in themselves: The Jew finds his love for his seven sons again in his love for the Christian child, the Sultan finds his beloved brother's son in the pardoned Templar, and the Templar finds in Recha the sister with whom he has felt "enmeshed" and "one texture with her being" from the very first moment (III/8; B 9, 562). And neither of these good deeds is the result of conscious deliberation; they are all of a kind which, as Nathan says, are "so seldom" *our* deeds (V/4; B 9, 607): Nathan experiences the adoption of the Christian child as a grace bestowed upon him by Providence, Saladin is guided by the spontaneous sympathy aroused in him by the physiognomy of the Templar, and the Templar blindly follows Recha's voice (I/1; B 9, 488), becoming a "riddle" to himself during the act to which he "gave no thought" (I/6; B 9, 513).

The linking of these good deeds into a fortuitous combination of circumstances is a visionary glimpse of the reality of which Lessing speaks in the announcement of *Nathan*. The story about the reunion of a family divided by religious wars takes a potentially tragic turn because Daja cannot reconcile it with her faith to conceal Recha's origin from the Christian girl and is carried away to reveal the secret to the Templar, and because this Templar, who misinterprets his love for his sister as erotic love, believes he has found the true reason for Nathan's unwillingness to give him his daughter as a wife in the adoption of the Christian child by a Jew.

The scene in which Nathan first suspects that the Templar and Recha might be brother and sister is concluded with the ominous words: "The searcher's eye / Not seldom finds more than he wished to find" (II/7; B 9, 536). – This is one of the quotes through which Lessing lets the thinking mind know what sort of game is being played here. Lessing's *Nathan* is not only an averted tragedy, but, more specifically, an Oedipus drama redirected towards a happy ending. After all, Oedipus is the hero who, in his search for Laius' murderer, finds himself.

Oedipus and *Nathan* share not only the analytical approach – the on-stage action essentially consists in the revelation of the backstory and the characters' true identities – but also the central motif of the belief in oracles. In a posthumous text with the strange title *Womit sich die geoffenbarte Religion am meisten weiß, macht sie mir gerade verdächtig* (roughly "What revealed religion holds most dear is what makes me suspicious"), Lessing uses *Oedipus* as an example for how the Greeks knew how to prevent the "foolish desire of mankind to foresee their fate in this life" through "suitable fabrications of the inevitable" (B 8, 663–64). The desire to know one's own fate in this life is foolish because it robs the future of its openness; this also applies to the question of what awaits us after death: If we worry "about a future life", we lose "the present one". Accordingly, Lessing's reservations against the belief in oracles are simultaneously reservations "against all revealed religion":

> Even if it were true that there was an art to know the future, we had better not learn this art. Even if it were true that there was a religion that gave us certain knowledge about the next life, we had better not listen to this religion. (B 8, 664)

This is nothing less than a rejection of the certainty of salvation in Christian faith. The belief that through Christ's sacrifice, man has gained eternal life is "suspicious" to Lessing. The exultation of St Paul in the First Epistle to the Corinthians – "O death, where is thy sting? O grave, where is thy victory?" (1 Corinthians 15:55) –, the happiness of eternal redemption that Luther finds testified in the Scriptures: Lessing cannot share it. People who know they are in possession of the truth and who are certain of their salvation are in danger of failing to do right or, even worse, of doing wrong for the sake of faith.

In the preface to *Nathan*, Lessing points out that "the disadvantage that revealed religions bring to the human race can never have been more striking to a reasonable man than in the times of the Crusades" (B 9, 665). The embodiment of "pious frenzy" (II/5; B 9, 532), as the Templar, reformed by the experience of war, calls it, is the figure of the Patriarch, who expects the pardoned man to murder his rescuer in order to earn a "crown in Heaven" (I/5; B 9, 507). The fact that it is precisely this fixation on heavenly reward that obscures the sight of what is truly good is the clou of the religious criticism acted out in Lessing's play, and for which *Oedipus* and the Ring Parable provide the material.

In *Oedipus*, it is the Oracle of Delphi that tempts Laius to abandon his son, and that tempts Oedipus, who has been saved by a merciful shepherd, to flee his foster parents, just so he can unwittingly return to the place where his destiny is fulfilled. It might be allowable to read

Sophocles' tragedy as an expression of scepticism towards the Attic "can-do attitude" (CM, 39) – and Lessing probably did so. The egocentric self-empowerment, which is only aware of its own salvation, is replaced by conscious self-restraint, to which the acknowledged good obliges; the child murder at which Laius fails so disastrously is replaced by the motif of the rescue of the orphaned child by the childless Jew. This makes *Nathan* a drama of fatherhood: Nathan is Recha's "sire in truth" because he – as the Templar knows – sees "the form divine" in her and makes it come alive through his education (V/3; B 9, 604).

There is another prophecy at the centre of the Ring Parable, which is the heart of *Nathan*: The ring, which is passed down in a long succession of generations from father to favourite son, has "the magic power that he who wore it, / Trusting its strength, was loved of God and men" (III/7; B 9, 556). This magical quality of the ring is most blatantly apparent in the late medieval ring parables of the *Gesta Romanorum*, a collection of exemplary stories and legends. Here, the one true ring actually exists, performing miracles and, if need be, putting this miraculous power to the test, and there is the one true heir, besides two brothers willingly deceived by the father. In the novelistic Ring-Parable tradition Lessing oriented himself on, which has found its most elaborate expression in Boccaccio's *Decameron* (1351), the emphasis is not on the question of the true religion – this question is only the means to an end, with which a sultan sets a trap for a Jew in order to extort money from him. In the *Decameron*, the story is meant to demonstrate how to use clever talk to extricate oneself from a precarious situation. Boccaccio, however, already supplements this deception motif, which is dominant in his source, the collection of novellas *Il Novellino*, with a sequel in which the sultan and the Jew make friends. Lessing picks up on this friendship motif.

Unlike in Boccaccio, however, his Saladin wants to know the truth "in truth" (III/6; B 9, 554). Thus, it is in fact a play about the question of the truth of the revealed religions. This is why Lessing restores the ring's power to work miracles; he does, however, significantly modify this motif: He ties the effectiveness of the ring to the attitude of its wearer and expands the story with a sequel in which the sons accuse each other of fraud and go to court.

With this sequel, the question of the appropriate interpretation of the ring is moved to the centre of attention. Lessing's version of the Ring Parable is, therefore, more than just a simple parable about the equality of the three monotheistic book religions; it is a parable that thematises the parabolic quality of religious discourse (cf. GTN 3, 410–11). In the monologue in which Nathan reflects on how to answer the Sultan, he shakes his head at Saladin wanting to have the truth at nominal value. With this, Lessing picks up on the distinction between the spirit and the letter, which he had put forward in the Fragments Controversy, in order to expose the literal belief in the Holy Scriptures as a misunderstanding of the book religions. Nathan's solution is aimed in the same direction: "Not only children can be quieted / With fables" (III/6; B 9, 554) – stories are the indispensable medium for the experiences religions speak of; for their knowledge is not knowledge one can possess but an interpretation of human life, which is validated by experience. If we believe that with the possession of the Holy Scriptures, we are in possession of an exclusive truth, we deceive ourselves. This is what happens to the brothers: The ring is received "from hands beloved" (III/7; B 9, 555), it is a token of love. When the father, who loves all of his sons equally, has this ring replicated by an artist so that no one (not even he himself!) can distinguish the rings from each other, he does so out of love. And when the sons quarrel over who has the genuine ring, they again do so out of love: They cannot believe that they have been deceived by "such a loving father" (III/7; B 9, 558). The irreconcilable dispute arising from the "unbeguiled, / Unprejudiced affection" (III/7; B 9, 559) of the father for his children and the love of the children for this father is the scandal that preoccupies Lessing. The ring is valuable not as a unique object but as a symbol of parental love, which for Lessing is non-exclusive. Only those who know they are loved can become capable of love and thus bring forward the power of the ring. What psychology calls "basic trust", Lessing's play calls "submission to God's will". In the Old Testament, this submission is embodied by Job. Among Lessing's posthumous works, there is a note: "*Islam*: an Arabic word which means the surrender of oneself to God's will" (B 9, 660).

In a letter to his brother Karl, Lessing pointed out that he had added a "very interesting episode" (Aug 11, 1778; B 12, 186) to Boccaccio's story. This episode is the story about Recha's adoption, which Nathan tells to "simple piety" alone, embodied by Bonafides, because only he can understand "the deeds / God-fearing man can force himself to do" (IV/7; B 9, 596). In this story, the motifs of charity and of fatherhood overlap; in it, an experience takes shape that virtue is its own reward because it frees the virtuous from the egocentrism of their desires. The sons in the Ring Parable are "deceived deceivers" (III/7; B 9, 559), since they insist on the promise the father has given them, thereby destroying the power of the ring.

The Ring Parable interprets the dramatic plot and needs to be interpreted within the dramatic plot. Lessing's anti-tragic play allows for the reunion of a family that has been divided by religious wars, by translating the drama of mis-recognition told by the Ring Parable into a drama of recognition – a sequence of anagnorisis scenes –, in which the "voice of nature" (III/10; B 9, 571) overcomes all separations. In the finale, Lessing once more draws attention to this play of (mis-)recognition: With the words "his heart / Knows nothing of it! – We're imposters!" (V/8; B 9, 625), Recha recoils from the Templar when at first, he refuses to recognise her as a sister. No less telling are the words addressed to the Templar by Saladin, which conclude the play: "Just see that scoundrel here! / He knew some of the truth [about his origins, R. V.], and yet he could / Consent to make me murder him!" (V/8; B 9, 627). They remind us of the catastrophe of parricide, which was at the centre of the Greek tragedy and happily avoided in Lessing's dramatic poem.

Nonetheless, the full intellectual richness of *Nathan* becomes apparent only when it is placed in the context of Lessing's late social and religious philosophy, as evidenced in his writings on the nature of Freemasonry and the "education of the human race". In *Ernst and Falk*, he addresses the risks and side effects of socialisation; in the *Education* treatise, he reconstructs the history of revealed religions as an unforeseeable yet purposeful process.

Dialogues for Freemasons: *Ernst and Falk*

"There's nothing better than *thinking aloud* with a friend" (B 10, 14). This programmatic commitment to a casual exchange of ideas opens the dialogues between Ernst and Falk about the true nature of Freemasonry. The key question is about the "civil society of human beings in general" (B 10, 24) and the risks and side effects inevitably associated with the socialisation of man. Civil society, according to Lessing's central idea, "cannot unite people without dividing them" (B 10, 30). This dialectic of union and division also manifests itself on the levels of state, religion and social class; it turns people, who as *mere* human beings "are attracted to one another by virtue of their common nature" (B 10, 28), into *such* a human being and *such* a human being: "Germans and French, Dutch and Spanish, Russians and Swedes" (B 10, 28), "Jews and Christians and Turks" (B 10, 29), people of "exalted rank" and "social inferiority" (B 10, 33). As such, they are in danger of encountering members of other groups with caution or reservation – "cold, reserved, and distrustful" – and coming "into collision" with them (B 10, 28).

Falk's socio-philosophical analysis presents the attentive friend with an unavoidable dialectic. Nevertheless, the realisation that even the best of all possible political constitutions has adverse effects is no cause for bitterness; Falk does not want to make civil society contemptible to Ernst – quite the contrary: It is only within civil society that it is possible to "cultivate" reason, which can counteract the unwanted evils of coexistence in a state (B 10, 31). Even an objectively distanced study of them is a means of reconciling ourselves with the inevitable, because it soothes the mind by making it realise the natural course of things: What "in days of depression" may give cause to grumble against "Providence and virtue", can make the socio-philosophically 'enlightened' "calm and happy" (B 10, 37).

Falk's apologia for the fallibility of human inventions is a theodicy in terms of social philosophy – and therefore, it is not the last word. Accepting the inevitable paves the way for another insight: Since people "can only be united through division! and only through incessant division can they remain united" (B 10, 31), there always need to be people "who have already transcended those divisions" (B 10, 40), i.e., who have detached themselves from the exclusive commitment to the shared values held by the group they belong to. The point Falk is making is this: These people are the Freemasons. Their concern is to "reduce as far as possible the divisions which so much alienate people from one another" (B 10, 34). However desirable this may be, it cannot be decreed by "civil laws" because it would "in fact transcend the boundaries of each and every state". The deeds of the Freemasons, which are proof of their convictions, are 'works of supererogation' – *opera supererogata* (B 10, 32).

The term *opus supererogatum* is from the Gospel of Luke (Luke 10:35; cf. JvL, 132), where it refers to the generosity of the Good Samaritan, who not only helps the Jew that has been attacked by robbers, but also pays for the cost of his care. It is not by chance that this term is at the centre of the *Dialogues*: The Christian commandment of neighbourly love is based on the experience of a common human nature; Lessing's social philosophy attempts to take the consideration of this experience to a cosmopolitan level.

On the evening of October 14, 1771, Lessing had been admitted to the Hamburg lodge 'Of the Three Golden Roses' – however, it was not to go further than this inauguration. For the arcane rituals of Freemasonry, their "words and signs and customs" (B 10, 16), Lessing had no use, even less so for their economic behaviour and for the rivalry between the lodges (cf. B 10, 53–54). The perspective from which Lessing characterises the nature of Freemasonry is of an explicitly socio-philosophical nature, and he claims it to be the only one "from which healthy eyes can distinguish a true image (rather than a mere phantom as it appears to defective eyesight)" (B 10, 12).

True Freemasonry is an anthropological datum, rooted in human nature no less than the inclination to feel attracted to those who are familiar to us because they speak the same language, inhabit the same territory, share the same fate, possess the same manners and customs, have the same faith and orient themselves by the same values – it manifests itself in the experience of spontaneous kinship. This enables Falk to say: "Freemasonry has always existed" (B 10, 16) – it is the indispensable counterpart to the regulations imposed by the state that give a stable form to social coexistence, and it depends "not on *external associations*, which can so easily degenerate into *civil regulations*, but on the shared sentiments of kindred spirits" (B 10, 57).

The dialogues between Ernst and Falk are, therefore, primarily addressed to the Masonic lodges themselves – or rather to all who are seriously interested in the nature of Freemasonry. They are, as the subtitle says, *Dialogues for Freemasons* (*Gespräche für Freimaurer*; B 10, 11). Ernst, who has followed the far-sightedness of his friend Falk and joined a lodge, is disillusioned at the realisation that it does not live up to its claim of "admitting to their order every worthy man of the right disposition, irrespective of nationality, irrespective of religion, and irrespective of social class" (B 10, 40). He only finds in it the civil divisions it wants to counteract. Instead of "thinking beyond all social gradations", the members of the lodge keep to themselves and are self-sufficient "in such good company among ourselves" (B 10, 52).

The connection between Lessing's social and his religious philosophy is palpable. In either case, he distinguishes between "scheme, guise, outward garb" (B 10, 54) and inner truth – between lodge and Freemasonry, between Church and faith (B 10, 53). Since the lodge is not Freemasonry, but only its outward form as a social institution, one can be a Freemason "without being *called* a Freemason" (B 10, 37). And: since faith is not the Church, one can be a Christian without being called a Christian (cf. B 8, 453). The true Christian has recognised that the Christian faith finds its true purpose in the *opus supererogatum* of charity.

The dialogues between Ernst and Falk follow the epigram's logic of "*expectation* and *resolution*" (B 7, 188), riddle and solution. Their beginning is marked by the mysterious sentence that the "true deeds" of the Freemasons "are their secret": They "are aimed at making all that are commonly described as good deeds for the most part superfluous" (B 10, 21). This secret cannot be expressed by the true Freemason without reservations, because the one to whom it is communicated must necessarily already have a sense for the true meaning of the words, in order to be able to grasp them appropriately. That there are "truths which are better left unsaid" is the insight of a wise man: "The wise man *cannot* say what is better left unsaid" (B 10, 25).

"*Thinking aloud* with a friend" is a gentle initiation. Ernst proves a true Freemason because he is able to follow his friend's hints and allusions and to identify the deeds commonly referred to as good. The heroic deeds of political and religious martyrs – "whatever costs blood is certainly not worth shedding blood for" (B 10, 56). They are dispensable because unprejudiced openness to interpersonal encounters overcomes the separations brought into the world by civil society, without having to abolish the state, the Church, or social gradations themselves.

Lessing's social philosophy is radically individualistic in its conception: It creates a model of how conflicts emerge. Lessing's dramas are centred around this idea from the very beginning, whether by staging a tragic escalation or the fortunate avoidance of the same. The ethos of Freemasonry takes the stage in the motif of friendships between people across group boundaries: in the Samaritan act of the travelling Jew, in the rescue of the true freethinker by the true theologian, in the philanthropic generosity of Tellheim, and last but not least in the three good deeds that are at the heart of *Nathan*.

Falk describes the work of the Freemasons as a form of cultivation in the original sense of the word. Counteracting the evils "even the happiest citizen cannot do without" means preparing the ground for Masonic "awareness": "to encourage it to germinate, to transplant the seedlings and remove the weeds and superfluous leaves" (B 10, 37). – All this takes time: "A thousand thousand years" the modest judge in the Ring Parable has predicted for "bringing to the fore" the "magic powers of the stones" in their rings (III/7; B 9, 559). Such a time horizon is also expected in Lessing's Freemason dialogues:

> The true deeds of the Freemasons are so great, and so far-reaching, that whole centuries may elapse before one can say 'This was their doing!' They have nevertheless done all the good that has so far existed in the world – mark my words: in the *world!* – And they continue to work on all the good that has yet to come in the world – mark my words – in the *world*. (B 10, 21)

The Education of the Human Race

In the *Counter-Propositions* to the *Fragments* of Reimarus, Lessing had published 53 paragraphs of an allegedly anonymous work, in which he drafts a history of the Jewish-Christian book religions. It is entitled *The Education of the Human Race*. When Lessing publishes the work in 1780, it comprises 100 paragraphs. Lessing, however, does not present himself as the author, but as the editor. With good reason.

The Freemason Falk knows that all development takes time: "Don't worry, the Freemason calmly waits for the sunrise, and lets the candles burn as long as they will and can" (B 10, 56). Patience is also the virtue on which the *Education* treatise relies, reckoning with unforeseeable periods of time. In the preface, Lessing almost emphatically confesses to the error inherent in all humanity:

> Why should we not see in all the positive [i.e. revealed] religions simply the process whereby the human

understanding in all places can alone develop, and will develop further still, instead of reacting with either mockery or anger to one of them? [...] Can God's hand be at work in everything except in our errors? (B 10, 74)

This commitment to human fallibility is a commitment to history and to the principle of evolution. Reality is a process. This applies to the species as well as to the individual. In a posthumous fragment, Lessing toys with the idea that "more than five senses are possible for human beings" (cf. B 10, 229–32): The evolution of our sensory perceptions may not yet be complete – just like the intellectual and moral development of mankind. This development, however, has a cultural dimension, and this is the point Lessing makes in the *Education* treatise: He parallels the history of revealed religions and their influence on morality with the education and social development of the individual.

Lessing admired in Leibniz that he had "tried to lead each individual along the path to truth on which he found him" (B 7, 483). This principle of "accommodation" (cf. MF 1, 427–28), the adaptation of the doctrine to the capacity of the pupil, is what Lessing sees at work in the history of revealed religions: He regards the texts of the Old and New Testaments as records in which a cultural learning process can be traced. However, this view requires a standpoint located beyond the standpoint of the revealed religions themselves.

This is the reason for Lessing's pretence that he was merely the editor, and not the author, of this treatise. As he has done in the Fragments Controversy, Lessing tries to fend off the accusation of partisanship and to argue from a non-partisan standpoint. In this, he also follows Leibniz, not wanting to call Leibniz's "best of all possible worlds" doctrine *his* doctrine (B 7, 484): The *Theodicy* tries to overcome such a particularistic standpoint and consider the way of the world from a divine perspective.

The same is true of the *Education* treatise, which takes a look at the history of moral consciousness without pursuing partisan interests of its own, but – like Nathan the Wise – with "mankind's true interests" (III/5; B 9, 552) in mind. In the preface, therefore, Lessing characterises the author as a traveller, who – as if at a liminal moment in history – looks back at the path mankind has taken, and who – like the Freemason Falk, spreading the "wings" of his "imagination" (B 10, 47) – turns his gaze into an immeasurable distance, in which he sees "a soft evening glow" (B 10, 74). The future itself remains unknown to him, but his speculations try to anticipate it.

In his *Counter-Propositions* to Reimarus, Lessing had claimed: "Revealed religion does not in the least presuppose a rational religion, but includes it within itself" (B 8, 319). The *Education* treatise is also committed to this principle: Reason is not superior to revelation but tries to uncover its truth-apt contents. That the written records of revealed religions are in need of, and able to cope with, such an interpretation, is presupposed by Lessing. What is under discussion is the interpretation of human life in a comprehensive sense, i.e., (1) how we shall understand reality as a whole, (2) how we want to understand ourselves as part of this reality, and (3) what consequences this has for our behaviour. The idea that there is "*salvation*" (B 9, 196) in finding conceptions "more worthy of God and more beneficial to the human race" (*Axioms*; B 9, 83), has already been crucial for Lessing in the Fragments Controversy; "better and more precise conceptions of the divine being, of our own nature, and of our relations with God" (§ 77; B 10, 95) are the telos of the *Education* treatise, too. The treatise attempts to consider the history of Judaism and of Christianity developing from Judaism from the standpoint of a clever educator, and to read the Holy Scriptures of the revealed religions as "primers" (§ 26, § 64) which successively reveal the divine origin of reality to the students, thus making their actions 'fruitful'.

The education of the human race takes place in three phases: It begins with the Old Testament, its orientation towards divine commandments and prohibitions, and the principle of reward and punishment (cf. § 16; B 10, 78). It finds its continuation in the Christian doctrine of the immortality of the soul, which brings the principle of self-care into the world and directs the attention away from worldly well-being to the "purity of the heart with a view to another life" (§ 61; B 10, 90). And it finds its fulfilment in the "time of a *new, eternal Gospel*" (§ 86; B 10, 96), which does not need to fix the "capricious gaze" of man on future salvation, because it knows that doing good deeds is its own reward – not in the future, but in the very moment of the deed. For the insight into what is not only good for me, but good in itself, can lend a determination that grows from the experience of being genuinely committed to one's will, which means to be at peace with oneself.

The Jewish philosopher Baruch de Spinoza, whose *Ethics* – alongside Leibniz's *Theodicy* – were a significant inspiration for Lessing, calls the moral good, which is under discussion here, self-satisfaction, "acquiescentia in se ipso": "Self-satisfaction is the joy which is produced by contemplating ourselves and our own power of action" (BdS, 467). The insight that moral satisfaction lies in doing good "because it is good" (§ 85; B 10, 96), was the heart of the Job scene, which Lessing recreated in *Nathan*. And it is the clou of the interpretation that Nathan's judge puts forward for the symbol of the ring: There are no genuine or fake rings, only self-fulfilling and self-destructive ways of wearing them. The only true way of wearing the ring is the one that emulates the father's "unbeguiled, / Unprejudiced affection" (III/7; B 9, 559): It frees its wearer from the "selfishness of the human heart" (§ 80; B 10, 95).

The education of the human race is a process of moral evolution in a comprehensive sense, concerning good *understanding*, good *motives*, good *behaviour*. The effort for an appropriate interpretation of the religious tradition is itself part of this process: It expands the capacity of the human mind and prepares the ground for the formation of character. Lessing's "speculations" understand themselves as "the *most fitting* exercises of all for the human understanding, so long as the human heart is at all capable of loving virtue for its everlasting salutary consequences" (§ 79; B 10, 95). Without training on "spiritual objects", the human mind would not attain that "complete enlightenment" which is necessary to produce the "purity of heart which enables us to love virtue for its own sake" (§ 80; B 10, 95).

Therefore, the *Education* treatise reads the life story of Jesus not as a fulfilment of the prophecies mentioned in the Old Testament, and it does not regard the miracles we read about as a validation of his teaching – even if they may once have contributed to the acceptance of this doctrine (§ 59). Lessing replaces these "proofs of the spirit and of power" by hermeneutic detective work: In the Old Testament, he looks for and finds "preparatory exercises" (§ 44), "allusions" (§ 45) and "pointers" (§ 46) that anticipate the New Testament doctrine of the immortality of the soul. In a second step, he makes it his business to translate the "revealed truths" of the New Testament – the doctrine of the Trinity (§ 73), of original sin (§ 74) and of the Son's satisfaction (§ 75) – into "truths of reason" (§ 76; B 10, 94), making visible the contents accessible to human reason even without the guidance of revelation. Thus, the New Testament now becomes a legacy that cannot simply be taken literally but needs to be interpreted appropriately, because it is a figurative, parabolic text, and as such, like the opal of the ring, it "sheds a hundred colours fair" (III/7; B 9, 555).

The argumentative strategy of the *Education* treatise shows most impressively how Lessing thinks in categories of learning, and how decisively he places independent thinking at the centre of such learning. His entire literary production follows his poetics of self-experience, and his philosophy of religion understands the history of the book religions as a school of moral insight. Religion is void unless it becomes lived experience. This experience cannot be told; it needs to be acquired in a process of enlightenment about one's own errors and prejudices. If we want to "learn to calculate", we must not be content with the mathematics teacher revealing the solution to us; the solution can only serve us as a "guideline" to orient ourselves while calculating. The same applies in the case of the revealed religions – their truths have been revealed in order to be appropriated by reason: "They were, so to speak, the result of the calculation which the mathematics teacher announces in advance, in order to give his pupils some idea of what they are working towards" (§ 76; B 10, 94).

The parallel between the education of the human race and the social development of the individual has its limits: The process of individual perfection ends with death. This end becomes an intellectual challenge for Lessing in the last sections of his *Education* treatise. The strictly arguing sequence of paragraphs takes on the character of an enthusiastically excited speech: first a prayer, finally an inner monologue. Lessing's last thoughts are dedicated to the New Testament doctrine of the immortality of the soul, a question he had already encountered in philosophical form in Leibniz's *Monadology* and in Charles Bonnet's text on the *Palingénésie philosophique* (1769). Palingenesis, transmigration, rebirth: Lessing does not commit himself. He practises philosophical speculation.

For the human race, the "time of fulfilment" (§ 85; B 10, 96) is still far away: We do not live in an "*enlightened age*" but in an "age of *enlightenment*" (IK 2, 59), as Kant will put it. Enlightenment is an open cultural process. If education has a *goal*, if it is to be not only for the benefit of mankind but also for the benefit of the individual, this process must not simply break off. The telos of education is "cultivation": the insight into the "inherent values of reality" (RS, 48), which purifies the heart and empowers the individual to do good "because it is good" (§ 85; B 10, 96). – One life, however, is not enough to reach this perfection.

Part II

Consequences

Lessing as a Public Figure

Lessing died on February 15, 1781, in his apartment in Brunswick. In one of his last letters, addressed to Moses Mendelssohn, he reminisces about shared moments and thanks his friend for the appreciation he has shown him in his last letter. On this letter, he says, he is

> still chewing and *nibbling*. The juiciest word here is the noblest. And indeed, my dear friend, I need such a letter very much from time to time, if I am not to become completely despondent. I do not think you know me as someone hungry for praise. But the coldness with which the world lets certain people know that nothing they do is right is, if not fatal, at least debilitating. (Dec 19, 1780; B 12, 370)

Lessing led an unprecedented public life, seeking publicity and initiating public debates: "I am not aware of ever having written a line to anyone that could not be read by the whole world" (Jan 8, 1773; B 11/2, 497), he once wrote to Eva König. When he complains in his letter to Moses Mendelssohn about the coldness shown to him, it is not a complaint about lack of praise, but about lack of resonance – and about the fact that the "fermenta cognitionis" he has disseminated (HD 95; B 6, 655), particularly the "fermentations" (B 10, 221) of his religio-philosophical polemics, found no creative echo.

"Fermenta cognitionis" – thought-provoking ideas: Lessing's complaint that his publications have not 'fermented' thinking is based on his conviction that reason can only thrive in critical confrontation with the thinking of others. The cultivation of reason, as the Freemason Falk puts it, is only possible in civil society (cf. B 10, 31); the soil upon which it thrives is the printing press.

The idea that Enlightenment is a collective process requiring freedom of the press will also be emphasised a few years after Lessing's death by Kant in his famous answer to the question about the nature of Enlightenment. And Johann Gottfried Herder will write a continuation of Lessing's Freemason dialogues in his *Letters for the Advancement of Humanity* (*Briefe zur Beförderung der Humanität*), no. 26, accentuating in particular the dimension of media theory in Lessing's social philosophy: In fact, the society of Freemasons is the "*society of all thinking people in all parts of the world*". Their "Chairman" was Gutenberg – his invention of the movable-type printing press had initiated the emergence of a media sphere across regional and social borders, where the "spirits" can communicate without being dependent on an "assembly of bodies" (JGH, 139).

Lessing himself had envisaged such a media theory of Enlightenment in the preface to his treatise *How the Ancients Portrayed Death* (*Wie die Alten den Tod gebildet*):

> Granted that as yet truth has been established through no contest; yet nevertheless truth has gained by every controversy. Controversies have stimulated the spirit of investigation, have kept prejudice and authority in constant convulsion; in brief, have hindered varnished untruth from taking root in the place of truth. (B 6, 717)

This corresponded to Lessing's intellectual profile. He was entirely focused on testing traditional opinions and common-sense plausibilities for their validity. His friends testified that "in speculative matters", in particular, "the truth found was not worth as much to him as the exercise of the mind in seeking to find it" (RD, 72) – indeed, he had greater pleasure in "asserting a nonsensical proposition with acuity than in hearing the truth poorly defended" (RD, 65).

This practical approach might be the most characteristic feature of Lessing's nature and, equally, the key to his work. Nourishing the "spirit of investigation" through controversy, fathoming the truth of religion with prudent doubt, training intuitive cognition through fabulation, becoming more compassionate and more cheerful by watching plays – it is *practice* that Lessing exemplifies in his writings: a practice of *thinking*, willing to put all certainties up for discussion, having learnt that error is an integral part of intellectual development; a practice of *faith* that recognises how any form of religious interpretation of the world proves itself only in lived experience and is realised in doing good; a practice of *poetry* that understands itself as a critical modernisation of ancient poetry, and that wants to be understood as such. If there is a project to which Lessing felt committed, it was the education of the human race by training – in conversation, and even more in reading and writing – the ability of the individual to educate oneself.

Both as a religious philosopher and as a poet, Lessing was fascinated by what was at the beginning and how it was not only handed down but also corrupted in the process of cultural transmission: the religion of Christ, which he defended against the Christian religion; the art of Greek tragedy, the ethos of which he re-emphasised despite the traditional reduction of the classics to formal conventions and sensational subjects. When he writes in the conclusion of the *Hamburg Dramaturgy* that "My first thoughts are surely not a jot better than the average man's; and the wise thing for the average man to do with those first thoughts is to keep them under wraps" (HD 101–04; B 6, 682), this also means: Lessing's dramatic work, despite its theatrical effectiveness, demands too much prior philological knowledge to be easily accessible to the viewer and reader. Misunderstandings are inevitable. Lessing is one of the founding fathers of modern dramatic poetry, which finds its subject not in a number of sensational chains of events but in the dynamics of the human mind; still, the understanding of this dramatic quality and the thought experiments that constitute it has always posed problems for the audience.

Even his contemporaries could not come to terms with his art of critically revising and reinventing the master plots of literature – the stories about the struggle of virtue against vice, of the sacrificial death for one's fatherland, of the martyrdom of persecuted innocence. This is especially true for Lessing's tragedies, which are still regarded as founding texts of the genre of *bürgerliches Trauerspiel*, but which actually have nothing more in common with the plethora of trivial family dramas emerging in the following decades than the fact that their conflicts are not situated in the context of a struggle for political power. As research has shown (cf. CMö), what dominates the latter is precisely the kind of virtue-vice based moralism that Lessing had problematised.

The history of Lessing's influence is essentially a history of misunderstandings – regardless of whether people were well disposed or hostile towards him: Johann Jakob Dusch, whom Lessing had attacked several times in his *Letters on Literature*, published two lengthy *Letters on "Miss Sara Sampson"* (*Briefe über "Miß Sara Sampson"*), in which he cannot frown enough upon the uneventfulness of the drama (cf. St, 55–56), because he is unable to comprehend Lessing's exemplary plot construction. The playwright and popular philosopher Johann Jakob Engel, who will develop Lessing's reflections into his *Ideas for a Theory of Acting* (*Ideen zu einer Mimik*, 1785/86), puzzles in his *Letters on Emilia Galotti* (*Briefe über Emilia Galotti*) over why Odoardo Galotti stabs his daughter instead of the Prince (JJE 2, 115–17) – unaware that the alternative he envisages between filicide and tyrannicide is the very one that is overcome by Lessing's modernisation of the Virginia myth.

The reactions to *Philotas* have already been evidence of the lack of comprehension that met Lessing's art of perspectivism, his attempt to make the characters' blindness the object of perspectival representation. Lessing's friend Johann Wilhelm Ludwig Gleim felt it incumbent on himself to versify *Philotas*, and in doing so, he turned Lessing's play into its very opposite: He reverts to telling the patriotic story of a struggle between unscrupulous aggressors and heroic defenders of the fatherland, which Lessing's drama had already annihilated from a cosmopolitan perspective (cf. GTN 3, 213–27). Lessing's avowed adversary, the Swiss playwright and literary theorist Johann Jakob Bodmer, also proceeds in the same way; he feels challenged by Lessing's drama to write one about Polytimet, the son of Aridaeus, and he is equally unable to perceive the mirrored structure of the conflict (cf. GTN 3, 227–39).

However, Lessing is not only the first German poet whose literary oeuvre has provoked a kind of secondary literature, but also the first German poet whose oeuvre has been philologically examined on a large scale. Lessing himself had begun early on to work on his image as an author by editing his *Writings* (1753–55); his brother Karl, who acted as Lessing's first biographer and published his posthumous works, was also the first to edit his *Complete Writings* in collaboration with Johann Joachim Eschenburg and Friedrich Nicolai (1793–1825). Standards were subsequently set by Karl Lachmann, who had made a name for himself with critical editions of the *Nibelungenlied* (1826) and the songs of Walther von der Vogelweide (1827), and who now applied the critical method he had developed to Lessing's writings (1838–40). The key idea for his epoch-making edition was the idea of the *one* text, as originally intended by the author, which has to be reconstructed by a critical examination of the sources. The third, revised and expanded edition of Lessing's *Complete Writings* prepared by Franz Muncker (1886–1924) eventually became the standard edition well into the 20th century. Despite the now outdated editorial principles and certain editorial deficiencies, it is still unsurpassed as a complete edition (cf. MF, 56–60).

A particularly vivid example of the meticulousness with which Lessing's work was philologically examined in the 19th century is the lifework of the anatomist and private scholar Paul Albrecht, who made it his mission to expose Lessing as a plagiarist. In six self-published volumes (1888–91), he provides endless lists proving that "there are no *original* thoughts in Lessing at all, that everything we like about him is the product of *other* brains" (PA 1, 3). In particular, Lessing's dramas are turned into cleverly made-up patchwork: "For example, the Young Scholar [...] consists of 107, Minna von Barnhelm of 319, Miss

Sara Sampson of 436, Emilia Galotti of 499, Nathan the Wise of 340 scraps just stitched together" (PA 1, 3). What makes Albrecht's judgement most remarkable is the fact that Lessing, like hardly any other author, had admitted to making literature out of literature and even pointed out his sources in key quotations. "Shakespeare wants to be studied, not plundered" (HD 73; B 6, 549), he declares in the *Hamburg Dramaturgy*. And this, of course, applies equally to his relationship with the ancients, of whom he considered himself a student.

The meticulousness with which Lessing's life and work were explored by 19th-century positivist literary scholarship attests to the appreciation Lessing received as a German national poet. This appreciation is also evident in the establishment of Lessing as a literary classic that had to be read in school; and the revaluation of German classes at grammar schools, in turn, contributed significantly to engraving Lessing in cultural memory (cf. CG 1–5).

The 19th century not only laid the foundations for the study of Lessing's life and work, it not only made Lessing a classic author for schools and seminars – the 19th century also shaped the legends and narratives relating to Lessing which German philology still grapples with today. They reflect the singularity and "misunderstandability" of this oldest classic of German literature (cf. GTN 1, 238–48), revealing a peculiar discrepancy between the timeless appreciation of the person and the puzzled frowning upon his dramatic work.

Pre-Classicist and Pioneer

Lessing had already been perceived as an intellectual authority by his contemporaries. This rank was never disputed during his lifetime and remained equally undisputed after his death. No biography of Lessing can go without the words of praise with which Friedrich Schlegel and Goethe honoured him: "*He himself was worth more than all his talents*" (St, 178), it is said in Schlegel's great character portrait from 1797. "A man like Lessing is what we need," Goethe remarks in his conversations with Eckermann, "for what was it that made him so great but his character, his perseverance!" (St, 254). The appreciation of Lessing as a person knows no boundaries: No German can pronounce his name "without something of an echo sounding in his chest" (St, 262), Heinrich Heine declares. To the theatre critic and journalist Alfred Kerr, Lessing is a "high-ranking civilian" (St, 437). "If we knew nothing about Lessing but his life, we would already have reason enough to pay homage to this flawless man, this great fighter" (GLJ, 20), Ricarda Huch writes in the *Book on the Occasion of the Goethe and Lessing Anniversaries 1929* (*Buch des Goethe-Lessing-Jahres 1929*). – *On Humanity in Dark Times* (*Von der Menschlichkeit in finsteren Zeiten*; St, 486) is the title Hannah Arendt gave to her speech on being awarded the Hamburg Lessing Prize in 1960. And so on, ad libitum.

What applies to the person does not apply in equal measure to his oeuvre. Heine's enthusiasm is tentative: The philosophical and theological fighter Lessing is "more important" to him "than his dramaturgy and his dramas" (St, 264). Even during his lifetime, Lessing's dramas give rise to doubts as to the quality of their art. And this ambivalence continues to shape the image of Lessing among the following generations. In the 19th century, German philology, in establishing itself, begins to tell the history of its subject and to review the Germans' literary heritage in order to consider it as evidence of their cultural achievements. Lessing is a main protagonist in this history. He stands at the beginning of everything – he is, as Heinrich Heine has written, "the founder of modern German literature (*Originalliteratur*)" (St, 260), the master dramatist who plants the standard.

Accordingly, this is also how Erich Schmidt, perhaps the most renowned literary historian of the late 19th century, sums up the matter. In the second edition of his groundbreaking Lessing biography, he describes Lessing's life and work as the beginning of German literature: "Among 18th-century German writers, Lessing is the only one before Goethe and Schiller whose personality and works still appear to us today truly alive and present" (St, 397). Klopstock, "the father of a new, heavily armoured and high-flying poetic language", who used to be considered on a par with Lessing during his lifetime; Wieland, the witty novelist whose *History of Agathon* (1766/67) had once been epoch-making; Herder, the great cultural intermediary, who left his traces mainly in aesthetics and philosophy of history – according to Erich Schmidt, all of them are fading from the memory of "the wider public" (St, 397). Lessing, on the other hand, is not. Lessing lives on, but even he has had to pay "the toll of mortality" (St, 397). While the "big three" among his dramatic masterpieces – *Minna*, *Emilia* and *Nathan* – are still shining bright "in the sky of the German theatre" (St, 398), the other plays and all of Lessing's minor works are already enshrouded in "the dust of the past" (St, 397).

A particularly telling portrayal is by literary historian Hermann Hettner, who introduces the chapter on Lessing in his *Literary History of the 18th century* (*Literaturgeschichte des achtzehnten Jahrhunderts*) with the often-quoted words:

> The heart of the German swells when he speaks of Lessing. Lessing is the manliest (*mannhafteste*) character in German literary history. His life and strife were an unending war and victory. [. . .]
>
> In all those magnificent developmental struggles through which the eighteenth century raised the German people so surprisingly quickly from the disgrace of the most pitiful humiliation to the most educated and free-thinking people on Earth, Lessing always stood in the front line. Wherever he went, he planted the standard of the new era – so firm and unshakeable that Gustav Kühne aptly remarked, in view of the aberrations of later generations, how nowadays, in many ways progress means nothing other than going back to Lessing. [. . .]
>
> What Lessing has been to the German drama as a playwright, what he has been to it as a philosopher of art, is illuminated most clearly by the fact that between Gottsched's *Dying Cato* (*Sterbender Cato*) and Goethe's and Schiller's immortal dramatic masterpieces, not more than one lifespan had passed. What made this miraculous turnaround possible? There is only one answer: This lifespan was Lessing's. (HH 2, 486–87)

Hettner situates Lessing's oeuvre in a transitional phase of German literary and cultural history: Lessing is the one who overcomes the dilettantism of Gottsched and his era, paving the way for Goethe and Schiller – he is the "pre-classicist" (WB 2) of German literature. The idea of an epochal turning point that coincides with Lessing's life and work was prefigured in the chapter on German literature in Goethe's *Truth and Poetry*, in which Goethe portrayed Lessing against the background of the "empty epoch" (TaP I/7; MA 16, 291). This idea was to establish itself as a narrative throughout literary history, and is paralleled by the idea of Enlightenment being overcome by the Storm and Stress generation and perfected by Weimar Classicism.

In his aesthetic studies on modern drama (1852), Hermann Hettner accordingly declares Schiller and Goethe to be the measure of all things and recommends their work for imitation by modern poets; Lessing's oeuvre, on the other hand, is degraded to the product of a moralising bungler and trivial dramatist, in which everything boils down "to the most homespun morality":

> *Miss Sara Sampson* and *Emilia Galotti* revolve solely around the very extreme of the conventional moral commandment of virginal chastity, *Minna von Barnhelm* revolves around painful delicacy in financial matters, and even *Nathan* is, fundamentally, nothing more than a moral sermon on tolerance. (HH 1, 72)

The same Lessing who had declared sexual intercourse to be "the most intimate love in all of nature" (B 4, 451) in his notes on Burke's *Philosophical Enquiry into the Origin of our Ideas of the Sublime and Beautiful*, is denounced by Hettner as a poet who regards his heroines' virginal chastity as the epitome of moral integrity.

The legend of the morally bigoted dramatist finds its counterpart in the legend of the manly fighter (cf. JS). Manliness is viewed as Lessing's virtue, the will to fight as his greatest strength. However, this overlooks the fact that Lessing, of all people, had a particularly keen sense for the destructive and self-destructive potential of male self-assertion, and that in his eyes, true masculinity proved itself in fatherhood. Lessing is the fighter and pioneer par excellence: He fights for the liberation of German literature and culture from the cultural dominance of France, for the political and social emancipation of the bourgeoisie from the absolutist state, and for the self-assertion of modern thinking against traditional religious interpretations of life and the world.

The metaphor of Lessing the fighter was coined as early as the 18th century. It is already to be found in Johann Gottfried Herder's great obituary (1793), where Lessing's "manly love of truth" (St, 130) is praised and he is engraved in cultural memory as a "noble seeker, recogniser, defender of truth" (St, 133). This is picked up on by Heinrich Heine, who refers to Lessing in his great essay on *The Romantic School* (*Die romantische Schule*, 1833) as a "literary Arminius" who has freed the German theatre from the "foreign rule" of the French (St, 260). This metaphor – "heightened into the heroic", as Erich Schmidt mockingly remarked in 1899 – determines the image the nation has of Lessing: He has become their "hero and patron saint of intellectual freedom" (St, 398). Thanks to Franz Mehring and his book on *The Lessing Legend* (*Die Lessing-Legende*, 1893), in which he opposes the ideological appropriation of Lessing as a poet of the Frederician era, Lessing is established as one of the "intellectual pioneers of the German bourgeoisie" (St, 403); his ostensible moralism is regarded as the ideological weapon of the rising bourgeoisie against the vice-ridden nobility – a narrative that was adopted both by German philology in the GDR and the politicising German philology in 1970s West Germany, and that still resonates in today's textbooks.

Whether moderate or militant, differentiated or diffuse – in whatever way the Lessing-the-fighter metaphor is taken up, it pits the man against his work: "As a dramatist, Lessing was supreme intellect; he lacked the poetic imagination from which figure after figure emerges, to live independently of its creator" (St, 411). Such was the verdict of Franz Mehring, and with good reason: The 19th-century image of Lessing is shaped by the image of Enlightenment as a whole: secularisation, bourgeoisification, belief in reason. The history of Lessing's canonisation is part of a more comprehensive canonisation process, the protagonists of which are Goethe and Schiller. The reinvention of poetic literature by the 'Goethe generation' was not without its consequences for the perception of Lessing's literary work.

Lessing and Goethe

Lessing and Goethe never met. When Goethe learns of Lessing's death, he is affected. On the very same day, he writes to Charlotte von Stein: "Hardly anything could have happened to me more fatal than Lessing's death. Not a quarter of an hour before the news came, I was making plans to visit him. We are losing much, much more in him than we think" (Feb 20, 1782; as cited in WB 3, 5).

This sounds as if fate had prevented what was long overdue. In fact, there would have been plenty of opportunity for Goethe to meet Lessing, but, at least as a young student, he had deliberately avoided him (cf. TaP II/8; MA 16, 352). There is something ominous about the fact that Goethe could not approach Lessing and Lessing could not approach Goethe: It illustrates how, with Lessing, not only something new began, but also something old came to an end. With Goethe's writings, a new literature is born, and as much as Lessing's dramas can be understood as realisations of a literary modernisation programme in their own right, they remain alien to the generation that steps onto the literary stage after him.

For this young generation, Lessing first becomes an inspiration as the discoverer of Shakespeare. For Lessing, Shakespeare was the epitome of a playwright who actualised Aristotle's *Poetics* in an equally unorthodox and exemplary way. He regards him as the embodiment of genius, which "has internalised a sample of all rules" (HD 96; B 6, 657). To the 'Goethe generation', Shakespeare is the liberator from all dramaturgical conventions – even those Lessing had still felt obliged to, considering them as exemplary realisations of elementary dramatic principles. Lessing had understood the unity of time as a mimesis of our moral existence, referring to the ancient idea that man is but a "creature of a day"; Goethe sees Shakespeare as a spirit that has freed itself from the shackles of the rules and is now showing him the way out into the open:

> I did not hesitate even for a moment to renounce the regular theatre. It seemed to me that the unity of place was so carcerally fearful, the unities of action and of time annoying fetters to our imagination. I jumped into the free air, and only then did I feel that I had hands and feet. And now that I saw how much injustice the lords of the rules down in their hole have done to me, how many free souls are still writhing inside, my heart would have burst if I had not announced a feud against them and sought daily to beat down their towers. (MA 1.2, 412)

When in his speech *On Shakespeare's Day* (*Zum Schäkespears Tag*, 1771), Goethe confidently proclaims that, "We have in us the germ of the merits we appreciate" (MA 1.2, 411), this commitment is a tribute to his own "discerning genius" (MA 1.2, 412) that has made him see how true to life Shakespeare's dramas are: "Nature! Nature! nothing so nature as Shakespeare's people" (MA 1.2, 413), is his enthusiastic motto.

With this naturalness, the discernment of which the young Goethe owes to his own genius, Lessing's dramas cannot compete. Goethe appreciates them for their dramaturgical refinement, praising *Minna von Barnhelm* for its masterful exposition (cf. St, 233), but even so, Lessing's plays appear to him as "mere invention (*nur gedacht*)", as he writes to Herder (Jul 10, 1772; HA 1, 133). This expression is aimed at *Emilia Galotti*, whose literary quality he later characterises ambivalently in a letter to Zelter:

> In its day, this play arose from out of the deluge of Gottsched, Gellert, Weiße, etc. as the island of Delos did, that it might compassionately receive a goddess in labour. We young folks took courage from it, and so became greatly indebted to Lessing.
>
> In the present stage of culture, it can no longer be influential. If we look into it narrowly, we respect it, as we do a mummy, because it gives us a proof of the high and ancient dignity of the person preserved. (Mar 27, 1830; St, 257–58)

Looking back on his own lifetime, Goethe shows reverence towards Lessing's work, but he only considers it as a testimony of a past literary epoch that is worth preserving. In his conversations with Eckermann, he defends Lessing again by placing his literary oeuvre in its historical context: "Rather pity the extraordinary man for being obliged to live in such a pitiful time that it afforded him no better materials than are treated in his plays" (Feb 7, 1827; St, 254).

However, Lessing did not find his materials in the social reality of his time but in literature itself, and he found in these materials the topics that were on his own mind – above all, misanthropy and "irascibility" (B 9, 692), problematising their damage to relationships and their self-destructive power, not least because they were familiar to him. In one of the few autobiographical testimonies still available today, he attributes them to the inheritance from his father, who "in the heat of passion so easily" acted too rashly and who had hoped to have changed for the better at least in his son (B 9, 693).

Lessing's topics, even if not drawn from current events, are of general and also of personal interest. What does not occur to him, however, is to display his own life and biographical experiences in his literature. For Goethe, on the other hand, this is his declared programme; he is the inventor of a kind of literature that focuses on the writer's own experience of life and finds its raison d'être in the ability to do so: "All [...] that has been confessed by me," he says in *Truth and Poetry*, "consists of fragments of a great confession" (TaP II/7; MA 16, 306). This confession applies first to Goethe's early poetry, but above all, it is the defining characteristic of *Werther*.

The debate over Goethe's *Werther* is particularly revealing as to the chasm that separates Lessing from the 'Goethe generation'. Like the epistolary novels by Richardson and Rousseau, *Werther* also became a European bestseller, and it did so because its author had found a language for the inner experience of the love dramas in which he got entangled, a language that enabled him to give authentic expression to this experience. The medium in which the young Goethe invented himself as a writer was the letter. Therefore, it is no coincidence that Goethe's *Werther* is an epistolary novel, and no more is it a coincidence that his sorrows are the Sorrows of *Young* Werther and that the audience of the novel consisted of young men and young women. *Werther* is an outstanding literary testimony of a new, mixed-gender youth culture, in which Lessing himself had no share and which was, in fact, alien to his generation.

Lessing is sceptical about it all: Although he appreciates the aesthetic merits of the novel, he is concerned whether "such a sentimental product might not cause more harm than good", because the readers "could easily mistake the poetic beauty for the moral one" (to Eschenburg, Oct 26, 1774; B 11/2, 667). Apart from the fact that Lessing was prejudiced against the novel due to his acquaintance with young Jerusalem, whose suicide had inspired Goethe, he did not sympathise with the idea of "love as passion", an idea which has *Werther* for its literary founding text. He was suspicious of love stories because they reduce the spectrum of interpersonal relationships to the phase of infatuation, and because in their trivial form, they inappropriately moralise sexuality. Werther's suicide is understood by Lessing as a consequence of the "Christian education" that – unlike classical antiquity, which he considers exemplary – "knows so well how to model a physical need into a matter of spiritual perfection": "Do you really think," he writes to Eschenburg,

> that a Roman or Greek youth would have taken his life in *this* way and for *this* reason? Certainly not! They knew how to guard themselves against the transports of love by quite different means; and in Socrates's day, such an ἐξ ἔρωτος κατοχή [possession by love], which drives them to τι τολμᾶν παρὰ φύσιν [venture something against nature], would hardly have been forgiven even to a girl. (Oct 26, 1774; B 11/2, 667)

Lessing's rejection tells us a lot, not least because Goethe's novel claims to provoke the very compassion that is central to the *Hamburg Dramaturgy*: "To his spirit and character you cannot refuse your admiration and love; to his fate you will not deny your tears" (MA 1.2, 197), the editor's preface says. And Werther himself points out in conversation with Lotte's fiancé Albert that any judgement about a morally reprehensible act first needs to consider the "underlying motives of our actions" (MA 1.2, 233). Goethe's novel, like Lessing's drama, is a form of *Bewusstseinspoesie*; unlike Lessing, however, he does not appoint his audience as judges of his characters, but justifies even extreme states of consciousness like the 'madness of love' heightened into an experience of existential loneliness, because they are an expression of the *conditio humana*.

Goethe reads Lessing's *Emilia*, which is left open on Werther's desk (cf. MA 1.2, 299), as a love drama – he takes it for granted that Emilia does secretly love the Prince (cf. FWR 2, 663–64). And he also reads Lessing's *Minna* as a love story, praising its exposition, but disapproving of the third act, where the love plot loses momentum in favour of the episodes central to the play about the soldier's fortune (cf. FWR 2, 663).

However great the differences between Lessing and Goethe may be where aesthetics is concerned, they closely resemble each other in questions of religious philosophy. The young Goethe attracts notice in Leipzig by not going to church – as Johann Christian Kestner, Charlotte Buff's fiancé, testifies, he is "not enough of a liar" to do that: "He has a high regard for the Christian religion, but not in the form our theologians present it in" (GG 1, 62). Goethe has Faust evade Gretchen's innocent question about his faith, because this question cannot be answered directly: "Who dare express Him? / And who profess Him, / Saying: I believe in Him! / Who, feeling, seeing, / Deny His being, / Saying: I believe Him not! / The All-enfolding, / The All-upholding, / Folds and upholds he not / Thee, me,

Himself? / [...] The Name is sound and smoke" (MA 6.1, 635–36). In answering thus, he is, again, close to Lessing, who avoided being pinned down by Goeze on a confession of faith, and repeatedly countered his opponent, who never tired of demanding such a confession, by asserting that the language of images and parables is not an aesthetic deception but an authentic way to communicate about questions of faith.

The work in which Goethe most clearly follows in Lessing's footsteps is his *Iphigenia*, which has always been perceived as a drama about true humanity and placed on a par with Lessing's *Nathan*. *Iphigenia*, too, is a religio-philosophical drama. At its centre is the Tantalus myth, whose parallels to the Judaeo-Christian myth of the Fall of Man are impossible to miss, particularly in the Song of the Fates. This myth is about the hubris of Tantalus, who, having been invited to dine with the gods, tests them by serving them his own son for a meal; and it is about the revenge of the gods, who banish the sinner to the Orcus, condemn him to eternal torment and impose a curse upon his descendants, which manifests itself in the form of child sacrifice and parricide from generation to generation. The Song of the Fates accuses the gods, their despotism – "Eternal dominion / They hold in their hands / And o'er their wide empire / Wield absolute sway" – and their arbitrariness: "From races ill-fated, / Their aspect joy-bringing / Oft turn the celestials, / And shun in the children / To gaze on the features / Once lov'd and still speaking / Of their mighty sire" (IV/5; MA 3.1, 208).

This interpretation of human suffering as consequence of a Fall from Grace and of a fate imposed by divine powers scandalises Iphigenia – after all, she herself has escaped from being sacrificed by her war-bound father Agamemnon thanks to the benevolent intervention of the goddess Diana. At the same time, it leads her into temptation: Faced with the agonising choice of either sacrificing her brother Orestes, who is stranded on the island, to the goddess Diana in her capacity as priestess, or betraying King Thoas, to whom she is gratefully indebted, and helping Orestes steal the goddess's image, a "revulsion" threatens to grow in her and tear apart her "tender breast". In this situation, she sends a desperate prayer to the gods, in which everything is at stake and which is spoken in the spirit of the religious enlightenment Lessing had already pursued: "Save me, and save your image in my soul!" (IV/5; MA 3.1, 207).

Goethe's drama also revolves around the question of the truth of "religion as such" (B 2, 264), and he also links this question to the question of the images of God that are concretised in religious myths. "To recognise one God, to try to form the worthiest ideas of him, to take account of these worthiest ideas in all our actions and thoughts" – this is how Lessing defines the "most comprehensive definition of all natural religion" (B 5/1, 423). The behaviour that makes human beings pleasant to one another is a reflection of the divine and at the same time, its realisation. Goethe's poem on the Divine (*Das Göttliche*) expresses it thus: "Hail the unknown / Higher beings / We sense! / That man be like them; / That his example teach us / To believe in them." And: "Let the noble man / Be helpful and good! / Tirelessly, he shall work towards / What is useful and right, / And be to us an image / Of those beings we sense!" (MA 2.1, 90–91).

In *Iphigenia*, it is the imagery of Greek mythology that Goethe uses as his poetic material to formulate and answer his question. The answer is: The stories of sin and retribution, of redemption and damnation are not stories about an extra- and superhuman reality but a reflection of a psychological and interpersonal reality. They testify to the human desire for revenge and to the martial self-assertion of masculinity in the struggle for life or death: "Who to the gods ascribe a thirst for blood / Do misconceive their nature, and impute / To them their own inhuman dark desires" (I/3; MA 3.1, 175).

Religious enlightenment is based on the insight into this projection mechanism of religious myths; and it culminates in lived practice, which demands "purity of heart", as it is called in the *Education* treatise (§ 80; B 10, 95). Iphigenia knows: "'tis through the heart alone [the gods] speak to us"; and she also knows that "the raging tempest" of the heart "drowns" this "still, small voice" only too easily (I/3; MA 3.1, 174). Correspondingly, the voice of reason in *Nathan* is also quiet and gentle; reflective contemplation is required in order to hear it, because reason *is* the ability to pause and reflect: "'tis heard by all, / Whate'er may be their clime, within whose breast / Flows pure and free the gushing stream of life" (V/3; MA 3.1, 214).

Just as Nathan frees himself from the "hate / Irreconcilable" he has "sworn" to the Christians (IV/7; B 9, 596), Iphigenia frees herself from the "profound hate" (IV/5; MA 3.1, 207) towards the gods, which is her inheritance, by unconditionally entrusting herself to Thoas. It is no coincidence that this conscious alternative to the mythical interpretations of interpersonal conflicts is brought forth and exemplified by a woman. – In Lessing's works, too, the truly virtuous heroes are pious and worldly-wise women like Minna, "soft, effeminate" men like Aridaeus (8; B 4, 34), and fathers like Nathan, who have learned to distinguish between egocentric cleverness and the true benefit of the people. Iphigenia's "unheard-of deed" (V/3; MA 3.1, 213) also saves her male interaction partners from getting hopelessly entangled in the reaction patterns of revenge which the Tantalus myth is all about.

An Unpoetic Poet

Goethe's reinvention of literature by the development of forms of expression that emulated the expressivity of everyday language and the intimacy of inner speech, and the "literary revolution" (TaP III/11; MA 16, 523) of his generation, which produced the concept of the poetic genius, were responsible for Lessing's being perceived as an "unpoetic poet".

There are innumerable accounts attesting to this. Everyone praises Lessing's critical acuity, the conciseness and polemical power of his style – and yet they cannot bring themselves to grant him the status of a true poet. "I have never been able to admire Lessing very much, as far as I know him as a poet," Johann Georg Heinzmann confesses in 1785, candidly judging that Lessing's dramas were always "among the best German plays", but none of them bore "the stamp of actual poet-genius": "His creative power was more an acquired role than nature, and he possessed to the highest possible degree the art of imitating genius [...] without having it himself" (St, 148).

In his *Preliminary Studies for Life and Art* (*Vorstudien für Leben und Kunst*, 1835), the Hegelian Heinrich Gustav Hotho regards it as a proved fact that "Lessing was no poet in the deeper sense of the word" (St, 267). He too concedes to Lessing the status of "the real founder of our new dramatic poetry", but again, he too considers that the vividness of Lessing's dramatic language is merely a surrogate for a naturalness that Lessing lacks:

> Indeed, from every word of the epigrammatically pointed dialogue, there speaks the most lucid mind with all its acuity only too clearly, and even the tones of feeling and of surging passion owe themselves to his antithetical considerations; but so cleverly is the game of hide and seek played, with laborious diligence, in these works of art, that they succeed in giving anyone who is not completely at home in the realm of poetry the deceptive appearance of naturalness. (St, 267)

The image of the unpoetic poet is the image of the 19th century, which was entirely under the spell of Weimar Classicism. The topos was established around 1800, and the extensive Lessing portrait created by the Romantic Friedrich Schlegel to honour Lessing's philosophical and critical spirit was of supreme importance. Schlegel doubted that Lessing had "had poetic sense and artistic feeling" (St, 179). His dramatic "magnum opus", the "admired and certainly admirable" *Emilia Galotti*, he calls "a great example of dramatic algebra", a "masterpiece of pure reason produced with sweat and pain", which nevertheless does not and cannot penetrate "the heart", "because it has not come from the heart" (St, 182). Schlegel's aim is not to belittle Lessing's work, but to him, its literary uniqueness does not spring from its poetic nature, but is evident in an inimitable "*mixture of literature, polemics, wit, and philosophy*" (St, 189). All the characters in his dramas, the servants as well as their mistresses and masters, *Lessingise* (St, 185): They speak with alertness, with presence of mind, with laconic pointedness – and this is sustained down to every smallest turn of dialogue.

For example, when the young Templar realises how he has imperilled Nathan by visiting the Patriarch, he explains himself with the words: "I imagined that this child / Which you had shrewdly wrested from the Christians / You would be loath to yield to them again. / To keep it short and sweet, I thought I might / Just put the dagger at your throat" (V/5; B 9, 609). Nathan's response to this confession is as brief as it is pointed: "Ah, sweet? / What would be sweet in that?" (V/5; B 9, 609). Such are the sequences Schlegel has in mind when he speaks of Lessing's characters "Lessingising". The idiomatic phrase "short and sweet" refers not to the conveyed message, but to the act of conveying it, which is kept brief. But Nathan takes the phrase literally, or rather: Lessing makes Nathan take the Templar at his word, thus giving him the opportunity to give witty expression to a central moral-psychological insight. The Templar's act was one of rashness, into which he was tempted by his egocentrism, and this rashness nearly has fatal consequences.

This incisive wit is the outstanding characteristic of Lessing's dramatic style. Its full charm is played out in the comedies and therefore was probably appreciated mainly by authors who were active in the field of comedy themselves. Hugo von Hofmannsthal – whose comedies (*An Impossible Man*, *The Incorruptible Servant*) follow Lessing's tradition insofar as they centre the comic play around the virtuous protagonist – held a speech on the occasion of Lessing's 200th birthday, in which he praised the "incomparable intensity" peculiar to this "wittiest" art of dialogue, with its "watching each other's words, passing replies back and forth" and "fencing with the intellect (and with the heart masking as intellect)" (St, 453). Hofmannsthal is also aware that Lessing's dramatic language cannot be compared to Goethe's: "Nothing of the breathing, soulful element that Goethe later introduced into the language of the theatre, nor anything of the dark sounds of nature that the Storm and Stress movement brought up." All of Lessing's characters, he concludes, "speak in sharp antitheses, in pointed phrases, as if they were all thinkers" – and just this is the characteristic charm of this language: "It has such an intellectual life within itself that it turns the play into something indestructible" (St, 452–53).

This tone of Lessing's can be found everywhere, even in his most intimate remarks, such as the letters concerning the deaths of his son and wife, which have moved both his contemporaries and posterity deeply. In them, Lessing's incomparable physiognomy is revealed: his witty laconism and the astute play with antitheses, which corresponds to his adeptness at staging his public disputes as a didactic and dialogical process. In the Lessing year of 1929, Thomas Mann accordingly attempted to put an end to the never-ending dispute over Lessing's status as a poet. He does so by questioning the standard itself by which Lessing's literary oeuvre is measured: Lessing's "modernity and contemporaneity," Mann's argument goes, "seems to me to be grounded in the very fact that the all-too-German concept of poetry cannot encompass him, that it does not fit him because it is insufficient" (St, 449). Lessing is a solitary figure who does not need to conform to any standard because his style makes him unmistakable: "Do you really have to be a poet if you are a Lessing?" (St, 449).

Lessing and Schiller

Schiller, too, had an ambivalent relationship with Lessing; like Goethe, his literary work constitutes a break in literary history. What Schiller seeks is pathos – he is the poet of the sublime. Already in his early dramas, he combines the intimacy of the chamber play, following Lessing's tradition, with the grand gesture of the opera stage, which had fascinated him since his youth. He ties in with Lessing, but goes beyond him, shaping our understanding of tragedy in a way that would also impact our understanding of Lessing's work to this day.

If we are to believe Goethe, Schiller "did not really love Lessing's dramas" (*On German Theatre*; MA 11.2, 163). This harsh judgement is softened by the actual proximity of the young Schiller to Lessing's dramatic work, but above all to his writings on dramatic theory, about which he says in retrospect: "There is no question at all that among all Germans of his time, Lessing was clearest about questions of art, the one who thought about it most astutely and at the same time most liberally and who most unswervingly focused on the essentials" (to Goethe, Jun 4, 1799; MA 8.1, 699). Schiller's Mannheim speech on what a "good permanent theatre" can achieve (1784), composed with great rhetorical verve, is indebted to Lessing's idea that the moral effect of the theatre cannot be separated from the pleasure of seeing a display of human life and participating in it. Also, the idea of an *Aesthetic Education of Man* (*Über die ästhetische Erziehung des Menschen*), which Schiller will develop in the homonymous letters after his encounter with Kant's philosophy, finds its precursor in Lessing's ethical-aesthetic programme. Like Lessing, Schiller is convinced that the poetic representation of human life is indispensable for the cultivation of fellow feelings and thus for human self-formation – even and especially where literature does not limit itself to imitating exemplary or vicious behaviour.

How much Schiller is intent on exploring the limits of what is humanly possible, thus cultivating a human consciousness free from moral prejudices, is clear from his early fascination with the figure of the criminal, prominently displayed in the "true story" of the *Criminal from Lost Honour* (*Der Verbrecher aus verlorener Ehre*, 1786) and in the *Robbers* (*Die Räuber*, 1781).

As a narrator, he pursues a poetic programme, the proximity of which to Lessing's poetics of pity is impossible to miss. The story of the poacher, murderer and bandit chief Christian Wolf promises to respect the "republican freedom of the reading public". It should enable them to consciously follow his fatal actions. To do so, the readers must become familiar with the hero, so that they can see him "not only *perform*, but *will* his action" (NA 16, 8); for only in this way can "that wholesome alarm" arise in them "that warns too secure health", which sees in the criminal not its equal, but merely "a creature of another species". Only what awakens an "obscure consciousness of similar peril" (NA 16, 8) in us can move instead of alienate us. If this is not the case, the story fails its purpose of "being a school of cultivation", limiting itself instead to satisfying the audience's "curiosity" (NA 16, 8).

The narrator Schiller shows his criminal being drawn into a vortex of passions, but at the same time he also gives him a human grandeur that surpasses Lessing's ethical-aesthetic programme, because the "great force" that has been in motion in "every great crime" (NA 16, 7) gives rise to sublime emotions. While Lessing had banished the villain from the stage, because a person who does evil for evil's sake would appear to him as nothing but the "miserable last resort of an insipid mind" (HD 2; B 6, 196), Schiller gives his villain the power to want and assert his wickedness. The poacher Christian Wolf, who has served his prison sentence, has to experience how even the children avoid him and decides in defiance and despair to do "something bad": "Formerly I had sinned from *necessity* and *levity*, now it was from free choice, and for my own pleasure" (NA 16, 14–15). When he surrenders to the courts "of [his] free choice" (NA 16, 29) at the end of the story, he rises above all sensuous considerations and gains a moral grandeur in which the subject's freedom of will is revealed.

Already in his preface to the *Robbers*, Schiller had emphasised that he wanted to place vice "before the eyes of men in its colossal magnitude":

> Every man, even the most depraved, bears in some degree the impress of the Almighty's image, and perhaps the greatest villain is closer to the most upright man than the petty offender; for the moral forces keep even pace with the powers of the mind, and the greater the capacity bestowed

on man, the greater and more enormous becomes his misapplication of it; the more responsible is he for his errors. (NA 3, 7)

The fact that a person who pursues a goal exerts a great fascination on us was also clear to Lessing: "We love anything with a purpose so much that it affords us pleasure regardless of the morality of that purpose" (HD 79; B 6, 579), he says in the *Hamburg Dramaturgy*; but the power as such, which Schiller admired, being the source of all deeds, was not worthy of admiration to him. The voice of reason, which Lessing's dramas make heard, is not powerful but gentle.

Like Lessing, Schiller is one of the founding fathers of the modern psychological drama. He, too, pursues the purpose of exhibiting the psycho-logic of the human heart on stage and "tracing out the innermost workings of the soul" (NA 3, 5) – such is the expression he uses in the preface to the *Robbers*. And for Schiller, too, the question of man's position in the whole of creation is at stake. His dramatic work, his aesthetics and his philosophical writings are intended as contributions to the interpretation of human existence after the decline of institutionalised revealed religions.

The cultural consequences of a literary culture whose full development has made the belief in the literal truth of religious myths brittle, are not only at the centre of the philosophical poem about *The Gods of Greece* (*Die Götter Griechenlandes*, 1788), but also the *Philosophical Letters* (*Philosophische Briefe*, 1786).

In *The Gods of Greece*, Schiller contrasts a world that has been deprived of its soul by the natural sciences with the anthropomorphic imagery of myth: "Then, through a veil of dreams / Woven by song, truth's youthful beauty glowed, / And life's redundant and rejoicing streams / Gave to the soulless, soul – where'er they flowed / Man gifted nature with divinity / To lift and link her to the breast of love; / All things betrayed to the initiate eye / The track of gods above!" (NA 1, 190). And he praises the colourful diversity of ancient cult religions and the way in which, to quote Lessing, "the ancients portrayed Death": "Before the bed of death / No ghastly spectre stood – but from the porch / Of life, the lip – one kiss inhaled the breath, / And the mute graceful genius lowered a torch" (NA 1, 193).

In the *Philosophical Letters*, Schiller characterises his time as an age which "has witnessed an extraordinary increase of a thinking public, by the facilities afforded to the diffusion of reading", so that "few persons are willing to *remain* in the condition in which the *chance of birth has cast* them" (NA 20, 105). The religious enlightenment has freed reason from the spell of mythical thinking, but this liberation comes at a price: At the beginning of the correspondence, the enlightened Raphael has robbed Julius of his childlike faith, and with the devil, before whom he used to tremble, and the deity, to which he used to cling dearly, has also taken away his peace of mind. Julius tries to compensate for this loss with a philosophical confession of faith, substituting it for the revealed truth, in order to find again the "enthusiasm" that used to inspire and encourage him. The centre of his *Theosophy* is love, referred to as "sympathy" (NA 1, 169) in Schiller's *Hymn to Joy* – this is the force that makes the fragmented deity whole again: "Egotism erects its centre in itself; love places it out of itself in the axis of the universal whole" (NA 20, 123). Love is the gravity of the moral world; it guarantees the cohesion of creation.

The proximity of the *Theosophy of Julius* (*Theosophie des Julius*) to Lessing's *Education* treatise is palpable. Schiller knows, too, that human thinking is limited and that the language of religion is a language of images and parables: God is only a metaphor, not the thing itself; but the attempt of the human mind to "measure the supersensuous by means of the sensuous" and apply "the mathematics of its conclusions to the hidden physics of the *superhuman*" (NA 20, 127), is truth-apt nevertheless – retaining its value even when it errs: "Every facility of the reason, even in error, increases its readiness to accept truth" (NA 20, 129).

In the *Philosophical Letters*, it is the metaphor of gravity with which Schiller tries to conceptualise the moral world. In his dramas, the myth of the Fall of Man becomes his source of inspiration, as it already had been for Lessing. Schiller considers it "the greatest event in the history of mankind", because it made man moral and thus, free:

> The Fall of Man away from instinct, which indeed brought moral evil into Creation; however, only in order to make the moral good in it possible; that falling away is without contradiction the most fortunate and the greatest event in the history of mankind; his freedom traces itself from this moment [...]. (*Some Thoughts on the first Human Society*; NA 17, 399–400)

All the tragic heroes in Schiller's early dramas are heroes who succumb to the temptation of "eritis sicut Deus" (Genesis 3:5), entangling themselves in sin out of their arrogated greatness. This applies to Karl Moor (*The Robbers*), who approaches society with almost universal hatred and is finally forced to realise that two of his kind would shake creation to its very foundations. This applies to Fiesco (*Fiesco's Conspiracy at Genoa*), who is faced with the choice of becoming either Genoa's first servant or its tyrant, and who succumbs to this temptation at the cost of his murder – at least in the first version of the play. This also applies to the Marquis Posa (*Don Carlos*), who does not shy away from instrumentalising his friend in his enthusiastic fight for freedom, because he presumes to sport with the power of heaven: "I have created in my Carlos' soul, / A paradise for millions!" (IV/21; NA 7.1, 582) – "Of bounded mind, / Man, who is not omniscient, must not dare / To guide the helm of destiny" (IV/21; NA 7.1, 581).

"Seduction is the only true force" (V/7; B 7, 369) – Emilia's often-quoted dictum could also serve as a motto for Schiller's early plays. This is particularly evident in his domestic tragedy *Love and Intrigue* (*Kabale und Liebe*, 1784), which is considered exemplary of the genre alongside Lessing's *Emilia*, but, like *Emilia*, is in fact a genre of its own kind. *Love and Intrigue* takes the audience to the world of the court and its intrigues, exploring the psychology of power and seduction. Its actual hero is not Louise Miller, the town musician's daughter – although the tragedy was initially named after her –, but Ferdinand von Walter, the President's son.

Schiller interprets the lovers' first meeting as the rise of a new world: "The first moment that I beheld him [...] – oh! then was the first dawning of my soul! [...] I forgot there was a world, yet never had I felt that world so dear to me! I forgot there was a God, yet never had I so loved him!" (I/1; NA 5, 20/22). These are Louise's words. Ferdinand sees in her devoted gaze "the handwriting of heaven" (I/4; NA 5, 24) and presumes to elevate himself as the master of her fate: "Trust thyself to me! thou shalt need no other angel. I will throw myself between thee and fate – for thee receive each wound. For thee will I catch each drop distilled from the cup of joy, and bring thee in the bowl of love" (I/4; NA 5, 26).

In the finale, all this is turned into its very opposite: Ferdinand, who had claimed to "see through [Louise's] soul as clearly as through the transparent lustre" of a diamond (I/4; NA 5, 24), is blinded by the intrigue of the Secretary Wurm, Schiller's Marinelli – and unable to see that the love letter to the Court Marshal von Kalb that has been extorted from Louise, is intended to act on his passion like a "grain of leaven that will cause a destructive fermentation" (III/1; NA 5, 86). By it, he is driven to avenge creation: "Judge of the world, ask her not from me! She is mine. For her sake I renounced the whole world – abandoned all thy glorious creation. Leave me the maid, great Judge of the world! [...] The maiden is mine! Once I was her god, but now I am her devil!" (IV/4; NA 5, 126).

Schiller's main inspiration for the construction of Ferdinand and Louise's love story were two of Shakespeare's tragedies: *Romeo and Juliet* and *Othello*. From the tragedy of the "star-cross'd lovers", he borrows the motif of a family- or class-related conflict and the idea of a doomed fate that prevents the lovers from getting to each other. This is echoed in the lament of Louise, after she has been misjudged and poisoned by her lover: "A dreadful fatality has deranged the language of our hearts" (V/7; NA 5, 184). – *Othello*, on the other hand, provides Schiller with the template for a crime of passion, by means of which the deceived, blinded virtuous hero wants to restore the integrity of creation. Like Othello, Ferdinand loses faith in the world: "If she be false, O then heaven mocks itself" (III/3; WS, 299). Like Desdemona, Louise is the "cunning'st pattern of excelling nature" (V/2; WS, 373) – a "masterpiece of nature" (I/5; B 7, 300) which, according to Lessing's 'Othello' Odoardo Galotti, has "selected the wrong clay" (V/7; B 7, 369):

> They are tears for thy soul, Louise! tears for the Deity, whose inexhaustible beneficence has here missed its aim, and whose noblest work is cast away thus wantonly. [...] 'tis but a common sorrow when mortals fall and Paradise is lost; but, when the plague extends its ravages to angels,

then should there be wailing throughout the whole creation! (NA 5, 184)

Schiller accused Lessing of being the "supervisor of his heroes" rather than their friend (Apr 14, 1783; NA 23, 81). He himself identifies with his heroes – their hubris is familiar to him. In a letter to the librarian Reinwald, a friend of his, he confesses to finding himself in his literary characters (Apr 14, 1783; NA 23, 79). This imbues his dramas with their peculiar power. As he writes in his *Notice to the Audience* of his *Fiesco* (*Erinnerungen an das Publikum*, 1784), his plays are designed to make "the hearts of so many hundreds tremble, as by the almighty stroke of a magic rod, according to the poet's fancy", to "lead the audience's soul along by the reins", and to "propel it to heaven or hell, according to my wishes" (NA 22, 90–91). And the poet who does all this is he himself.

There could hardly be a greater contrast between that and Lessing's idea of writing for the "best and most enlightened people of his time" (HD 1; B 6, 191), in order to discuss his psychology of human conflicts and criticism of traditional interpretation patterns. Accordingly, in Schiller's writings on tragic theory from the 1790s pity is eventually pushed away from the centre of tragedy. It is regarded as a mere (sensuous) means of achieving a higher (supersensuous) purpose (cf. HJS, 51–52). This higher purpose is the experience of the sublime, which arises from admiration for the hero, who – unlike Lessing's heroes – is a middle character because he is human, a sensuous and a rational creature rolled in one: "The *sensuous being* must profoundly and violently *suffer*; there must be pathos, therewith the being of reason may be able to give notice of his independence and be *actively* represented" (*On the Pathetic*; NA 20, 196). In his *Letters* on *Don Carlos* (*Briefe über Don Karlos*, 1788), Schiller had interpreted the Marquis Posa's suicide as a form of enthusiastic self-elevation, and defended it from the character's point of view (cf. NA 22, 173–77); in his treatise *On the Sublime* (*Ueber das Erhabene*), written between 1793 and 1796, he sees the conscious submission to the inevitable as evidence of human greatness.

Schiller defines the feeling of the sublime as a "mixed feeling" – a combination of "*woefulness*" and "*joyfulness*" (NA 21, 42), which gives to humans the vivid experience that they can elevate themselves as moral beings above the constraints of the sensuous world. The woefulness affects the empirical self, the suffering sensuous creature; the joyfulness is nourished by the consciousness of freedom possessed by the individual as a rational creature. Art is to enable man to "assert his will" (NA 21, 39) by confronting him with human destinies, where the power of the moral will rises above all necessity. The stage on which such fates are being played out is world history. It exposes the need to "ensure one's well-being" (NA 21, 48) as an illusion of the small-minded. The true purpose of art is to immunise the mind against the inevitable fate with the help of an "artificial misfortune": "The pathetic [...] is an inoculation against unavoidable fate, whereby it deprives it of its malignancy and the assault of the same is led to the strong side of man" (NA 20, 41). Not the most compassionate human being is the best human being, but the one who has learned through the experience of the sublime to face the adversities of real life with serenity.

The examples with which Schiller occasionally illustrates his conception of tragic greatness tell us a lot about it. All of them are stories about someone's readiness to sacrifice their own life, the "highest interest of sensuousness", in the service of a moral duty (*On the Reason Why We Take Pleasure in Tragic Subjects*; NA 20, 141). With *The Pledge*

(*Die Bürgschaft*, 1799), Schiller has arguably erected his most influential monument to this ideal: "Too late? And no more action to take? / Vain life, since it cannot requite him! / But death with me can yet unite him; / No boast the tyrant's scorn shall make – / How friend to friend can faith forsake. / But from the double death shall know, / That truth and love yet live below!" (NA 1, 424).

How widely Schiller's idea of tragedy differs from Lessing's ethical-aesthetic programme is evident even in the smallest detail. Schiller opens his treatise *On the Sublime* with a quote from Lessing's *Nathan*: "No man needs must" (NA 21, 38). To the question that Nathan attaches to this maxim, and the small dialogue that arises from it, he pays no attention. Nathan: "No man needs must, and must a dervish, then? / What must he?" Al-Hafi: "What one warmly begs of him / And he admits is good: that must a dervish." The moral-philosophical point Lessing wants to make prompts Nathan to recognise the true human and the true friend in the dervish: "Now, by our God, you speak the truth. – Let me / Embrace you, man" (I/3; B 9, 498). Schiller has no use for this. He detaches the opening sentence from the epigrammatically pointed dialogue, turning Nathan's statement into a dictum that is to be understood as an expression of moral self-assertion: "The will is the species character of man, and reason itself is only the eternal rule of the same" (NA 21, 38).

There is a good reason for this. Lessing's *Nathan* is an anti-tragic alternative to the tragedy of Oedipus. Schiller, who highly esteemed the play but also viewed it sceptically, put it on at the court theatre in Weimar in 1801 in a revised version, which was to be crucial for the drama's later impact. Shortly thereafter, he made his own attempt at bringing the ancient tragedy to life: His *Bride of Messina* (*Die Braut von Messina*) is a tragedy in the tradition of

Sophocles' *Oedipus*, and at the same time a counterpart to Lessing's *Nathan* and Goethe's *Iphigenia*.

Schiller musters everything the ancient tragedy has to offer in terms of material and dramaturgy. He piles horror upon horror: infanticide, incest, fratricide, and suicide. And he idealises the drama by making the characters speak in dignified verses and adding a chorus to reflect on the plot. At the centre of Schiller's tragedy, there is again an ancestral curse and an oracle. The curse is directed against the Prince of Messina, because he had stolen his bride from his father, whose "awful curse" now pours out "Heaven's vengeance on the impious bed" (l. 964–66; NA 21, 53). The sons conceived in this bed have been alienated from each other by envy and hatred since childhood. When the Prince is prophesied by an "Arab, skilled to read the stars" (l. 1317–18; NA 21, 65), that his entire progeny will be destroyed if his wife gives birth to a girl, and a girl eventually is born, the father orders the child to be killed. The Princess, however, prevents the bloody deed and hides the girl in a convent. She, too, has had a dream interpreted for her: A monk promised her that this child would not bring a curse, but a blessing upon the family, uniting the sons "in bonds of tender love" (l. 1351; NA 21, 66).

This is part of the backstory to the on-stage action, which is revealed – as in *Oedipus*, on which Schiller had studied this technique – in the course of the play. The plot begins after the Prince's death on the day when the mother wants to reconcile the hostile brothers with each other and introduce to them their now grown-up sister. But one of them, Don Manuel, as if by chance, has already met her and secretly made her his bride; the other, Don Caesar, has also fallen in love with the very same young woman and is passionately courting her. When Don Caesar finds his brother in the arms of Beatrice, who has been abducted from the convent, he stabs him – only to recognise immediately the full extent of the tragic doom and take his own life: "The curse of old / Shall die with me! Death self-imposed alone / Can break the chain of fate" (l. 2640–41; NA 10, 118).

Curses and doom, oracles and omens are ubiquitous in Schiller's play; interpreting them is the futile attempt to be armed against fate. Schiller identifies this as the legacy of all religions – Greek polytheism, Christian monotheism, "Moorish superstition" –, which are gathered together in his Messina and present a "collective whole" for the imagination (*On the Use of the Chorus in Tragedy*; NA 21, 15). However, he does not address the question of the truth of religion, let alone of theodicy. In his treatise *On the Sublime*, he had declared it the purpose of tragedy to familiarise the audience with "the malice of the fates": with "the irresistible flight of good fortune, deceived security, triumphant injustice, and defeated innocence" (NA 21, 52). – However we may judge Don Caesar's suicide – as a great deed which raises the tragic hero above the fate that has horribly destroyed all hopes and dreams, or as the completion of a fatal delusion, from the spell of which he cannot free himself even in death –, Schiller's tragedy requires grand guilt and the grand gesture of a freely chosen death. The chorus comments on the end of the play "*after a deep silence*": "In dread amaze I stand, nor know / If I should mourn his fate. One truth revealed / Speaks in my breast; – no good supreme is life; / But of all earthly ills the chief is – Guilt!" (l. 2835–39; NA 10, 125).

Schiller's tragedy is not a religio-philosophical drama but a religious act in itself: an "act of worship" (KW, 154), which allows the individuals in the audience to recognise and experience their shared humanity on stage, "with every bond of destiny rent asunder – when man becomes his brother's brother with a *single* all-embracing sympathy, resolved once again into a *single* species" (NA 20, 100). This is how Schiller had imagined the liberation of the individual from their egocentric isolation in his speech about *The Theatre Considered as a Moral Institution* (*Die Schaubühne als eine moralische Anstalt betrachtet*). So close to Lessing's social philosophy, and yet so far from it.

An Untragic Tragedian

If Goethe made an unpoetic poet out of Lessing, Schiller made him an untragic tragedian. With Schiller, the reflection on tragedy as a literary genre takes an anthropological turn: The poetics of tragic plots, which Aristotle had elaborated and Lessing had rediscovered, is now transformed into a philosophy of the tragic, with standards that obscure our view of Lessing's work. This process takes place in the 19th century, condensing in the formula of "tragic necessity" and the idea of the inevitability and inescapability of the tragic fate. Plots in which the catastrophe – as in the case of Lessing – could have been avoided by prudent action can be no instances of true tragedy. The 19th century, indeed, is neither the first nor the only one blind and deaf to Lessing's art of representing the tragic delusion of the virtuous protagonist. Its perspective makes Lessing appear as a precursor to Schiller – a precursor, however, who seems to have missed his target.

This change of tragic theory from a poetics of self-inflicted misfortune to an anthropology or metaphysics of the tragic is particularly striking in the oeuvre of Friedrich Hebbel, whose "domestic tragedy" *Mary Magdalene* (*Maria Magdalena*, 1844) is unmistakably in Lessing's tradition. The work on this drama is preceded by an intensive study of Lessing's *Emilia Galotti*, which Hebbel finds to be too calculated: "The poet is schoolmastering the Muse's horse" (St, 286); the chance arrangement of individual steps into a tragic plot is lacking "the serious face of necessity" (St, 287); Emilia herself is "something like a contradiction" (St, 287) to Hebbel – he cannot find an approach to her character. The fact that in the moment of her fiancé's death the thing she feels most vividly "with regard to the lecherous assassin" is that she is seducible, does not seem natural to Hebbel, nor an expression of an "ordinary soul" (St, 287). To be truly tragic, the girl, "in holy terror of the demonic forces within her, with feminine bashfulness yet heroic courage, should have chosen death in her last free hour" (St, 287) – but Lessing lacked the poetic means to portray this. Hebbel's poetic imagination, therefore, seeks an alternative scenario, and he finds it in Emilia's "glowing sensuality, formerly lulled to sleep" (St, 288), which is awakened by the Prince and leads her into an inner conflict: "To have one man in her heart and walk down the aisle with the other, this would not agree with her piety, her purity of heart" (St, 288).

However, the tragic hero in Lessing's play is, in fact, not the daughter but the father; the deep inner conflict that Hebbel finds missing is a fantasy of the 19th century: "In Lessing, we are never shaken by the profound tragedy of a profound mind" (HH 1, 72), Hermann Hettner states in his aesthetic studies on modern drama (1852). The literary historian Gustav Kettner passes judgement on *Lessing's dramas in the light of their time and ours* (*Lessings Dramen im Lichte ihrer und unserer Zeit*, 1904): "Lessing does not yet reckon with the demonic violence and the oblivious happiness of a passion that fills up the whole personality, only with the dull power of sensual urges, which is felt as sinful from the beginning" (GK, 244–45). It almost goes without saying that Kettner sees the ideal of tragic greatness exemplified in Schiller's dramas, especially *Don Carlos* and the *Bride of Messina*.

> How completely different is the sacrificial death of a Posa, who departs with "O queen! how lovely still is life!", or of a Don Caesar, whose "arms enfold a treasure, to deck this earthly sphere, and make a lot worthy of the gods"! For Emilia, death is nothing but relief, her deed, ultimately, is merely an act of desperation. (GK, 245)

Hebbel agrees. In the programmatic preface to *Mary Magdalene*, he emphasises that the truly tragic "must appear as something conditioned by necessity from the outset, as something that comes with life itself, like death, and is not to be circumvented" (FH, 26). A tragic event is one that leads to catastrophe with fateful necessity. According to Hebbel, the domestic tragedy, on the other hand, has replaced tragic constellations with sad misfortunes. In any attempt to rehabilitate the genre, therefore, the catastrophe must not evolve out of mere "*externals*", especially not the "collision" of the bourgeois with the aristocratic world caused by "love affairs" – tragedy must be found *within* the bourgeois world: in the "stark narrowness" of its moral universe and the "*terrible fetters*" that confine *life*" in a fateful way (FH, 26).

The "most confined circle" of the lifeworld (*Lebenswelt*) recreated by Hebbel, which his heroine is irretrievably tied to, is governed by ideas of recognition and honour. Social status is its elixir of life, social ostracism is death itself.

Klara, who shares her fate with her sick mother, her selfish brother and her principled father, the carpenter Anton, in a craftsman's household, has been coerced into intimacies by her admirer Leonhard. Now, she is pregnant. When her brother Karl is suspected of theft and arrested for it (a social humiliation their mother does not survive), Leonhard, who has advanced to the position of tax collector, uses "consideration for his office" (II/5; FH, 75) as a pretext to break up with Klara and leave her to her fate. Her father makes her promise not to bring shame on him, threatening to take his own life if she does:

> The moment I notice that people are pointing fingers at you, too, I will – (*moving his hand to his neck*) shave, and then, I swear to you, I'll shave off the whole man. [...] For I can bear everything – I have proved that – everything, except shame! Put on my neck whatever yoke you want, just don't cut through the nerve that holds me together! (II/1; FH, 65–66)

Klara's first love Friedrich, who has made a career as secretary and to whom she is still attached, wants to marry her, but cannot get over having to "lower my eyes before the guy I'd like to spit in the face" (II/5; FH, 76). – And so, things take their inevitable course: Klara can "neither go back nor forward" (II/5; FH, 73). The pregnancy serves Hebbel as a lever to put his protagonist under pressure to act. To avoid becoming her "father's killer", she feels compelled to kill herself, and consequently her unborn child, instead (III/4; FH, 83). Ultimately, her only concern is not to make it look like a suicide.

The conflict Hebbel attributes to Emilia – "to have one man in her heart and walk down the aisle with the other" (St, 288) –, is here passed on to Klara. He develops the supposed motif of a class-related love drama by basing his tragedy on the "*internal*" conditions of the bourgeois world (FH, 26). In the dedicatory poem that prefaces the play, he declares that the poet has to display the "inner labyrinth" of the human mind intertwined with the "outer world", and "to represent in a clear image, / How both complement and illuminate each other" (FH, 32). Hebbel depicts Leonhard and Klara's sexual union accordingly, turning it into the actual root of the disaster: Klara has only yielded to Leonhard because she wanted to persuade herself of having forgotten Friedrich. When he went to university without keeping in touch with her, she had had to endure "scorn and ridicule from all sides": "That girl's still thinking of him! – She really believes his childish nonsense was meant seriously! – Does she get any letters? And Mother, too! [...] And my own heart. If he has forgotten you, show him that you, too – oh God!" (II/5; FH, 74). When Klara unexpectedly meets Friedrich again at a dance, Leonhard realises immediately that he is in danger of losing her to his rival, so he tries to "tie her closely" to him "with the final bond" (I/4; FH, 43): "And he stood before me! Him or me! Oh, my heart, my cursed heart! To prove to him, to prove to myself, that it was not so, or to stifle it if it were, I did what now – (*breaking into tears*)" (II/5; FH, 74).

Hebbel does everything to make sure there is no way out for his protagonist, and to destroy any hope of salvation at the same time. In the lifeworld staged in his tragedy, everybody has good reasons to blame the others and justify themselves. The perspective of the drama, which displays the "narrowness", i.e., the egocentrism of human behaviour, in a particularly drastic way, shows this "most confined circle" as a universal delusion. Its most succinct embodiment is Master Anton – a father who is as rough as the "old soldier" Odoardo Galotti, and who abuses his daughter as lovelessly as the musician Miller his Louise. In this social environment, where everyone is only looking for their own advantage, he has turned into a "bristly hedgehog":

> At first all my spines were directed inwards. They all pinched and pressed on my smooth skin for their amusement and were pleased when I flinched because the points penetrated my heart and entrails. But I didn't like that, so I turned my skin around, and now the bristles went into their fingers, and I had peace. (I/5; FH, 53)

In this world, pity is a mere pretence to mask contempt: "I can't bear a world where people have to be pitiful so they don't spit in front of me" (II/1; FH, 65). When Anton learns that Klara has thrown herself into a well, "her head horribly smashed on the edge" (III/11; FH, 93), he responds uncharitably: "She spared me nothing – we've all seen it!" And: "I can't make sense of anything anymore!" (III/11; FH, 94).

This Hamlet-like bewilderment about the world being out of joint, which ends the play, marks Hebbel's tragedy as an attempt to use the "most confined circle" for portraying not only an individual fate but a world whose social institutions have petrified into mere façades.

An example of how much Lessing's image in the 20th century is shaped by the understanding of tragedy established in the 19th century is Bertolt Brecht. Even though his conception of epic theatre regards itself as an alternative to Europe's entire Aristotelian dramatic tradition, his understanding is shaped by a tradition that finds the ideal realisation of tragedy in Schiller's oeuvre.

Brecht is the anti-Aristotelian par excellence and, as such, Lessing's antipode. He feels it incumbent on him to ban pity from the theatre, because it tempts the audience to sink into a narcotic state of trance where intellectual distance is called for and a critical view of social conditions is needed. Many of his plays discuss the tragic impotence of human fellow feelings: The young comrade in the *Lehrstück The Measures Taken*, Shen Te, the Good Person of Szechwan, Joan Dark, Saint Joan of the Stockyards – all of them are "martyrs of pity" (HJS, 11), characters who are moved by human misery and tempted by their own emotions to act irrationally.

Brecht's aversion to pity was essentially an aversion to the self-sufficient enjoyment of art, which he saw realised in a particularly drastic way in the "cannibalistic" drama (BB, 149) of Naturalism – that illusionistic dramaturgy of the "fourth wall", which suggests to the audience that they are observers of an intimate world involuntarily revealed to their gaze. And it was an aversion to the fascination with human greatness and "great individual experience" (BB, 149), which neglects the social conditions of human behaviour. Schiller's "grand, gigantic fate, which elevates the person when it crushes him" (*Xenia*; NA 1, 359), the idea of tragic necessity, which had fascinated the 19th century, were an abomination to Brecht. His project of epic theatre saw itself as a large-scale attempt to assert the ability of man to be the master of his own fate.

The study of classical philology, too, has long oriented its understanding of tragedy on "what has been the German understanding of tragedy since Schiller" (ASc, 193). What educated circles had considered "tragic" since the 19th century can be looked up, for example, in the *Damen Conversations Lexikon*, an encyclopaedia from 1838. With explicit reference to Schiller, it states: "We call tragic what presents to us human strength and greatness in the struggle with fate or in general with all that is fearsome, oppressive and tormenting in real life." And moreover: "At the sight of these struggles, our hearts are moved and touched, but at the same time elevated by the grandeur of the hero, who defies all blows of fate and only appears truly victorious when he is struck down" (DCL 10, 180).

Arguably, this Schillerian German understanding of tragedy has also informed the interpretation of Aristotle presented by the renowned classicist Wolfgang Schadewaldt in the 1950s. In a widely noted essay, Schadewaldt raised objections against Lessing's interpretation of Aristotle, emphasising the instinctive shock Aristotle meant by his formula of *eleos* and *phobos*: "woe and horror" (*Jammer und Schauder*), not "pity and fear" (*Mitleid und Furcht*), is what tragedy aims to evoke. And these primitive emotions are not intended to have a moral effect but to generate a kind of psychosomatic discharge and catharsis. Schadewaldt assigns to horror "the threatening, the overwhelmingly close, the 'monstrous' aspect of fate"; to woe, the "overwhelming power of suffering, which is destructive" (WSc, 169–70). – The reverberations of Schiller's theory of the pathetic and the sublime are hard to miss. Recent works on Aristotle's *Poetics* have rejected this interpretation and newly appreciated Lessing's philological achievement (cf. EK).

Legislator of the Arts

Lessing did not write novels. This is probably largely owing to the fact that the novel played only a marginal role in ancient literature, and none at all in ancient poetics. It is a product of literate culture. Over the course of the 18th century, it established itself in the canon of literary genres, even though literary theory still remained sceptical for a long time. Lessing had nothing to contribute to the poetics of the novel, but his writings on dramatic theory and media aesthetics have served as an inspiration for modern narrative literature. And for a good reason: They are part of a broader process of literalisation, in the course of which literature becomes aware of its own written nature and opens up new creative potentials for storytelling through writing.

With his media aesthetics of the mimetic arts, Lessing became a role model for Friedrich von Blanckenburg. In 1774, Blanckenburg, an officer who dabbled in questions of aesthetics, published his *Theory of the Novel* (*Versuch über den Roman*), which is considered the first significant poetics of the novel in Germany. In this undertaking, Lessing is his role model in two respects: firstly, as the author of the *Hamburg Dramaturgy*, which distinguishes the art of literary myth-making from mere historiography; secondly, as the author of *Laocoön*, whose interpretations of Homer are Blanckenburg's gold standard of the art of narrative writing.

The art of myth-making is the art of imagining events as a "concatenation of cause and effect" (FvB, 10). This art of concatenation, according to Blanckenburg, is also imperative for the novelist. In Christoph Martin Wieland's *History of Agathon*, which Lessing himself had praised as the "first and only novel for the thinking man" (HD 69; B 6, 531), Blanckenburg finds an exemplary realisation of this programme. The art of narrative writing is not the art of describing human passions but the art of representing them in the expressions and actions of the characters, not saying what they feel, but showing their feelings through their behaviour.

> Novelists usually confine themselves to merely *narrating* the passions and sensations of their characters. When they love, the novelists tell us that they love, and that settles the matter. [...] At most, they tell us what is going on, and we want to see more than that. The impression is very different when we see an effect develop before our eyes, from when we hear it narrated. Now, this flat, barren impression made by the mere *narration* of the event, which does not arouse our passions at all, can be avoided if the novelist knows how to transform this narration into action. (FvB, 493–94)

Like a drama, the illusionary qualities of which Lessing emphasises so strongly both in the *Hamburg Dramaturgy* and in *Laocoön*, a novel should establish an *"ideal present"* (FvB, 493), a Here and Now. It should depict "the emergence, continuation, and entire *coming into being* of passions", thus awakening the *"sympathy"* of the reader (FvB, 29–30), and not only entertain him in the *"pleasantest"* way, but also in the way "most *useful* for humanity" (FvB, 91–92).

The rejection of mere 'story-telling' in modern narrative literature has a long tradition behind it, which goes back to ancient rhetorics and the early European novella, where it is discussed under the heading of *evidentia*. Successful storytelling does not *tell* us what has happened, but *shows* it. In oral storytelling, which rhetorics primarily had in mind, this is not only expressed verbally: The narrator necessarily turns into an actor who makes his characters come alive through facial expression, gestures, intonation. Writing, on the other hand, deprives the author of the possibility to embody his characters; and it is this limitation of means to activate the reader's imagination which is responsible for the fact that written storytelling has had to resort to descriptions instead.

A reflection on the limits of poetry is, therefore, a reflection on the aesthetic limitations imposed on storytelling in narrative writing. – Consequently, the solution which Lessing had found in Homer and which Blanckenburg suggests to the novelist, is more than just some phenomenon that concerns literary history. Homer's epics stem from an oral storytelling tradition, which is preserved in written records. In their art of translating everything into action, Lessing discovers a basic principle of storytelling, which is also a basic principle of literature. Since literature imitates human actions, and since human actions are performed primarily in speaking, literature has to be measured by whether it succeeds in making its characters speak in such a way that they gain a profile as persons. The characters' speech becomes poetic when the speakers do not merely exchange information but, in speaking, present themselves as persons, i.e., when the speech is merely the perceptible part of a broader psychological and interpersonal dynamic.

Even more clearly than Blanckenburg, playwright Johann Jakob Engel recognises that Lessing's writings on dramatic theory and media aesthetics should be read as founding texts of a literature that represents the human mind. In his treatise *On Plot, Dialogue, and Narration* (*Über Handlung, Gespräch und Erzählung*, 1774), Engel asserts that all actions originate from "the thinking and feeling soul" (JJE 1, 201), and this soul reveals itself in the literary character's manner of speaking:

> It is unbelievable how well the soul knows how to impress itself into the words, how well it knows how to use the speech as its mirror, in which it is entirely represented, down to the finest and most delicate features. The logical proposition, or the mere general sense, extracted from the words, is always the least part of them; the composition of the expression as a whole, which gives us an exact idea of the specific state of the soul when forming the thought, is everything. (JJE 1, 233)

This, too, is a variation on Lessing's dictum that the poet should not lose himself in descriptions, but represent characters in action (cf. JJE 1, 238–39). In the theory of the novel in the 19th century, this is a ubiquitous maxim: The novelist Friedrich Spielhagen recurs to it in his essay on *Objectivity in the Novel* (*Über Objectivetät im Roman*, 1864) when referring to the poetic qualities that a literary text gains by letting the characters speak and thus keeping them "continuously active" (FS, 190). This insight has not lost any of its validity to this day. Even modern guides to the art and technique of storytelling are conscious of being indebted to Lessing when they emphasise that "lengthy descriptions" tire the reader and that the art of creating literary characters consists in stimulating the imagination "through typical details and hints" (FG, 90). Storytelling becomes vivid when it neither reports nor describes, but shows: "Show, don't tell," is the title of the pertinent chapter in the widely-read guidebook *Stein on Writing*, which introduces aspiring writers to the art of storytelling (cf. SS, 122–28).

However, Lessing's media theory of poetic literature not only has a technical side; it also pursues an ethical-aesthetic programme. His reflections on theatre and the limits of painting and poetry are also a vindication – a vindication of mankind and the images we make of ourselves. Lessing defends them against the objections of misanthropic resentment and nihilistic self-disempowerment. In this respect, Lessing may be considered the forerunner of Poetic Realism, whose art of storytelling claims to represent the human world as a world of beings capable of recognising and pursuing truth.

For a principal witness to this ethical-aesthetic programme, we can look at Fontane. In his programmatic essay on *Our Lyric and Epic Poetry since 1848* (*Unsere lyrische und epische Poesie seit 1848*, 1853), he understands the modernity of his epoch as "a return to the only correct path", which "*Lessing's* beautiful, up-to-now unmatched realism" had pointed out to literature (TF 1, 238). For Fontane, too, the crucial question is how to make the characters speak. His novels are conversation novels not only in a technical sense – poor in sensational events, but rich in states of consciousness that can be gauged from the manner of speaking: "In the end, an old man dies and two young people marry; – that's about all that happens on 500 pages. Of complications and solutions, of conflicts of the heart or conflicts generally, of tensions and surprises, there is nothing in it," his often-quoted comment on *The Stechlin* (*Der Stechlin*, 1898) says. And: "Nothing but chatter, dialogue, in which the characters reveal themselves, and with them the story" (TF 2, 650).

Fontane, too, is committed to an aesthetic programme that makes a point of preserving personal dignity. This ethos of realistic storytelling is evidenced particularly in his reflections on Émile Zola. In his notes on Zola's novel *La fortune des Rougon*, Fontane is mainly provoked by the fact that it appears to be "a negation of the individual's *free will*" (TF 1, 538). In Zola's world – according to Fontane's diagnosis –, man has "no soul that *by its own power*, in spite of all weakness and all temptation, can do great, beautiful, virtuous, heroic things"; his actions are influenced by physical stimuli, a "special composition of blood", his "*nerves*" that determine him, and "his *senses*":

> If anything special happens that gets on his nerves, or if he sees or smells anything special, he is subject to the impressions of it, so that it can be said: This or that unfortunate moment, this or that temptation could have been avoided but for the smell of a soap kettle, which happened to strike his senses.
>
> This is not entirely stupid; I do not deny that in the majority of cases, he is right. But all this is not the role of art. Art must argue and affirm the opposite. And if you cannot do this, you have to remain silent. (TF 1, 538–39)

These are harsh words, and it is not by chance that they remind us of the almost desperate determination with which Lessing banishes the figure of the villain from the theatre in his *Hamburg Dramaturgy*. In Lessing's eyes, the "abominable" has no place on the stage, because the "examples of such undeserved and terrible fates" only confuse the mind: "Away", therefore, "with them from the stage! Away with them, if only it were possible, from all books!" (HD 79; B 6, 578). – When Fontane rejects Zola's naturalism no less harshly, he argues in a very similar way. He emphasises the *exemplary* character of literary representation – its proximity to "real life" and its aesthetic distance: The novel, according to Fontane's credo, should be "an undistorted reflection of the life we lead" (TF 1, 568), and it should give to this life the "intensity, lucidity, clarity, and completeness", consequently the "emotional intensity" that Fontane understands as "the transfiguring power of art (*die verklärende Aufgabe der Kunst*)" (TF 1, 569).

In his study of Zola's novel *La conquête de Plassans*, Fontane specifies this concept of realism by addressing the difference between what occurs in the world and what art should represent. Anything can happen, Fontane does not doubt that, but he does not consider this an aesthetic argument. Literary representation is ultimately committed to beauty, or "beautifulness (*Schönheitlichkeit*)", as Fontane says; and whether or not something is beautiful, is shown by whether or not its representation allows of the reader's "joyful participation" (TF 1, 548). The argument with which he defends his aesthetic programme could also have flown from Lessing's pen:

> In a certain sense, at least from the moral point of view, we demand average people who only get caught up in "exceptional situations" because of a particular concatenation of circumstances. We must understand the person and recognise them as one of our own, that is the first condition; and the second condition is that, when the "exceptional situation" occurs, we regard it as an exceptional situation, but at the same time we must also feel that *we*, under the same circumstances, would have let the same exceptional situation arise. Representations that consistently show an "exceptional case", in which *everything* strikes us as foreign,

the character as well as his deed, do not belong in art. In their presence, our compassion falls away: The absolute good and evil leaves us cold because it is no longer human. (TF 1, 547)

This is the programme of the art of perspectival representation in a nutshell, as Lessing, following in Aristotle's footsteps, had outlined it in the *Hamburg Dramaturgy*. Fontane answers the question of what realities are suited for poetic representation at all, by measuring the quality of the literary representation against the experience it opens up to the reader. Fontane's ethical-aesthetic programme is also a rejection of an art of description that uses an abundance of sensational details to attempt to "make an impression" (TF 1, 539) but remains without Gestalt qualities. "What Zola brings forth," Fontane criticises, "is an interesting but confusing back and forth, in which it is difficult to find one's way" (TF 1, 539).

However, Lessing's *Laocoön* is not only reflected in the programme of Poetic Realism, but also became a repeatedly cited reference text for art theory itself. Wilhelm Dilthey, accordingly, referred to Lessing in his seminal essay from 1906 as the second great "legislator of the arts" after Aristotle (WD, 34). *Laocoön* is an indispensable factor in the aesthetic discourse of the 19th century – during the second half of the century, more than fifty editions are published.

Already their contemporaries were fascinated by the debate between Winckelmann and Lessing. Herder, who critically comments on Lessing's reflections on the temporality of the arts in the first edition of his *Critical Groves* (*Kritische Wäldchen*, 1769), uses them as a starting point to distinguish between painting and sculpture in a study entitled *Sculpture* (*Plastik*, 1778). Goethe picks up on Lessing's formula of the 'fruitful moment', developing his own theory of the "highest moment of expression" (MA 4.2, 74). His Laocoön treatise, which is published in the first issue of his and Schiller's periodical *Propylaea* (1798), is considered *the* programmatic text of Classicism. Goethe detaches the moment represented by the group of statues from the narrative context and directs the attention to the inherent movement of the depicted bodies: to the "contrast of struggle and flight, of action and suffering, of energy and failing strength" (MA 4.2, 82). And he draws attention to the Gestalt qualities of the sculpture: to the interplay "of symmetry and variety, of repose and action, of contrast and gradation", which "in spite of the high pathos of the representation, produce an agreeable impression, and by their grace and beauty temper the storm of passion and suffering" (MA 4.2, 77–78). All this makes the Laocoön Group an exemplary work of art that rejects the "modern notion that a work of art must have the appearance of a work of nature" (MA 4.2, 77).

There can be no doubt that Lessing's primary interest was not in "painting" but in poetry. In this respect, *Laocoön* became a widely discussed standard work of media aesthetics, which found a particularly astute reader in the literary theorist Theodor A. Meyer. His study on *The Stylistic Principles of Poetry* (*Das Stilgesetz der Poesie*, 1901) explicitly regards itself as an "aesthetic commentary on Lessing's *Laocoön*" (TM, 24). It claims to rethink Lessing's question about the linguistic nature of poetry, the central argument being that not "articulated sounds in time" are the medium of poetry, but "our conceptions (*Vorstellungen*), in the way that they are expressed in articulated sounds" (TM, 28). Such conceptions are generated when we relate the successive signs to each other. In fact, Meyer's opponent is not really the author of *Laocoön*, but 19th-century aesthetics, notably represented by Friedrich Theodor Vischer, who had rejected Lessing's concept and declared not language itself but the "imagination" to be the medium of literature. According to Vischer, poetry is "the art of inner perception" ("die Kunst der innerlich gesetzten Sinnlichkeit"; TM, 30); language is only a means to activate the imagination. Meyer cannot agree with this thought: "Language in poetry," he objects, "is not a vehicle for inner perceptions (*Sinnenbilder*)" (TM, 74), it has its own logic. It abstracts from the sensory abundance of the phenomenal world, focusing only on specific characteristics of the objects and processes it refers to. And this focus is impressed upon poetry:

> In it, the phenomenal world is not brought to our minds as it actually is, in image, motion and sound, but entirely in the manner in which it appears in the processing by our imagination, in all the thought-ness and mind-ness of the imagination and the abstract abbreviation, summary and fragmentation this makes possible. And this abstract hint of reality, this extract from reality which has been concentrated, intellectualised (*ins Geistige umgesetzt*) and permeated by the purely intellectual (*vom rein Geistigen durchsetzt*), is not stretched and inflated back into its real shape, nor do we restore its phenomenal appearance which has been destroyed by language, but in the form in which we receive it, it conveys its content to us. (TM, 88–89)

If poetry is vivid (*anschaulich*), it is not in an extra-aesthetic sense, in which 'vivid' means as much as 'perceptible'; in the aesthetic sense, the perceptible only becomes vivid if we can experience it as an expression of life (cf. TM, 32). Literary texts are aesthetically meaningful when they evoke the impression of life and increase our awareness of being alive.

Friend of Spinoza

Lessing was one of the leading intellectuals in Europe. The leitmotif of his life was the question of the truth of religion and the authentic interpretation of religious tradition. His literary as well as his philosophical oeuvre is nothing but an attempt to fathom this truth and assert it with the strongest possible determination. As a religious philosopher who wrote poetry and a poet who reflected on religious philosophy, he has had an enormous impact on the history of human thought.

With the publication of the Reimarus fragments, Lessing had provoked the most momentous religio-philosophical dispute of the 18th century; unintentional, yet no less momentous was another dispute that arose over a statement by Lessing, which was made public by the popular philosopher and writer Georg Friedrich Jacobi after Lessing's death. It concerned the philosophy of Spinoza, which Lessing had evidently endorsed in a conversation with Jacobi.

Jacobi's work *On the Doctrine of Spinoza in Letters to Herr Moses Mendelssohn* (*Über die Lehre des Spinoza in Briefen an den Herrn Moses Mendelssohn*, 1785) has made history. Goethe referred to it in *Truth and Poetry* as an "explosion which revealed and brought into discussion the most secret relations of men of worth; – relations of which they perhaps were not themselves conscious, and which were slumbering in a society otherwise most enlightened" (TaP III/15; MA 16, 681). Hegel characterises it as a "thunderclap", which had descended "out of the blue" (H 2, 315–16), and even considers the publication of the letters on Spinoza the beginning of modern German philosophy: According to the authoritative judgement of Hermann Timm, "there is no second event in recent intellectual history with a similarly broad impact" (HT 2, 6).

The Dutch philosopher Baruch de Spinoza had already been considered the epitome of an atheist before the 18th century. His philosophy dismisses the concept of a personal deity as a naïve anthropomorphism and challenges his contemporaries with the idea that our images of God are images that we make of God. (If triangles or circles could speak, they would say that God is eminently triangular or circular.) Spinoza's philosophy exposes the egocentric perspective on the world, which considers "all natural things as means to our own advantage" (BdS, 83) and judges everything according to whether it meets our needs or is contrary to them. And it exposes the naïve notion that God is the creator of this world in which everything happens for our weal or woe. Nature, however, has no final cause – final causes are "mere human figments" (BdS, 85); attributing them to the will of the gods or of one deity means seeking refuge with a being that is not of this world, from lack of knowledge about the true nature of things.

Following a deeply human intuition, René Descartes had distinguished between two substances in his *Meditationes de prima philosophia*: corporeal substance (*res extensa*) and mental substance (*res cogitans*). This substance dualism was rejected by Spinoza: Thought and extension are attributes of one and the same substance, referred to as "God" by Spinoza: "*Quicquid est, in Deo est, et nihil sine Deo neque concipi potest.*" – "*All that is, is in God, and nothing can be or be conceived without God*" (BdS, 30–31). Lessing recognised this rejection of an extramundane deity in the yet unpublished *Prometheus* poem by Goethe, which Jacobi had shown to him during his visit to Wolfenbüttel in July 1780. Prometheus, the culture hero of Greek mythology, scoffs at Zeus and the gods, addressing a blasphemous prayer to them:

> I know of nothing more wretched
> Under the sun than you gods!
> Meagerly you nourish
> Your majesty
> On dues of sacrifice
> And breath of prayer
> And would suffer want
> But for children and beggars,
> Poor hopeful fools.
> Once too, a child,
> Not knowing where to turn,
> I raised bewildered eyes
> Up to the sun, as if above there were
> An ear to hear my complaint,
> A heart like mine
> To take pity on the oppressed. (MA 1.1, 230)

Lessing famously commented that,

> The point of view from which the poem is written is my own point of view... I have no more use for the orthodox concepts of the deity; they give me no satisfaction. Ἓν καὶ Πᾶν! [One and all!] I know nothing else. That's also the sense of this poem; and I must confess that I like it very much. (HS, 77)

To Jacobi's astonished remark that in this case, Lessing "would be pretty much in agreement with Spinoza", the latter replied that, "If I must call myself after anyone, I know of no one else" (HS, 77). And: "You should rather make friends with him properly. There is no other philosophy than that of Spinoza" (HS, 78).

The contemporaries did not doubt the purport of the reported conversation; those who knew Lessing could, as Herder or Elise Reimarus testified, practically hear him speak, but nonetheless, Lessing's friends could not believe that such had been his words. Moses Mendelssohn, to whom Jacobi's letter was addressed, was alarmed by the Spinozist legacy of Lessing alleged in it. He felt compelled to protect his deceased friend's name from Jacobi's defamatory insinuation and defend him publicly: first in his *Lectures on God's Existence* (*Vorlesungen über das Dasein Gottes*, 1785), also known as *Morning Hours* (*Morgenstunden*), then again in a written work addressed *To Lessing's Friends* (*An die Freunde Lessings*, 1786). In his *Lectures*, Mendelssohn not only attempted to refute Spinoza's pantheism (chap. XIV), but also advocated for Lessing and the "doctrine of divine Providence and governance" (chap. XV), for which he considered *Nathan* to be the key witness: Mendelssohn reads it as "a kind of *Anti-Candide*" (HS, 35; B 9, 1231); while Voltaire in his satirical novel on "optimism" had tried everything to undermine faith in Providence, Lessing's "panegyric to Providence" (HS, 36; B 9, 1232) reinstated this faith.

Mendelssohn's interpretation of *Nathan* certainly places too much of the burden of proof on the dramatic poem. Spinoza's rejection of an anthropomorphic image of God, which is also evident in Goethe's poem, was part of a broader ethical project that found its telos in a theory of a reasoned and rational life. Lessing could agree with Spinoza on this point, too. Like Spinoza, throughout his life he pursued the idea that it is the rational insight into the nature of things and the nature of what is truly good, that is able to direct the human will and provide orientation to human life. This point was also discussed in the conversations with Jacobi: "I see that you would like to have a free will," Lessing is purported to have said, confessing in the same breath that he had "no desire for a free will" (HS, 82) – a confession that can already be found in Lessing's comments on Karl Wilhelm Jerusalem's *Philosophical Essays* (*Philosophische Aufsätze*, 1776), which he had edited, and that might equally have flown from Spinoza's pen: "Compulsion and necessity whereby our conception of the best operates – how much more welcome are they to me than the bare capacity to act now one way and now another under the same circumstances! I thank the creator that I *must*; that I must act for the *best*!" (B 8, 168).

"Hen kai pan" became the motto of all those poets, philosophers and intellectuals who would no longer be satisfied with the institutionalised religions' traditional answers to the question about the meaning of human existence, and who nevertheless would not give up regarding individual human life as embedded within a horizon that exceeds that life. These included, among others, the students at the Tübinger Stift, namely the young poet Friedrich Hölderlin and the aspiring philosophers Schelling and Hegel. For them, the encounter with

Spinoza's philosophy was a revelation, for to all of them, as Schelling wrote to Hegel, "the orthodox conceptions of God were no longer valid" (as cited in HT 1, 90). In his lectures on the *History of Modern Philosophy* (*Geschichte der neueren Philosophie*, 1827), Schelling considered it hopeless to "proceed towards truth and perfection in philosophy" unless you "have at least once in your life immersed yourself in the abyss of Spinozism" (FSc, 54); according to Hegel, you could be either a Spinozist or no philosopher at all (cf. H 2, 163–64).

In the Tübinger Stift, Hegel was considered "Lessing's confidant" (as cited in HT 1, 90). Traces of his intimate knowledge of Lessing can still be found in Hegel's philosophy of history. His main inspiration was Lessing's *Education* treatise, which, with its recourse to Joachim of Fiore's triadic model of history, had opened up new paths. The idea that world history is "the real *theodicy*", which Hegel will unfold in his *Lectures on the Philosophy of History* (*Vorlesungen über die Philosophie der Geschichte*, 1837; H 1, 540), is based on Lessing's idea that the education of the human race *is* the self-revelation of God, and that history is the actualisation of reason – even if it does not always travel straight: "It is not true that the shortest line is always the straight one" (§ 91; B 10, 98), he writes in the *Education* treatise. Hegel will recognise in it the "*cunning of reason*" (H 1, 49).

Lover of Theology

Lessing was not a professing Christian – no more than his Nathan was a professing Jew or his Saladin a professing Muslim: "Nathan's attitude towards *all* positive religion," Lessing clarifies, "has all along been *my own*" (B 9, 665). In his *Education* treatise and in a fragment written in 1780 about the "religion of Christ", the question of the divinity of the Jewish itinerant preacher Jesus of Nazareth remains unanswered: "Whether Christ was more than a human being is a problem. That he was a true human being – if he was a human being at all – and that he never ceased to be a human being is not in dispute" (B 10, 223). Jacobi reports in his letters on Spinoza that "with the idea of a personal and absolutely infinite being in the unchanging enjoyment of its supreme perfection", Lessing had associated "such an impression of *infinite boredom* that it caused him pain and anxiety" (HS, 95–96).

Even though his scepticism made it impossible for him to commit to "any one dogma" (B 9, 57), Lessing remained faithful to the topic of religion throughout his life. But as in his studies on classical antiquity, he was most interested in the beginnings, and this interest in origins was again linked to a polemical impulse against the traditional understanding of cultural heritage. Lessing felt committed to the original teachings of Jesus of Nazareth, devoting himself to defending the "religion of Christ" against the "Christian religion", that is, against what had become of these teachings in the process of transmission and dogmatisation of a canon of Holy Scriptures and religious doctrines.

In fact, Lessing's true legacy lies in the field of religious enlightenment. As such, both Protestant and Catholic theology took note of his writings – in some part approvingly, in some part critically distanced. References to his religio-philosophical writings can be found in all surveys of the topic (cf. AS, WT). The theological encyclopaedia *Lexikon für Theologie und Kirche* describes Lessing as one of the "most incorruptible and influential figures in German intellectual history" and attributes to him a "momentous significance" for the development of Protestant theology (GR, 980). In particular, the Tübingen School surrounding David Friedrich Strauss owed much to him. Theologians as significant as Karl Barth grappled with the position that Lessing developed in the Fragments Controversy (cf. JK).

Far more significant, however, than Lessing's influence on theology was the effect his work had on the educated. As a "lover of theology" (B 9, 57), he made a point of questioning the monopoly of the Church on determining the nature of religion. The theologian and religious historian Emanuel Hirsch has therefore described Lessing's oeuvre as a "turning point" and a "disruption to our literary, intellectual and religious history" (EH, 120), classifying his religio-philosophical writings alongside Kant's oeuvre as "that particular piece of German Enlightenment" which "has remained alive beyond the eighteenth century" (EH, 121).

The history of Lessing's religio-philosophical influence begins with the Fragments Controversy, continues with the debate over his Spinozist legacy, and remains alive to this day in the discussion about the ideal of humanity in *Nathan* and the conflict-ridden relationship between the three major book religions – painfully condensed in the history of European Judaism and the baleful part Germany has played in it.

Kant, in his preface to the *Critique of Pure Reason* (*Kritik der reinen Vernunft*, 1781), rejected all metaphysical speculation and drew a line between questions the human mind can answer and questions that must remain unanswered because they "transcend *every faculty of the mind*" (IK 1, 11). Why is there something rather than nothing? Where do we come from? Where are we going? – We do not know and we cannot know, but neither can we stop asking these questions of ourselves. Kant's philosophy of religion stays expressly "within the bounds of bare reason" (*Die Religion innerhalb der Grenzen der bloßen Vernunft*, 1793). Lessing was aware of these limits, which is manifest in his often-quoted renunciation of the "possession" of truth in favour of the ever-erring but "ever-active quest for truth" (B 8, 510), to which he gave expression in the course of the Fragments Controversy. Nevertheless, he did not regard the natural limits set to human knowledge as a commandment for him to limit his thinking, but – for the very reason that metaphysical questions are "questions to which *the very nature of reason gives birth*" (IK 1, 11) – as an incentive to extend these limits of thinking as far as possible and, thus, consciously cultivate the ability to disregard our own egocentric interests.

Lessing's attitude towards religion was no less critical than the epistemological position Kant was to develop – from his *Nathan*, he hoped that at least one in a thousand readers "learns from it to doubt the evident truth and universality of his religion" (to Karl Lessing, Apr 18, 1779; B 12, 247). His studies on religious tradition, however, served to enlighten religion about itself; they were intended as enlightenment about deceptions that are deeply rooted in human nature: thinking in terms of reward and punishment, longing for a certainty of salvation, and not least tying faith to sacred texts and ritual practices.

Lessing's 'a-theistic' philosophy of religion reached a wider audience thanks to *Nathan* and his re-interpretation of the Ring Parable. The publication of the book immediately triggered ambivalent reactions, being enthusiastically received in private circles, whereas in public, critical reservations and sometimes violent rejection predominated. The poet Johann Wilhelm Ludwig Gleim reports to his "dear, worthy" friend that "judgements of malice and stupidity I have heard in abundance" (Jul 22, 1779; B 9, 1197). Although the drama was praised in reviews as "quite worthy of Lessing and his reputation", they kept silent on the "moral attitudes" and "opinions" articulated in it (B 9, 1196). In his *Lectures on God's Existence*, or *Morning Hours* (1785), Moses Mendelssohn portrayed the awkwardness also encountered by Lessing himself: The malicious gossip,

> once limited to the student dens and bookshops, now penetrated into the private houses of his friends and acquaintances, whispering in everyone's ears: Lessing has affronted *Christendom* [...]. The friend and acquaintance had been welcome everywhere but now, wherever he turned, he found sullen countenances, reserved, frosty glares, cold welcomes and premature exits; he saw himself

abandoned by friends and acquaintances and exposed to all of the persecutions of his pursuers. (St, 37; B 9, 1232–33)

The Breslau physician Baltasar Ludewig Tralles, inexpert in literary matters, voiced his righteous anger in his *Miscellaneous Frank and Christian Remarks on Herr Gotthold Ephraim Lessing's New Dramatic Poem Nathan the Wise* (*Zufällige altdeutsche und christliche Betrachtungen über Hrn. Gotthold Ephraim Lessings neues dramatisches Gedicht Nathan der Weise*, 1779), concluding that *Nathan* advocated the "coldest indifference towards all religions" (as cited in B 9, 1182) – a reproach that was raised several times in the public debate, but also prompted enlightened minds like Christian Gottfried Schütz, Professor of Poetry and Eloquence at Jena University, to openly profess the "indifferentism" of the Ring Parable (as cited in B 9, 1215).

The fascination and the discomfiture caused by Lessing's dramatised philosophy of religion are also evident from the *Nathan* imitations and travesties (cf. HSt, HFW). Particularly illuminating is a sequel in blank verse written by the Meiningen court preacher Johann Georg Pfranger, entitled *The Monk of Lebanon* (*Der Mönch vom Libanon*, 1782). Pfranger had already been a passionate participant in the Fragments Controversy and responded to Lessing's provocation with a treatise *On the Resurrection of the Dead* (*Über die Auferstehung der Todten*, 1776). His concern for the salvation of souls is again the impulse that shapes Pfranger's "addendum" to *Nathan*. Pfranger passes this concern on to Saladin: The Sultan is on his deathbed, lamenting that he has been seduced by the "shimmering wisdom" of Nathan's tale into doubting the truth of religion:

> [...] for as soon as the mind
> Begins to doubt, so does the conscience, too. –
> From doubting to denial, it is but
> A short step: How soon this is done! – –
> O doubts! O doubts! When will be revealed
> From you the truth to my spirit? – Where am I? –
> If everything is true – oh! then everything is false!
> God loves them all – and God deceives
> Them all! – Nathan! Nathan! O where
> Has your shimmering wisdom led me!
> Oh! Now, how weak! Feeble slumber of death
> Hinders every striving towards a glimpse of truth! –
> God! Guide me through the dark road –
> Up to the light! Forgive! – forgive! – me, too! – (JGP, 13)

Saladin's fear of death is the fear of a sinner who has too carelessly gambled away any hope of redemption along with his faith. In his distress, a mysterious monk comes along to save the day, first by giving him medicinal herbs, then, however, by restoring his faith in the healing power of the true ring. The mysterious monk, who wins Recha's love and Nathan's friendship, is none other than Assad, Saladin's brother, presumed dead. Pfranger completes Lessing's story by returning to its beginning, which was Assad's conversion to Christianity (which had brought suffering to the family and death to Saladin's sister Lea); this conversion is now completed in the conversion of the whole family, for which Assad's return has set the course.

Heinrich Heine, in his essayistic *History of Religion and Philosophy in Germany* (*Zur Geschichte der Religion und Philosophie in Deutschland*, 1834), ranked Lessing alongside Luther, because he "roused to its very depths the German nation" (St, 262). The actual achievement of this second Luther was to free religion from the "yoke of the letter" (B 9, 50), which had come into being through the *sola scriptura* principle propagated by the first Luther (cf. St, 264–65). The ties that bind faith to the Holy Scriptures are severed, with the Scriptures being understood as figurative and parabolic texts.

Pfranger, however, insists on Biblical literalism. His monk implores Recha to seek salvation in the Gospel of Jesus: "O! read it / You will love Him, Recha!" (JGP, 61), "Read! And love Him!" (JGP, 71). Pfranger does not problematise the claim to exclusivity raised by each of the revealed religions – he takes it for granted that all people are children of God and that it is possible for everyone to find happiness: "In His sphere / Every creature can be happy. This is how / The incomprehensibly good Father of All / Has arranged it" (JGP, 67). What really puzzles and upsets him is Lessing's demythologisation of religion: "We are saved from the grave / Not by an angel, nor a man: only by God's power" (JGP, 207). And this power is granted by the right faith alone, which only the testimony of the resurrection of Christ can establish.

"Lessingiasis" and "Nathanology"

In the later understanding of *Nathan*, Lessing's challenging enlightenment of religion is lost sight of – almost as if the question of a reliable interpretation of life had become obsolete. It is replaced by the discomfiture about the figure of the noble Jew, who had always been met with scepticism, and the fascination this figure has always exerted. Lessing's dramatic poem is canonised as one of the central texts of the European tolerance discourse.

For educated Jews, it initially has the status of a promise: August Wilhelm Schlegel reports that Mendelssohn's "kin in religion" came to see "their Nathan" at a performance of the play in Berlin in 1802 (as cited in HFW, 253). In the 19th century, the interpretation of the play increasingly merges with the socio-political process of Jewish emancipation (cf. BF, 17). As the author of *Nathan* and a friend of Mendelssohn's (who is considered the model for Nathan), Lessing becomes an advocate and example of successful integration.

This is particularly evident in the *Memorial Book* (*Gedenkbuch*) published in 1879 by the Union of Judæo-German Congregations to celebrate the 150th birthday of both Lessing and Mendelssohn, as well as the centenary of the publication of *Nathan*. In Lessing's "gospel of tolerance", the editors find "the alliance of friendship between the two great fighters for truth and freedom of conscience embodied in such a noble and lasting way" (LMG, preface). The book is a collection of essays and studies from the preceding 50 years and strives to establish the myth of a German-Jewish 'cultural nation' (*Kulturnation*) that has taken literary form in *Nathan*: "The Christian and the Jew join hands in brotherhood. And the glorious intellectual blossom of this covenant is called: Nathan" (LMG, 3). Such are the words of Emil Lehmann, President of the Jewish Community in Dresden.

Hostilities follow soon enough. The German entrepreneur and writer Hector de Grousilliers declares the equality of religions to be an "empty phrase" (HdG, 13), calling on the Jews in Germany to acknowledge allegiance to Germany – just as the historian Heinrich von Treitschke, who writes an article on *Our Prospects* (*Unsere Aussichten*, 1879), provoking what is now known as the Berlin Antisemitism Controversy.

The rejection of Lessing and his "flat Jewish piece" – which is how Eugen Dühring, an economist dabbling in philology, refers to *Nathan* (St, 390) – becomes downright grotesque in the 1880s. In a treatise on *The Jewish Question as a Racial, Moral, and Cultural Question* (*Die Judenfrage als Racen-, Sitten- und Culturfrage*, 1881), Dühring 'unmasks' Lessing as a Jew "in terms of blood" (St, 390), who owes his reputation to nothing but the "most unashamed Jewish advertisement" (St, 395) in the press and feuilletons:

His authorial manners and his intellectual affectations are Jewish. His literary products give evidence everywhere of Jewishness in form and content. Indeed, what one could call his chief works are fragmentary works and reveal the incompleteness peculiar to the Jews even in style and presentation. [...] In the form and in the external aspect of writing, Lessing is accordingly everywhere Jewish. (St, 391)

Following in Dühring's footsteps, Sebastian Brunner, a Catholic clergyman from Vienna and key figure in the Catholic antisemitism discourse, takes the field in 1890. After Dühring had 'unmasked' Lessing as a Jew, Brunner declared him to be a Judas who betrayed Christianity to the Jews because he, habitually in need of money, let himself be bought (SB, 125). What Brunner resents is the rampant *Lessingiasis and Nathanology*. His opponents are the four "evangelists of the Lessing cult" (SB, 1): Theodor Wilhelm Danzel and Gottschalk Eduard Guhrauer, Wendelin von Maltzahn and Robert Boxberger, whose studies on Lessing are among the great positivistic research achievements of the 19th century. All this leaves the belligerent clergyman unimpressed. He is inspired by the idea of defending the Christian faith against the zeitgeist. His undivided appreciation, therefore, is reserved for the Meiningen court preacher Pfranger, whose *Monk of Lebanon* he praises as the work of a man "determined *to stand up heroically for Christ, the Redeemer of the world*, and bravely endure the mockery of his contemporary enlighteneers (*Aufklärlinge*)" (SB, 132).

In the controversies over Lessing's *Nathan*, a question that regularly comes up is how realistic the drama is. Brunner refers to Lessing's hero as a "theatre Jew" (SB, 97), contrasting him with the true Jew, who he considers has taken shape in Shylock, the usurer in Shakespeare's *Merchant of Venice*: "Shylock is the historical Jew from the New Testament – Nathan is an *ephemeral stage figure*" (SB,

97). And: "Nathan is a fiction of Lessing's, in which he, as a connoisseur of Jews, could not believe himself. Shylock is a portrait painted from life" (SB, 11).

Be that as it may, Nathan is, and continues to be, a "theatre Jew" indeed for the Jews living in Germany: a beacon and promise for some, mere fiction and attractive illusion for others. As educated circles in Germany celebrate Lessing's 200th birthday in 1929 (cf. WB 1), the *Jewish Review* (*Jüdische Rundschau*), the organ of the German Zionists, dedicates a special issue to this classic author, recalling what *Nathan* has meant to Jews. Reports of Jews in the ghetto who knew *Nathan* by heart (cf. SM, 36) are juxtaposed with sceptical reflections accusing Lessing of wanting to "Germanise and humanise (*eindeutschen und einmenschen*)" (ES, 35) the Jews. Such is the argument of the Israeli religious philosopher Ernst Simon, who wrote an article entitled *Lessing and Jewish History* (*Lessing und die jüdische Geschichte*), attempting to counter the conventional image of Nathan, as a "model of noble humanity in Jewish garb" and "a brilliant antithesis to Shakespeare's Shylock" (ES, 35), with an unconventional interpretation that reveals Lessing's true image of Jews. Simon points out that Lessing did not portray Nathan as an orthodox Jew, but as one who wants neither to be "a Jew outright" nor "not to be a Jew" (III/6; B 9, 554). This influential temptation to deny one's own Jewish identity is what Simon sees as Lessing's legacy. This, he argues, is the true "key to Nathan's historical position":

> *He did not shape an adequate past and present, but brought about a future in imitation of him.* The almost canonical status that Lessing's "Nathan the Wise" holds in the process of German-Jewish assimilation has made his emancipatory vision of the future an educational role model. No living Jew has begotten "Nathan", not even as a mere model; but Nathan has, in conjunction with social, political and

intellectual development, created hundreds of thousands of pseudo-Jews in his image. (ES, 35)

Anecdotal details reveal how much Lessing's *Nathan* also shaped the image of a humane Germany – again, a deceptive image. The Hungarian playwright and director George Tabori recounts that in 1932, his aunt could only reconcile herself to the fact that her Jewish nephew was going to study in Berlin because in her eyes, Lessing's *Nathan* vouched for the integrity of Germany: "If it weren't for this play, I wouldn't let you go to Germany, I'd rather throw myself under your train" (GT 1, 34). As late as October 1933, the Cultural Federation of German Jews attempted to put on *Nathan* – an attempt already met with scepticism by the *Jewish Review*, which feared that the performance might presume to remind the Germans of the true German spirit, or even aim to "cocoon the German Jews in a world of *illusions* in the approved fashion" (NN, 365).

To the Nazis, the play was a nuisance. The Cultural Federation being allowed to put it on in Berlin was probably owing to the fact that it was unwittingly classified as a "Jewish play". On German stages, *Nathan* was banned until 1945. – After 1945, in contrast, the play served to invoke the tradition of a different Germany. Four months after the fall of the Third Reich, the Deutsches Theater in Berlin is reopened with a production of *Nathan*. In the 1945/46 season, the drama is played at several German theatres (cf. BF, 146).

What follows is hackneyed edification and disillusionment. Edification overlooks the bitter aspects of the play and ignores its polemical dimension, which is directed against the self-misunderstanding of religions and its disastrous consequences. Disillusionment necessarily follows suit. The author Angelika Overath has impressively described the experience of falling into the trap of triviality when discussing *Nathan*: "What I was beginning to write was a more or less bottomless and ultimately irrelevant kind of multiculti nonsense, which had nothing to do with the Ring Parable" (AO, 22). Tolerance kitsch and multiculti nonsense are inevitable when Lessing's dramatic poem is reduced to ideological messages. They are the domain of political soapbox speeches. Against the backdrop of the catastrophes of the 20th and 21st centuries, disillusionment seems to be the only way to save Lessing's drama from mindless appropriation.

In George Tabori's *Nathan* adaptation from 1991, the lasting influence of the drama itself is what is reflected upon. Tabori calls it *Nathan's Death* (*Nathans Tod*). He drastically shortens the original text, rearranges parts of it, expands it with passages from Lessing's letters and writings, and gives it a framework by setting Nathan's house on fire: Tabori brings to life the story of the pogrom that Nathan tells to the friar Bonafides, by referencing the parable of the burning palace, which Lessing recounts in the context of the Fragments Controversy to contradict Goeze (cf. B 9, 41–44). This parable is told by Nathan at the beginning of the play – at its end, when Nathan's house is burning and his children are dying inside, he recalls it once again.

Lessing's parable compares the Christian religion to an old palace, whose "simplicity and grandeur" arouse admiration, but whose architecture – "from outside somewhat perplexing, from inside full of light and coherence" (GT 2, 3) – is nevertheless confusing to the experts. Lessing uses the Palace Parable to distinguish the religion as such from the Bible and the theologians' doctrines, and to declare the Anonymous Author's Biblical criticism as attacks that are not aimed at religion itself, but rather at the human attempts to understand its "plan" (GT 2, 3). And there are many such plans. When the fire alarm is given, all the experts rush forward to save their respective plans and argue about which part of the palace is on fire at all. The palace itself is left to its fate. In Lessing's version, everything turns out to be a false alarm: "the terrified watchmen had mistaken the northern lights for a conflagration" (GT 2, 4). In Tabori's play, the palace does burn, and no one is saved. Carrying his children and Recha out of the house, Nathan recalls the story once again: "Look, neighbour! here, she is burning. / Here is the best place to fight the fire. / Let them extinguish it here if they want to. / I don't extinguish it here. / Nor do I here. Nor do I here" (GT 2, 36–37).

Every success in Lessing's play is turned into its opposite in Tabori's drama: failure everywhere. Saladin sets a trap for Nathan, the young Templar delivers him to the Patriarch, Christians set Nathan's house on fire, Recha dies in the fire, and Nathan himself dies "on all fours, like an animal" (GT 2, 41). The bleak finale blends together the character and his author: Nathan is tired of life – Tabori has him speak Lessing's words, as recorded by Georg Friedrich Jacobi: "Oh, it has turned green so often / Before – I wish it would turn red for a change" (GT 2, 40–41; cf. RD, 526), and quotes from a letter from Lessing to Elise Reimarus, the Fragmentist's daughter: "Though I went home in a hurry, I / Arrived with reluctance. / For the first thing I found there was myself" (GT 2, 40; cf. early Nov, 1780; B 12, 350). Among Nathan's dead children, there is also Lessing's son, who died shortly after birth. Again, Tabori weaves Lessing's own words into his adaptation, quoting from the letter in which Lessing informs his friend Eschenburg of his child's death: "Here, the smallest one, a / Little rascal. My joy was / Only brief. And I was so loath to lose him. / For he had such good sense! such / Good sense! I know what I am saying. – / Was it not good sense that they / Had to drag him into the /

World with iron forceps? – that he was so soon / Revolted by it?" (GT 2, 41; cf. Dec 31, 1777; B 12, 116).

Nathan dies, words from the *Education* treatise on his lips, which are not only powerless against weariness and bitterness, but which seem to mock themselves: "No – it will come, it will / Certainly come, the time of / Fulfilment, when man – / Let me not despair of you, –" (GT 2, 41; cf. § 85; B 10, 96). The final word of the play is the Patriarch's: With a glass of champagne, he toasts Saladin, the monks and the Mamluks: "Finally it is fading, / This ridiculous song of his / That silly tale / About some ring / We'll never hear it again" (GT 2, 41–42). "*Handshake, hug, kiss – kiss*". Sittah, standing aside, commits suicide.

Tabori's *Nathan*, "freely adapted from Lessing", is a play that needs to be performed on stage (cf. BF, 153). The text itself is economical with words, a mere script. And it might only be understandable to those familiar with Lessing's dramatic poem. A conceptually similar, but significantly more complex attempt to address the lasting influence of the drama in a drama and confront the author with how his characters have taken on a life of their own, is undertaken by the director Elmar Goerden in his play entitled *Lessing's Dream About Nathan the Wise* (*Lessings Traum von Nathan dem Weisen*, 2002). Following the model of Luigi Pirandello's metafictional *Six Characters in Search of an Author* (1921), Lessing is visited on stage by his own characters and embroiled in "discussions about impact and responsibility" (EG, 12). The characters make suggestions about "this and that", agreeing to "almost nothing" (EG, 12): Recha wants to "appear" more in the play and requires a "love scene" (EG, 47–48); Daja outs herself as a member of the "Anonymous Antisemites" (EG, 52); the young Templar is conspicuous by his antisemitic obstinacy. The Friar demands a play in which "everyone has the same right to be different" (EG, 78). And the Patriarch keeps showing up to enquire whether the Ring Parable has been told yet.

The centre of the drama, which combines scenes from *Nathan* with passages from Lessing's letters and writings as well as quotes on the history of Jewish emancipation and the question of Jewish identity into a multi-layered collage, is the encounter of Lessing/Nathan with Shylock. Shylock is Nathan's shadow, his "dark brother" (EG, 88), the literary symbol par excellence of antisemitism and, as such, Nathan's declared enemy. He considers the shining light depicted by Lessing as the Jews' "shitty answer" to Mother Teresa (EG, 29), the "whitewashed lucky beggar" (EG, 36) and "the antisemites' good conscience" (EG, 38) – a literary fiction that has demanded of Judaism to deny itself and be "something special" (EG, 37) in order to be appreciated: "You should have been our brother, not our role model to the taste of others!" (EG, 38).

This play about the disillusionment of a dreamer is prefaced by a motto from Hans Henny Jahnn's speech on the occasion of the Hamburg Lessing Prize in 1956. It is entitled *Lessing's Farewell* (*Lessings Abschied*) and portrays a poet who is embittered and stricken by his illness: "He inhabited a realm of spirits: [...] The barren, grey, unfulfilled hours overwhelmed his constitution with their incessancy. [...] With horrifying clarity, attacking his inner dignity, the bouts of hypersomnia began to show, too" (EG, 9; cf. HHJ, 21, 23, 25).

The conclusion could not be clearer: the Nathan of the 21st century is a failed Nathan. Even in young adult literature, there is no escape. Mirjam Pressler's award-winning novel *Nathan and his Children* (*Nathan und seine Kinder*, 2009), which unfolds the story Lessing had presented on stage in a series of monologues from multiple perspectives, has Nathan fall victim to Christian assassins.

Pressler's Nathan is a broken man, barely escaped from insanity and scarred for life by the pogrom in which his family was murdered. His credo, which saves him day after day from losing his mind, is: "God is distant, but humans are near!" (MP, 48) – "God is out of reach, and the only way we can be close to him is by loving his creatures" (MP, 54). Since children have need of love, as Lessing's friar Bonafides says (cf. IV/7; B 9, 595), Pressler comes up with a counterpart to the story of the orphaned Christian child's adoption by the orphaned Jew: An unnamed foundling boy – he, too, scarred by fire –, who lives in Nathan's house, is adopted by Nathan's childless steward Elijahu as his own: "Everyone needs their place in the world, a place where they belong, and people in whose midst they find warmth and security" (MP, 53).

Nathan's words lead right into the heart of the Ring Parable. Its narration in the novel is ingeniously framed by Al-Hafi's retrospective monologue. Al-Hafi is the silent witness of the delicate conversation between Saladin and Nathan, and he interprets it as what it is in Lessing's version, and what it has been throughout the novella tradition of the Ring Parable: a trap designed for Nathan, which he cleverly avoids. The enthusiastic chess player Al-Hafi comments on the individual statements in the conversation like on a game in which Nathan slowly but surely checkmates Saladin, thus winning his friendship. But there is no trace of triumph. In Nathan's eyes, there is "a deep sadness" (MP, 164) – he knows that the story he has told the Sultan is "just a story, just a dream" (MP, 166). And it is presented as such in the novel – a dream, in reference to Martin Luther King's famous speech: "I have a dream that one day this nation will rise up and live out the true meaning of its creed" –

> "I have a dream that one day humanity will rise up and live out the true meaning of its creed. I have a dream that one day the sons of Jews, Muslims, and Christians will be able to sit down together at the table of brotherhood. I have a dream that one day even this city will be transformed into an oasis of freedom and justice." His voice dropped, lowered. "But it is just a dream. Reality is different." (MP, 166)

While Mirjam Pressler has her Nathan capitulate in order to at least strike some sparks of pathos from his resignation, Elfriede Jelinek remains without illusions. Her polyphonic "secondary drama" *Slag Heap* (*Abraumhalde*, 2009) was composed as somewhat of a missing link between Lessing's *Nathan* and her own "comedy of economics" *The Merchant's Contracts* (*Die Kontrakte des Kaufmanns*, 2009), and it flatly rejects any message of salvation. Jelinek links Lessing's text with centuries of text and thought in order to create an associative sequence of words that plays on loop like a barely audible background noise or a litany, commenting, counteracting and thus disturbing the peace of the toothless classic.

Lessing Dies

In 1850, a five-volume novel is published in Leipzig, bearing the succinct title *Lessing*. Its author, the private scholar, novelist and popular science writer Hermann Klencke, brings his hero to life by skilfully referring to the extensive material compiled by 19th-century Lessing philology.

What is particularly striking is how Klencke portrays Lessing's death: A few days before his death, Lessing's bookseller hands him "a play by a certain *Schiller*, entitled 'The Robbers'", and he has to learn that with this work, "a new era of theatre has begun" (HK 5, 504). His friend Eschenburg comforts him with the words, "You, my dear Lessing, will at any rate have prepared the ground for him" (HK 5, 504). This sentiment springs entirely from a 19th-century perspective. Lessing's death marks the end of an era. He himself knows it to be so: "I cannot call my life happy, for I worked for a nation whose character it is to have none – but if I hear a new literary epoch marked with my name, then may God grant that a new, coming generation recognises me, for I have always felt so lonely" (HK 5, 505). As "the apostle of a new future of our German literature", he is recognised and honoured by his friends: "He will live on in the belated realisation of his visionary striving!" (HK 5, 507).

The dying Lessing in the eyes of the 19th century is a poet who has outlived himself and fulfilled his task in history. The 20th and 21st centuries strike different notes: The Lessing who comes alive in their literary fiction can look back on his own future.

Heiner Müller grapples with the disastrous state of German intellectuals in his dramatic triptych *Gundling's Life Frederick of Prussia Lessing's Sleep Dream Scream* (*Leben Gundlings Friedrich von Preußen Lessings Schlaf Traum Schrei*, 1977). He, too, sees Lessing as a transitional figure: Like Brecht, he stands "at the end of a period and creates a new one" (HM 2). Müller presents a Lessing who is disillusioned and has lost faith in history:

> My name is Gotthold Ephraim Lessing. I'm 47 years old. I have one or two dozen puppets stuffed with sawdust which was my blood, dreamed a dream of theatre in Germany and reflected publicly on things which did not interest me. That's all over. Yesterday I saw a dead fleck on my skin, a patch of desert: the dying is beginning. (HM 1, 533)

Müller's grotesque play graphically demonstrates how the veneration of Lessing as Germany's classical poet silences the poet, who is dreaming of a German theatre. Attendants, who *"arrange busts of poets and thinkers all over the stage"*, *"encase Lessing in a Lessing bust"*, which stifles *"his muffled cry"* (HM 1, 535–36).

More intimate, but no less telling, is the portrait of the dying Lessing drawn by Christoph Hein (*Ein Wort allein für Amalia*, 2020). He has Lessing's stepdaughter Amalia König, as a very old widow, tell the story of Lessing's death in a letter. Hein's Lessing, too, is a disillusioned, misanthropic, resentful character who admonishes himself to be kind to people (cf. CH, 66), a dramatist who regrets having involved himself with the theatre (cf. CH, 57), a man humiliated by his social dependencies, struggling with his despondency (cf. CH, 65). The true Lessing, according to Christoph Hein, is Lessing the Dervish (cf. CH, 59), whom he has denied all his life and who only awakens in the delirium of his final hours: "What a man that would have been! He also fulfils a duty, the duty to himself. Do you know a higher one?" (CH, 59).

So, what remains? Which Lessing can we let die? From which images of Lessing can we conscientiously detach ourselves? The notions of Lessing the pioneer, Lessing the pre-classicist, Lessing the champion of tolerance – they do not do him justice. They are distorted images of an unredeemed culture that finds its intensities only in struggling and striving for recognition, and that can counter the struggle only with moral kitsch.

Lessing was not a preachy author. He became and becomes visible in his style, which had already been praised during his lifetime, the critical energy of which makes every reading of Lessing an extraordinary experience. He became and becomes visible in his presence of mind, with which he unmasks the perspectival blindness of the human heart. He becomes visible in his ability to take a comprehensive view of reality – especially where it shows its ugly face and reveals the hidden depths of the human soul.

In his *Vindication* of Simon Lemnius, who had been maliciously persecuted by Luther, Lessing comments on the "vilenesses" the great reformer indulged in, with the words: "God, what a terrible lesson to beware of pride! How far anger and revenge degrade even the most honest, the holiest man!" (B 3, 280) – only to wonder in the same breath: "But, would a less vehement temperament have been capable of accomplishing what Luther has accomplished? Certainly not! Let us therefore admire the wise Providence that even knows how to use the faults of its tools!" (B 3, 280).

He expresses himself along the same lines in a letter to the widowed Eva König, after she had complained to him about a maid who had got excessively drunk during the arduous journey to Vienna:

> In the end, it was probably better that the little creature had her own affairs, that she loved and drank, respectively, the first fellow and wine she came across – than if she had been a good sensitive girl who would not have let her mistress out of her sight and would have cried with her. Thanks to the former, you were torn from your own thoughts; the latter would have encouraged your grief. You will say that I have a special gift for finding something good in something bad. I do indeed; and I am prouder of this than of anything I know and can do. You yourself, as I have often noticed, possess a generous measure of this gift, which I cordially recommend you to apply everywhere; for nothing can make us more content with the world than this. (Oct 25, 1770; B 11/2, 79)

This art of perspectivism or, as Lessing puts it, the "gift for finding something good in something bad", is practised in all of his texts. For example, in *Nathan*, where they say, "Thanks to the patriarch..." (V/5; B 9, 611), the latter's attempt to find the apostatic Jew enables that same Jew to solve the mystery of Recha's origins. Lessing's art of perspectivism is a form of systemic thinking. It consists in the art of regarding even the dark sides of what is good with a sense of proportion, and it is the epitome of resilience, which is not deterred by the imperfections of man and the adversities of life. However adverse they may be – they always provide an opportunity to regroup in view of what is desirable and conducive to human life and coexistence. In the Fragments Controversy, Lessing will confront Goeze with the insight that whenever we move, we run the risk of crushing a worm. "Every movement in the physical world develops and destroys, brings life and death; brings death to this creature, *by* bringing life to another: Would you rather there be no death, and no movement? Or rather, death and movement?" (B 9, 197).

This keen awareness of the inevitable evils arising from human coexistence is particularly prominent in Lessing's way of conceptualising society. He juxtaposes the "civil society of human beings in general" with a culture of individuality, which turns the individual into a "*homo duplex*" (JA, 196–202) – one who has ceased to identify with the traditionally shared values of the group he belongs to because he has outgrown them. The price of tolerance is solitariness and the willingness to renounce any naïve certainty of salvation; its ethos is openness to encounters and sensitivity to the "inherent values" (RS, 48) of human reality. The only heaven that exists is the heaven people find within themselves and prepare for each other.

With all this, Lessing marks a beginning. His world is not yet the world of nation states and their mass-mediated "imagined communities" (Benedict Anderson). But his literary as well as his philosophical oeuvre has the potential to respond even to the challenges of our modern world, a world in which the dynamics of group formation – separation by unification – has reached unprecedented dimensions due to digital media. The answer to the manifold forms of "pseudospeciation" (JA, 201) lies in the voice of human nature that can only ever be experienced individually. This human nature is mentioned casually but insistently in Lessing's observations on Diderot's drama *Le Fils naturel* (1757). Its hero, Dorval, laments having wandered about among mankind for thirty years, "lonely, unacknowledged, neglected, without feeling the tenderness of any other human being or having met another person who sought mine in return" (HD 87/88; B 6, 621). Lessing rejects this idea most emphatically:

> Heaven forbid that I ever imagine the human species in any other way! Otherwise, I would rather wish to have been born a bear than a human. No – no person can be forsaken so long among other people. No matter where he has been tossed, as long as he falls among humans, he falls among creatures who, before he has even had time to see where he is, stand ready on all sides to link themselves to him. If not prominent, then lowly people; if not happy, then unhappy people! But they are people nonetheless. Just as a drop need only disturb the surface of water in order to be taken up by it and absorbed completely into it, whatever the water may be called, puddle or spring, river or lake, strait or ocean. (HD 87/88; B 6, 621–22)

What remains? In his acceptance speech for the Hamburg Lessing Prize, Botho Strauß stated that we cannot take up where Lessing left off. And he decreed that, "we do not need another Enlightenment. We are disintegrated to the core with enlightenment" (BS, 52). The opposite is true. Enlightenment, as Lessing conceptualised it, was and is a collective as well as an individual process, because it is about the question of how human potential can unfold in the best possible way. Along the same lines, Michael Hampe has recently advocated for a Third Enlightenment, defining it as an "educational process (*Bildungsbewegung*)" (MH, 83).

Education, however, "is the result of personal and collective efforts": "The primary goal of education is [...] the acquisition of a creativity that can make individual life meaningful and communities culturally sculpted" (MH, 83).

The Third Enlightenment Michael Hampe has in mind was and is Lessing's Enlightenment. Lessing's maxim of acting in accordance with one's "*individualistic perfections*" (B 2, 407) is evidence of the commitment to lead a life that is not just 'unthinkingly dreamt away', as he says in the *Anti-Goeze*, no. 4 (cf. B 9, 196), but is permeated by thought and thus a conscious and intensely lived life (cf. B 8, 137). Which is not without consequences: It contributes to reality remaining in flux, so that the last word about mankind has yet to be spoken.

Notes on the Bibliography

Sources quoted in the text are referred to using the authors' initials (first name/last name). In the case of authors of more than one work, the abbreviations are numbered as listed below; in all other cases, numbers refer to the respective volume of multi-volume works or editions. For the works of Gisbert Ter-Nedden, the acronym GTN is used.

The abbreviations for the Lessing edition by Wilfried Barner (B), the *Münchner Ausgabe* (Munich edition) of Goethe's works (MA), and the *Nationalausgabe* (national edition) of Schiller's works (NA) follow common conventions. Quotes from Lessing's dramas are cited with act and scene numbers, where applicable.

The compilations by Richard Daunicht (*Lessing im Gespräch*) and Horst Steinmetz (*Lessing – ein unpoetischer Dichter*) are referred to as RD and St, respectively. Moreover, I would like to highlight Wolfgang Albrecht's document compilations published by the Lessing Museum

Notes on the Bibliography

Kamenz (https://www.lessingmuseum.de), and the website of the Lessing Academy Wolfenbüttel (https://www.lessing-akademie.de), whose database makes available all of Lessing's writings, including his correspondence.

Where available, the translations of primary texts into English follow – and adapt, as appropriate – existing translations. For the list, see below.

Bibliography

Albrecht, Paul: Leszing's Plagiate. 6 Bde. Hamburg/Leipzig 1888–91. [PA]
Albrecht, Wolfgang: Lessing im Spiegel zeitgenössischer Briefe. Ein kommentiertes Lese- und Studienwerk. 2 Teile. Kamenz 2003. [WA]
Albrecht, Wolfgang: Lessing. Gespräche, Begegnungen, Lebenszeugnisse. Ein kommentiertes Lese- und Studienwerk. 2 Teile. Kamenz 2005.
Albrecht, Wolfgang: Lessing. Chronik zu Leben und Werk. Kamenz 2008.
Albrecht, Wolfgang: Lessing in persönlichen Kontakten und im Spiegel zeitgenössischer Briefe. Eine neue Quellenedition. Kamenz 2018.
Aristoteles: Werke in deutscher Übersetzung. Bd. 5: Poetik. Übersetzt und erläutert von Arbogast Schmitt. 2., durchgesehene und ergänzte Aufl. Berlin 2011. [A]
Äsop: Fabeln. Griechisch – deutsch. Hg. und übersetzt von Rainer Nickel. Düsseldorf/Zürich 2005. [Ae]

Assmann, Jan: Religio duplex. Ägyptische Mysterien und europäische Aufklärung. Berlin 2010. [JA]
Augustinus, Aurelius: Werke. Hg. von Carl Johann Perl. Bd. 16: Der Gottesstaat. De civitate Dei. Bd. 1. In deutscher Sprache von C. J. P. Paderborn u. a. 1979. [AA]
Barner, Wilfried: Lessing 1929. Momentaufnahme eines Klassikers vor dem Ende der Republik [1983]. In: W. B.: „Laut denken mit einem Freunde". Lessing-Studien. Hg. von Kai Bremer. Göttingen 2017, S. 109–23. [WB 1]
Barner, Wilfried: Der Vorklassiker als Klassiker: Lessing [1988]. In: W. B.: „Laut denken mit einem Freunde". Lessing-Studien. Hg. von Kai Bremer. Göttingen 2017, S. 225–38. [WB 2]
Barner, Wilfried: Goethe und Lessing. Eine schwierige Konstellation. Göttingen 2001. [WB 3]
Bender, Wolfgang F.: Hauptweg und Nebenwege. Studien zu Lessings *Hamburgischer Dramaturgie*. Berlin/Boston 2019. [WFB]
The Bible. New King James Version. URL: https://www.biblegateway.com.
Blanckenburg, Friedrich von: Versuch über den Roman. Faksimiledruck der Originalausgabe von 1774. Mit einem Nachwort von Eberhard Lämmert. Stuttgart 1965. [FvB]
Braun, Julius W. (Hg.): Lessing im Urtheile seiner Zeitgenossen. Zeitungskritiken, Berichte und Notizen, Lessing und seine Werke betreffend, aus den Jahren 1747–1781. Eine Ergänzung zu allen Ausgaben von Lessings Werken. 2 Bde. Berlin 1884/93. [JB]
Brecht, Bertolt: [Kölner Rundfunkgespräch.] In: B. B.: Gesammelte Werke in 20 Bänden. Hg. vom Suhrkamp Verlag in Zusammenarbeit mit Elisabeth Hauptmann. Bd. 15: Schriften zum Theater 1. Frankfurt a. M. 1967, S. 146–53. [BB]
Brunner, Sebastian: Lessingiasis und Nathanologie. Eine Religionsstörung im Lessing- und Nathan-Cultus. Paderborn 1890. [SB]

Das Buch des Goethe-Lessing-Jahres 1929. 100 Jahre Goethe. 200 Jahre Lessing. Braunschweig 1929. [GLJ]

Damen Conversations Lexikon. Hg. im Verein mit Gelehrten und Schriftstellerinnen von Carl Herloßsohn. Leipzig 1834–38. [DCL]

Daunicht, Richard: Lessing im Gespräch. Berichte und Urteile von Freunden und Zeitgenossen. München 1971. [RD]

Dilthey, Wilhelm: Gesammelte Schriften. Bd. 26: Das Erlebnis und die Dichtung. Lessing, Goethe, Novalis, Hölderlin. Hg. von Gabriele Malsch. Göttingen 2005. [WD]

Engel, Johann Jakob: Über Handlung, Gespräch und Erzählung. Faksimiledruck der ersten Fassung von 1774 aus der ‚Neuen Bibliothek der schönen Wissenschaften und der freyen Künste'. Hg. und mit einem Nachwort versehen von Ernst Theodor Voss. Stuttgart 1964. [JJE 1]

Engel, Johann Jakob: Briefe über Emilia Galotti. Vierter Brief. In: Der Philosoph für die Welt. Hg. von J. J. E. 2. Teil. Leipzig 1777, S. 101–24. [JJE 2]

Euripides: Medea. Griechisch/Deutsch. Übersetzt und hg. von Karl Heinz Eller. Stuttgart 1983. [E]

Fick, Monika: Lessing-Handbuch. Leben – Werk – Wirkung. 4., aktualisierte und erweiterte Aufl. Stuttgart 2016. [MF 1]

Fick, Monika: Vom Kriegs-Stand oder Lessings Komödie *Minna von Barnhelm* im Gegenlicht deutschsprachiger Soldatenstücke des 18. Jahrhunderts (2013). In: M. F.: Lessing und das Drama der anthropozentrischen Wende. Hannover 2021, S. 103–24. [MF 2]

Fischer, Barbara: Nathans Ende? Von Lessing bis Tabori. Zur deutsch-jüdischen Rezeption von „Nathan der Weise". Göttingen 2000. [BF]

Fontane, Theodor: Werke, Schriften und Briefe. Hg. von Walter Keitel und Helmuth Nürnberger. Abteilung III: Erinnerungen, ausgewählte Schriften und Kritiken. Bd. 1: Aufsätze und Aufzeichnungen. München 1998. [TF 1]

Fontane, Theodor: Werke, Schriften und Briefe. Hg. von Walter Keitel und Helmuth Nürnberger. Abteilung IV: Briefe. Bd. 4: Briefe 1890–1899. München 1998. [TF 2]

Gansel, Carsten: „Das Herz geht uns auf, wenn wir von Lessing hören oder ihn lesen" – G. E. Lessing im Kulturraum Schule um 1900. In: Mit Lessing zur Moderne. Soziokulturelle Wirkungen des Aufklärers um 1900. Hg. von Wolfgang Albrecht und Richard E. Schade. Kamenz 2004, S. 205–22. [CG 1]

Gansel, Carsten, Birka Siwczyk (Hg.): Gotthold Ephraim Lessings ‚Nathan der Weise' im Kulturraum Schule (1830–1914). Göttingen 2009. [CG 2]

Gansel, Carsten, Birka Siwczyk (Hg.): Gotthold Ephraim Lessings ‚Minna von Barnhelm' im Kulturraum Schule (1830–1914). Göttingen 2011. [CG 3]

Gansel, Carsten, Birka Siwczyk (Hg.): Gotthold Ephraim Lessings ‚Emilia Galotti' im Kulturraum Schule (1830–1914). Göttingen 2015. [CG 4]

Gansel, Carsten, Norman Ächtler, Birka Siwczyk (Hg.): Gotthold Ephraim Lessing im Kulturraum Schule. Aspekte der Wirkungsgeschichte im 19. Jahrhundert. Göttingen 2017. [CG 5]

Gellert, Christian Fürchtegott: Gesammelte Schriften. Kritische, kommentierte Ausgabe. Hg. von Bernd Witte. 7 Bde. Berlin/New York 1988–2008. [CFG]

Gesing, Fritz: Kreativ schreiben. Handwerk und Technik des Erzählens. Köln 1994. [FG]

Gleim, Johann Wilhelm Ludwig: Preussische Kriegslieder von einem Grenadier. Hg. von August Sauer. Heilbronn 1882. [JWLG]

Goerden, Elmar: Lessings Traum von Nathan dem Weisen. Stück und Materialien. Frankfurt a. M. 2002. [EG]

Goethe, Johann Wolfgang: Sämtliche Werke nach Epochen seines Schaffens. Münchner Ausgabe. Hg. von Karl Richter u. a. 21 Bde. München/Wien 1985–98. [MA]

Goethe, Johann Wolfgang von: Briefe. Hamburger Ausgabe in 6 Bänden. Hg. von Karl Robert Mandelkow. München 1988. [HA]

Goethe, Johann Wolfgang: Goethes Gespräche. Eine Sammlung zeitgenössischer Berichte aus seinem Umgang. Auf Grund der

Ausgabe und des Nachlasses von Flodoard Freiherrn von Biedermann ergänzt und hg. von Wolfgang Herwig. 5 Bde. in 6. Zürich 1965–87. [GG]

Gottsched, Johann Christoph: Versuch einer critischen Dichtkunst. Unveränderter reprografischer Nachdruck der 4., vermehrten Auflage, Leipzig 1751. Darmstadt 1982. [JCG]

Grousilliers, Hector de: Nathan der Weise und die Antisemiten-Liga. Berlin 1880. [HdG]

Hampe, Michael: Die Dritte Aufklärung. Berlin 2018. [MH]

Hebbel, Friedrich: Maria Magdalena. Ein bürgerliches Trauerspiel in drei Akten. Mit Hebbels Vorwort betreffend das Verhältnis der dramatischen Kunst zur Zeit und verwandte Punkte. Stuttgart 1986. [FH]

Hegel, Georg Wilhelm Friedrich: Werke in zwanzig Bänden. Bd. 12: Vorlesungen über die Philosophie der Geschichte. Frankfurt a. M. 1970. [H 1]

Hegel, Georg Wilhelm Friedrich: Werke in zwanzig Bänden. Bd. 20: Vorlesungen über die Geschichte der Philosophie III. Frankfurt a. M. 1970. [H 2]

Hein, Christoph: Ein Wort allein für Amalia. Berlin 2020. [CH]

Herder, Johann Gottfried: Werke in 10 Bänden. Bd. 7: Briefe zur Beförderung der Humanität. Hg. von Hans Dietrich Irmscher. Frankfurt a. M. 1991. [JGH]

Hettner, Hermann: Das moderne Drama. Aesthetische Untersuchungen. Braunschweig 1852. [HH 1]

Hettner, Hermann: Literaturgeschichte des achtzehnten Jahrhunderts. In drei Theilen. Dritter Theil: Die deutsche Literatur im achtzehnten Jahrhundert. Zweites Buch: Das Zeitalter Friedrichs des Großen. Braunschweig 1864. [HH 2]

Hirsch, Emanuel: Geschichte der neuern evangelischen Theologie im Zusammenhang mit den allgemeinen Bewegungen des europäischen Denkens. Bd. 4. Gütersloh 1952. [EH]

Horatius, Flaccus Quintus: Oden und Epoden. Lateinisch/Deutsch. Übersetzt und hg. von Bernhard Kytzler. Stuttgart 1981. [H]

Jahnn, Hans Henny: Lessings Abschied. In: Denken als Widerspruch. Plädoyers gegen die Irrationalität oder ist Vernunft nicht mehr gefragt? Reden zum Lessing-Preis. Hg. von Volker F. W. Hasenclever. Frankfurt a. M. 1982, S. 7–32. [HHJ]

Jelinek, Elfriede: Abraumhalde. URL: www.elfriedejelinek.com/farhalde.htm.

Kant, Immanuel: Werke in zwölf Bänden. Hg. von Wilhelm Weischedel. Bd. 3: Kritik der reinen Vernunft 1. Frankfurt a. M. 1968. [IK 1]

Kant, Immanuel: Beantwortung der Frage: Was ist Aufklärung? In: I. K.: Werke in zwölf Bänden. Hg. von Wilhelm Weischedel. Bd. 11: Schriften zur Anthropologie, Geschichtsphilosophie, Politik und Pädagogik 1. Frankfurt a. M. 1968, S. 53–61. [IK 2]

Kerber, Hannes: Die Aufklärung der Aufklärung. Lessing und die Herausforderung des Christentums. Göttingen 2021. [JK]

Kettner, Gustav: Lessings Dramen im Lichte ihrer und unserer Zeit. Berlin 1904. [GK]

Kim, Eun-Ae: Lessings Tragödientheorie im Licht der neueren Aristoteles-Forschung. Würzburg 2002. [EK]

Kleist, Ewald von: Cißides und Paches. In: E. v. K.: Sämtliche Werke. Hg. von Jürgen Stenzel. Stuttgart 1971, S. 135–52. [EvK]

Klencke, Hermann: Lessing. Roman. 5 Bde. Leipzig 1850. [HK]

Lessing, Gotthold Ephraim: Briefe, die neueste Literatur betreffend. Hg. und kommentiert von Wolfgang Bender. Stuttgart 1972. [GEL]

Lessing, Gotthold Ephraim: Werke und Briefe in zwölf Bänden. Hg. von Wilfried Barner u. a. Frankfurt a. M. 1985–2003. [B]

Lessing, Karl Gotthelf: Gotthold Ephraim Lessings Leben, nebst seinem noch übrigen litterarischen Nachlasse. 3 Bde. Berlin 1793–95. [KGL]

Lessing-Mendelssohn-Gedenkbuch. Zur hundertfünfzigjährigen Geburtsfeier von Gotthold Ephraim Lessing und Moses

Mendelssohn, sowie zur Säcularfeier von Lessing's „Nathan". Hg. vom Deutsch-Israelitischen Gemeindebunde. Leipzig 1879. [LMG]

Lüpke, Johannes von: Der fromme Ketzer. Lessings *Idee eines Trauerspiels „Der fromme Samariter nach der Erfindung des Herrn Jesu Christi"*. In: Neues zur Lessing-Forschung. Ingrid Strohschneider-Kohrs zu Ehren am 26. August 1997. Hg. von Eva J. Engel und Claus Ritterhoff. Tübingen 1998, S. 127–51. [JvL]

Meier, Christian: Die politische Kunst der griechischen Tragödie. München 1988. [CM]

Meisels, Samuel: Lessing im Ghetto. In: Jüdische Rundschau (Berlin), H. 6, 22.1.1929, S. 35–36. [SM]

Mendelssohn, Moses: Ausgewählte Werke. Studienausgabe. Hg. und eingeleitet von Christoph Schulte, Andreas Kennecke, Grażyna Jurewicz. 2 Bde. Darmstadt 2009. [MM]

Meyer, Theodor A.: Das Stilgesetz der Poesie. Mit einem Vorwort von Wolfgang Iser. Frankfurt a. M. 1990. [TM]

Molière: Le Misanthrope/Der Menschenfeind. Französisch/Deutsch. Übersetzt und hg. von Hartmut Köhler. Stuttgart 1993. [M]

Mönch, Cornelia: Abschrecken oder Mitleiden. Das deutsche bürgerliche Trauerspiel im 18. Jahrhundert. Versuch einer Typologie. Tübingen 1993. [CMö]

Müller, Heiner: Leben Gundlings Friedrich von Preußen Lessings Schlaf Traum Schrei. Ein Greuelmärchen. In: H. M.: Werke. Hg. von Frank Hörnigk. Bd. 4: Die Stücke. 2. Frankfurt a. M. 2001, S. 509–37. [HM 1]

Müller, Heiner: Wer wirklich lebt, braucht weder Hoffnung noch Verzweiflung. Gespräch mit Frank Feitler [17. Oktober 1985]. In: Programmheft „Mauser". Basler Theater. Spielzeit 1985/86. [HM 2]

N. N.: Warum „Nathan der Weise"? In: Jüdische Rundschau (Berlin), H. 59, 25.7.1933, S. 365. [NN]

Nicolai, Friedrich: Christoph Friedrich Nicolai's Bildniss und Selbstbiographie. Hg. von Michael Siegfried Lowe. Berlin 1806. [FN]

Nisbet, Hugh Barr: Gotthold Ephraim Lessing. His Life, Works, and Thought. Oxford 2013. [HBN]
Overath, Angelika, Navid Kermani, Robert Schindel: Toleranz. Drei Lesarten zu Lessings Märchen vom Ring im Jahr 2003. Göttingen 2003. [AO]
Ovidius Naso, Publius: Liebesbriefe. Heroides – Epistulae. Lateinisch – deutsch. Hg., übersetzt und erläutert von Bruno W. Häuptli. 2., überarbeitete Aufl. Düsseldorf/Zürich 2001. [O]
Petsch, Robert (Hg.): Lessings Faustdichtung. Mit erläuternden Beigaben. Heidelberg 1911. [RP]
Pfranger, Johann Georg: Der Mönch vom Libanon. Mit einem Nachwort hg. von Michael Multhammer. Hannover 2017. [JGP]
Pressler, Mirjam: Nathan und seine Kinder. Roman. Weinheim/Basel 2009. [MP]
Reemtsma, Jan Philipp: Lessing in Hamburg. 1766–1770. München 2007. [JPR]
Reimarus, Hermann Samuel: Apologie oder Schutzschrift für die vernünftigen Verehrer Gottes. Hg. von Gerhard Alexander. 2 Bde. Frankfurt a. M. 1972. [HSR]
Riemer, Friedrich Wilhelm: Mittheilungen über Goethe. Aus mündlichen und schriftlichen, gedruckten und ungedruckten Quellen. 2 Bde. Berlin 1841. [FWR]
Rohrmoser, Günther: Lessing, Gotthold Ephraim. In: Lexikon für Theologie und Kirche. Begründet von Michael Buchberger. 2., völlig neu bearbeitete Aufl. Hg. von Josef Höfer und Karl Rahner. Bd. 6. Freiburg i. Br. 1961, Sp. 980–81. [GR]
Schadewaldt, Wolfgang: Furcht und Mitleid? Zur Deutung des Aristotelischen Tragödiensatzes. In: Hermes 83 (1955), S. 129–69. [WSc]
Schelling, Friedrich Wilhelm Joseph: Zur Geschichte der neueren Philosophie. Münchener Vorlesungen. Hg. von Manfred Buhr. Leipzig 1966. [FSc]
Schiller, Friedrich: Werke. Nationalausgabe, im Auftrag des Goethe- und Schiller-Archivs, des Schiller-Nationalmuseums

und der Deutschen Akademie begründet von Julius Petersen, fortgeführt von Lieselotte Blumenthal u. ä., im Auftrag der Stiftung Weimarer Klassik und des Schiller-Nationalmuseums Marbach hg. von Norbert Oellers. Weimar 1943 et seq. [NA]

Schilson, Arno: Zur Wirkungsgeschichte Lessings in der katholischen Theologie. In: Das Bild Lessings in der Geschichte. Hg. von Herbert G. Göpfert. Heidelberg 1981, S. 69–92. [AS]

Schings, Hans-Jürgen: Der mitleidigste Mensch ist der beste Mensch. Poetik des Mitleids von Lessing bis Büchner. 2., durchgesehene Aufl. Würzburg 2012. [HJS]

Schmid, Christian Heinrich: Litteratur des bürgerlichen Trauerspiels. In: Deutsche Monatszeitschrift (Dezember 1798), S. 282–314. [CHS]

Schmitt, Arbogast: Zur Aristoteles-Rezeption in Schillers Theorie des Tragischen. Hermeneutisch-kritische Anmerkungen zur Anwendung neuzeitlicher Tragikkonzepte auf die griechische Tragödie. In: Antike Dramentheorie und ihre Rezeption. Hg. von Bernhard Zimmermann. Stuttgart 1992, S. 191–213. [ASc]

Scholz, Heinrich (Hg.): Die Hauptschriften im Pantheismusstreit zwischen Jacobi und Mendelssohn. Hg. und mit einer historisch-kritischen Einleitung versehen von H. S. Berlin 1919. [HS]

Schröder, Jürgen: Der „Kämpfer" Lessing. Zur Geschichte einer Metapher im 19. Jahrhundert. In: Das Bild Lessings in der Geschichte. Hg. von Herbert G. Göpfert. Heidelberg 1981, S. 93–114. [JS]

Schulz, Ursula: Lessing auf der Bühne. Chronik der Theateraufführungen 1748–1789. Bremen/Wolfenbüttel 1977. [US]

Shaftesbury, Anthony, Earl of: *Sensus Communis*: An Essay on the Freedom of Wit and Humour. In: E. o. S.: Characteristicks of Men, Manners, Opinions, Times. The Second Edition Corrected. London 1714, S. 57–150. [EoS]

Shakespeare, William: Othello, the Moor of Venice. Hg. von Michael Neill. Oxford 2006. [WS]

Simon, Ernst: Lessing und die jüdische Geschichte. In: Jüdische Rundschau (Berlin), H. 6, 22.1.1929, S. 35. [ES]

Sophokles: Aias. Griechisch/Deutsch. Übersetzt und hg. von Rainer Rauthe. Stuttgart 1990. [S]

Spaemann, Robert: Moralische Grundbegriffe. München 1982. [RS]

Spielhagen, Friedrich: Ueber Objectivetät im Roman. In: F. S.: Vermischte Schriften. Bd. 1. Aufl. Berlin 1868, S. 174–97. [FS]

Spinoza, Baruch de: Sämtliche Werke. Bd. 2: Ethik in geometrischer Ordnung dargestellt. Neu übersetzt, hg. und mit einer Einleitung versehen von Wolfgang Bartuschat. Lateinisch – Deutsch. Hamburg 1999. [BdS]

Stein, Sol: Stein on Writing. New York 1995. [SS]

Steinmetz, Horst (Hg.): Lessing – ein unpoetischer Dichter. Dokumente aus drei Jahrhunderten zur Wirkungsgeschichte Lessings in Deutschland. Frankfurt a. M./Bonn 1969. [St]

Strauß, Botho: Der Erste, der Letzte. Warum uns der große Lessing nicht mehr helfen kann. In: Die Zeit (Hamburg), Nr. 37, 6.9.2001, S. 51–52. [BS]

Stümcke, Heinrich (Hg.): Die Fortsetzungen, Nachahmungen und Travestien von Lessings „Nathan der Weise". Berlin 1904. [HSt]

Stockmayer, Karl Hayo von: Das deutsche Soldatenstück des XVIII. Jahrhunderts seit Lessings *Minna von Barnhelm*. Weimar 1898. [KHS]

Tabori, George: Ein Goi bleibt immer ein Goi … Zur „Nathan"-Inszenierung Claus Peymanns in Bochum 1981. In: G. T.: Unterammergau oder Die guten Deutschen. Frankfurt a. M. 1981, S. 29–35. [GT 1]

Tabori, George: Nathans Tod. Nach Lessing. Berlin 1991. © George Tabori, vertreten durch die Gustav Kiepenheuer Bühnenvertriebs-GmbH, Berlin. [GT 2]

Ter-Nedden, Gisbert: Lessings Trauerspiele. Der Ursprung des modernen Dramas aus dem Geist der Kritik. Stuttgart 1986. [GTN 1]

Ter-Nedden, Gisbert: Lessings Meta-Fabeln und Bodmers *Lessingische unäsopische Fabeln* oder Das Ende der Fabel als Lese-Literatur. In: Europäische Fabeln des 18. Jahrhunderts zwischen Pragmatik und Autonomisierung. Hg. von Dirk Rose. Bucha bei Jena 2010, S. 159–205. [GTN 2]

Ter-Nedden, Gisbert: Der fremde Lessing. Eine Revision des dramatischen Werks. Hg. von Robert Vellusig. Göttingen 2016. [GTN 3]

Thomas von Aquin: Über sittliches Handeln. Summa theologiae I–II q. 18–21. Lateinisch/Deutsch. Übersetzt, kommentiert und hg. von Rolf Schönberger. Einleitung von Robert Spaemann. Stuttgart 2021. [TA]

Timm, Hermann: Gott und die Freiheit. Studien zur Religionsphilosophie der Goethezeit. Bd. 1: Die Spinozarenaissance. Frankfurt a. M. 1974. [HT 1]

Timm, Hermann: Fallhöhe des Geistes. Das religiöse Denken des jungen Hegel. Frankfurt a. M. 1979. [HT 2]

Trillhaas, Wolfgang: Zur Wirkungsgeschichte Lessings in der evangelischen Theologie. In: Das Bild Lessings in der Geschichte. Hg. von Herbert G. Göpfert. Heidelberg 1981, S. 57–67. [WT]

Vergilius Maro, Publius: Aeneis. Lateinisch/Deutsch. Übersetzt und hg. von Edith und Gerhard Binder. Stuttgart 2008. [V]

Vollhardt, Friedrich: Gotthold Ephraim Lessing. Epoche und Werk. Göttingen 2018. [FV]

Wessels, Hans-Friedrich: Lessings „Nathan der Weise". Seine Wirkungsgeschichte bis zum Ende der Goethezeit. Königstein i. Ts. 1979. [HFW]

Wölfel, Kurt: Friedrich Schiller. München 2005. [KW]

Translations

Aristotle: Poetics. Translation by S. H. Butcher. URL: https://www.gutenberg.org/files/1974/1974-h/1974-h.htm.

Dühring, Eugen: On the Jews. Edited with an introduction by Alexander Jacob. Brighton 1997.

Goethe, Johann Wolfgang: The Auto-Biography of Goethe. Truth and Poetry: From my Own Life. Translated by John Oxenford. London 1848.

Goethe, Johann Wolfgang: Conversations with Eckermann. Being Appreciations and Criticisms on Many Subjects. With a preface by Eckermann, and special introduction by Wallace Wood. Washington/London 1901.

Goethe, Johann Wolfgang: Faust. Part One. Translated in the original metres by Bayard Taylor. London 1890.

Goethe, Johann Wolfgang: Iphigenia in Tauris. Translated by Anna Swanwick. Reading (PA) n. d.

Goethe, Johann Wolfgang: Letters to Zelter, With Extracts from Those of Zelter to Goethe. Selected, translated and annotated by A. D. Coleridge. London 1887.

Goethe, Johann Wolfgang: The Sorrows of Young Werther. Translated by R. D. Boylan. Edited by Nathen Haskell Dole. URL: https://www.gutenberg.org/files/2527/2527-h/2527-h.htm.

Goethe, Johann Wolfgang: Upon the Laocoon. In: The World's Best Essays. From the Earliest Period through the Nineteenth Century. Edited by David J. Brewer et al. Vol. 5. St Louis 1900, p. 1916–27.

Heine, Heinrich: Religion and Philosophy in Germany. A Fragment. Translated by John Snodgrass. Boston 1959.

Kant, Immanuel: An Answer to the Question: What is Enlightenment? Translated by Ted Humphrey. Indianapolis 1992. URL: https://www.nypl.org/sites/default/files/kant_whatisenlightenment.pdf.

Kant, Immanuel: The Critique of Pure Reason. Translated by J. M. D. Meiklejohn. London/New York 1900.

Lessing, Gotthold Ephraim: The Dramatic Works. Translated from the German. Edited by Ernest Bell. With a short memoir by Helen Zimmern. London 1878.
Lessing, Gotthold Ephraim: The Dramatic Works. Comedies. Translated from the German. Edited by Ernest Bell. London 1902.
Lessing, Gotthold Ephraim: The Hamburg Dramaturgy. A New and Complete Annotated English Translation. Translated by Wendy Arons and Sara Figal. Edited by Natalya Baldyga. New York 2019.
Lessing, Gotthold Ephraim: How the Ancients Represented Death. URL: https://de.scribd.com/document/512919909.
Lessing, Gotthold Ephraim: Laocoon. The Limits of Painting and Poetry. Translated by E. C. Beasley. With an introduction by T. Bubbidge. London 1853.
Lessing, Gotthold Ephraim: Nathan the Wise, Minna von Barnhelm, and Other Plays and Writings. Edited by Peter Demetz. Foreword by Hannah Arendt. New York 1991.
Lessing, Gotthold Ephraim: Philosophical and Theological Writings. Translated and edited by Hugh Barr Nisbet. Cambridge 2005.
Mendelssohn, Moses: Morning Hours. Translated with an introduction by Daniel O. Dahlstrom and Corey Dyck. URL: https://www.academia.edu/24034291/Morning_Hours_or_Lectures_on_Gods_Existence.
Müller, Heiner: Life of Gundling Lessing's Sleep Dream Cry. Translated by Dennis Redmond. URL: https://www.academia.edu/39708442/Plays_poems_and_prose_by_Heiner_Mueller.
Schiller, Friedrich: The Aesthetical Essays. URL: https://www.gutenberg.org/files/6798/6798-h/6798-h.htm.
Schiller, Friedrich: The Bride of Messina. Translated by A. Lodge. URL: https://www.gutenberg.org/files/6793/6793-h/6793-h.htm.
Schiller, Friedrich: The Criminal from Lost Honour. In: Tales from the German, Comprising Specimens from the Most

Celebrated Authors. Translated by John Oxenford and C. A. Feiling. London 1844, p. 34–50.

Schiller, Friedrich: Don Carlos. Translated by R. D. Boylan. URL: https://www.gutenberg.org/files/6789/6789-h/6789-h.htm.

Schiller, Friedrich: Fiesco, or the Genoese Conspiracy. URL: https://gutenberg.org/cache/epub/6783/pg6783-images.html.

Schiller, Friedrich: Love and Intrigue. URL: https://www.gutenberg.org/files/6784/6784-h/6784-h.htm.

Schiller, Friedrich: On the Pathetic. Translation by William F. Wertz, Jr. URL: http://wlym.com/archive/oakland/docs/SchillerOnThePathetic.pdf.

Schiller, Friedrich: On the Sublime. Translated by William F. Wertz, Jr. URL: https://archive.schillerinstitute.com/transl/trans_on_sublime.html.

Schiller, Friedrich: The Philosophical Letters. URL: https://www.gutenberg.org/files/6799/6799-h/6799-h.htm.

Schiller, Friedrich: Poems of the Second Period. URL: https://www.gutenberg.org/files/6795/6795-h/6795-h.htm.

Schiller, Friedrich: The Poems of Schiller. Third Period. URL: https://www.gutenberg.org/cache/epub/6796/pg6796-images.html.

Schiller, Friedrich: The Robbers. URL: https://www.gutenberg.org/files/6782/6782-h/6782-h.htm.

Schiller, Friedrich: Some Thoughts on the First Human Society following the Guiding Thread of the Mosaic Documents. Translated by Anita Gallagher. URL: https://archive.schillerinstitute.com/fid_91-96/963_schiller_human_society.html.

Schiller, Friedrich: Theater Considered as a Moral Institution. Translated by John Sigerson and John Chambless. URL: https://archive.schillerinstitute.com/transl/schil_theatremoral.html.

Sophocles: The Tragedies. Translated by Richard C. Jebb. Cambridge 1917.

GPSR Compliance
The European Union's (EU) General Product Safety Regulation (GPSR) is a set of rules that requires consumer products to be safe and our obligations to ensure this.

If you have any concerns about our products, you can contact us on

ProductSafety@springernature.com

In case Publisher is established outside the EU, the EU authorized representative is:

Springer Nature Customer Service Center GmbH
Europaplatz 3
69115 Heidelberg, Germany

www.ingramcontent.com/pod-product-compliance
Lightning Source LLC
LaVergne TN
LVHW021334080526
838202LV00004B/171